ANATOMY
OF A
SCIENTIFIC
DISCOVERY

ANATOMY
OF A
SCIENTIFIC
DISCOVERY

JEFF GOLDBERG

BANTAM BOOKS
TORONTO · NEW YORK · LONDON · SYDNEY · AUCKLAND

ANATOMY OF A SCIENTIFIC DISCOVERY
A Bantam Book / May 1988

LIBRARY OF CONGRESS
Library of Congress Cataloging-in-Publication Data

Goldberg, Jeff.
  Anatomy of a scientific discovery / Jeff Goldberg.
    p.   cm.
  Bibliography: p.
  Includes index.
                        ISBN 0-553-05261-6
  1. Endorphins—Research—History.   I. Title.
QP552.E53G65   1988
612'.822—dc19   87-31904
                                                        CIP

Published simultaneously in the United States and Canada

Bantam Books are published by Bantam Books, a division of Bantam Doubleday
Dell Publishing Group, Inc. Its trademark, consisting of the words "Bantam
Books" and the portrayal of a rooster, is Registered in U.S. Patent and Trademark
Office and in other countries. Marca Registrada. Bantam Books, 666 Fifth Avenue,
New York, New York 10103.

PRINTED IN THE UNITED STATES OF AMERICA

BP   0   9   8   7   6   5   4   3   2   1

This book is dedicated
to my mother and
in memory of my father.

ACKNOWLEDGMENTS

The events depicted in this book are drawn from interviews with the many men and women whose work has been responsible for the rapid growth of the endorphin research field and for its enduring promise. My task would have been unapproachable without the open and revealing accounts, encouragement, hospitality, and patience of the following scientists: Huda Akil, Kathy Acker, Sydney Archer, James Belluzi, Floyd Bloom, William Burroughs, Donald Catlin, Harry Collier, Brian Co, David DeWied, John Fothergill, Linda Fothergill, Robert Frederickson, Avram Goldstein, Roger Guillemin, Daniel Hauser, Graeme Henderson, John Hughes, Hans Kosterlitz, Heinz Lehmann, C.H. Li, Lars Lindstrom, John Liebeskind, David Margules, David Meyer, Barry Morgan, Howard Morris, Alan North, Fred Nyberg, Gavril Pasternak, Candace Pert, Dietmar Romer, Rabi Simantov, Eric Simon, Terry Smith, Derrick Smyth, Larry Stein, Solomon Snyder, Lars Terenius, Sidney Udenfriend, and Agneta Wahlstrom.

William Levy, David Walley, and other friends here and in Europe provided homes away from home during my research on the book; the writers Victor Bockris, Dean Latimer, Legs McNiel, and Miles gave much in the way of wise council; and my wife, Suzan, provided unshakable support.

I would like to thank especially my literary agent, Andrew Wylie, for his help initiating and launching this project; David Himmelstein for his valuable assistance on the final draft; and my editor, Peter Guzzardi, for his many constructive suggestions and his enthusiasm over the four years it has taken to reach the finish.

The best laid schemes o' mice and men
Gang aft a-gley;
An' lea'e us nought but grief and pain,
For promis'd joy.

"To a Mouse"
—Robert Burns

CONTENTS

SLAUGHTERHOUSE DAYS

In Aberdeen, on the northeast coast of Scotland, winter begins in early October and does not let up until May, or so it seems. On most days it rains.

In the fall of 1973 the old fishing and textile manufacturing city was being transformed into a kind of American frontier town by the discovery of offshore oil. Texas oil men roamed the streets in ten gallon hats and cowboy boots and the young men who worked the rigs came into town on the weekends like western movie extras, their pockets stuffed with cash, to drink and brawl themselves into oblivion. Oil was bringing prosperity and development to Aberdeen; new office buildings and shops were springing up among the grim granite edifices.

All the buildings in and around Aberdeen were made of granite mined from a nearby quarry—the building code of the "granite city" is still very strict in that regard. The stone sparkled with silica when the sun was shining but on Union Street, Aberdeen's historic main street, it was dull, dark, and gray at four o'clock in the morning.

The sidewalks were wet and empty, the store windows

unlit and gated, as John Hughes rolled through the predawn blackness, pedaling a push-crate bicycle that resembled an ice cream vendor's.

Hughes was thirty years old, a short, slight, bespectacled man, bookish-looking except for his swollen hands which looked like the hands of a boxer, or a murderer—flecks of blood had crusted under the cuticles and faintly stained his knuckles and fingertips. Most of his head was obscured by an orange woolen balaclava helmet that his wife, Mandy, had given him on the Christmas past.

Hughes turned left on Broad Street into the shadows of Marishal College where he stopped, slipped into the building, and silently made his way to his third-floor laboratory to collect what he needed: a supply of small plastic ziplock bags, a white lab coat, a gore-splotched hacksaw and hatchet, a short wooden-handled knife purchased at Woolworth's, and a bottle of Scotch whisky.

With everything safely stowed in the crate on the front of his bicycle, he pedaled toward the Market Street docks. The wind bit at his face and his glasses misted as he jolted over the wet cobblestones. The fishing fleet was casting off so Prince Edward quay was a site of bustling activity in the otherwise sleeping city. Gulls swooped in the wake of the boats and fought over the leavings of yesterday's catch.

Hughes stopped his bike at a warehouse whose owner reluctantly sold him a single block of dry ice, which, normally, could only be purchased in lots of ten. Hughes loaded the dry ice into the crate and pedaled slowly uphill, back past the Marks & Spencer department store on George Street. His final destination was still a mile away.

In 1908 the "killin' " house on the corner of George and Hutchinson streets first opened for business. The date was inscribed in the high granite walls above a wooden gate, along with the crest of the Butchers Guild—an axe, three knives, a castle—and its motto, *Virtute vivo:* "I live virtuously." This was the place where local farmers brought their pigs and sheep for slaughter, and the place John Hughes had come to collect his pig brains. The stone holding pens, pits, and the shelters for the workers had been constructed at the turn of the century, as had the floor of stone tiles—which covered part of the open field—and the system of drains and sewers beneath them which washed away the blood. The chains and pulleys and meathooks on overhead tracks were a more recent addition. There was no roof, and from the second floor windows on George Street the slaughtering process, as it proceeded through the morning, was inescapably visible.

Animals shuffled restlessly inside their wooden stalls while the butchers stood in groups near the warming wood fires on which cauldrons of water boiled. They talked in thick Scots accents, smoked cigarettes, and drank coffee; Hughes knew he must have seemed a weird bird to them: the little man who arrived every couple of days on a push-crate bicycle, put on a white lab coat, and spent the morning packing pig brains in dry ice.

To Hughes the pig brains were an absolute necessity. He needed a lot of them, and here they were free. He had tried explaining to the butchers that he was looking for a chemical in those pig brains, a chemical which resembled drugs derived from the opium poppy—a natural "morphine" produced from within the animal's own body which might, someday, unlock the mysteries of safe relief for human pain. A few of the butchers pretended to catch on, but Hughes quickly realized that gifts of whisky and a little money proved more effective tools of diplomacy than all his mad-sounding explanations.

He had been more successful communicating with the local veterinarian, the health inspector, and the supervisor of the abattoir, who were required by law to approve of the project before Hughes could begin work. Not that they really understood what he was talking about either, but they were willing to waive the meat-packing laws of the city in the interest of providing a few pig brains for science, especially since Scottish cuisine, for all its odd turns, did not run to pig brains.

When the killing started, Hughes stationed himself near the area where the pigs were corralled, on a stone bench under one of the shelters, out of the perpetual rain. One by one the animals were driven with sticks and electric prods into a narrow stone enclosure where a man stood poised, slightly above them, with a rifle. The huge, grunting creatures snorted menacingly at first, but as panic began to take hold their squeals became high-pitched, human-sounding. A single bullet exploded down and through the frontal lobes of each animal's brain and out the throat, dispatching it almost instantly. Fortunately for Hughes, the likeliest sources of the chemical he was after, the mid and back portions of the brain, were left intact.

The dead animals were hoisted up on pulleys, plunged into a vat of boiling water to loosen their hides, then fastened by their hind legs to a hook on a moving track. One of the men worked a chainsaw as the bloody carcasses clattered down the line, spilling guts in the mud, toward the bench where Hughes sat.

If Hughes's bribes had been successful—and if there was enough time—the butcher sliced off the pig's head with a single swipe of the chainsaw and nonchalantly brought it over. If the butcher was too busy, Hughes hacksawed the head off himself, carrying the grisly prize back to his bench. Seated again, he hatcheted the head open, reached in, and severed the brain with his Woolworth's knife. It took about ten minutes of manipulation to free the grapefruit-sized brain from the thick, sharp bone fragments of the skull, and by the time he finished, his hands were covered with grazes and cuts.

He dropped each brain into one of his plastic bags, placed it on the dry ice in the crate of his bicycle, and returned to his bench to repeat the procedure. The butcher lined up fresh heads, which Hughes would toss aside when he finished with them. By the end of the morning a pile of twenty or so would accumulate at his feet.

The sky lightened gradually. The sun, an unwarming, pale disk, rose at about eight, and all work came to a halt shortly after ten. Hughes collected his equipment and washed his hands at a cold water faucet. As the men began to leave for the Butcher's Arms or some other nearby pub, rats came out to scavenge the bloody refuse in the slaughterhouse's open field.

Hughes pedaled back through the monstrous Gothic archway of Marishal College at about ten-thirty. The sprawling building reminded him of the setting for a Frankenstein horror film: four prison-like wings—stark and gray as the rest of the city—enclosing a guardhouse and parking lot, dominated by the sooty clocktower, rising above the Michael Hall commissary. He parked his bicycle in a rack by the gate, lugged his bulky crate of brains and dry ice over to a small wooden door in the south wing, then up a winding staircase to the third floor.

John Hughes's morning routine was part of a risky scientific project on which he was gambling his entire career. That fall he was just beginning to isolate a crude chemical from his pig brains that was quite unlike anything scientists had ever seen. It was a naturally occurring compound, produced by cells within the brain and yet in laboratory tests it behaved with an uncanny similarity to morphine—the narcotic drug derived from the opium poppy.

Eventually, a number of chemicals in the brain and body would be found to have properties so akin to morphine that they would be given the name endorphins ("the morphine within"), but in the fall of 1973, Hughes's crude compound had no name. His coworkers in the lab were calling it "Substance X"—and very few people in the world, apart from Hughes, believed such a chemical even existed. If it did exist and if Hughes could get it pure enough, however, Substance X was bound to be of tremendous importance.

Drug companies were sure to be interested. There were still only two kinds of medicine available to treat the full gamut of human aches and pains in 1973: aspirin—and its close relative acetaminophen, the chief ingredient in Tylenol—and the family of opiates. Opiates were strong but addictive; aspirin was safe, but not strong enough to effectively treat migraine, arthritis, or the little understood syndrome of chronic pain.

There was a good chance that Substance X might provide a unique alternative. In fact, since it originated *in the body* and because animals are not born addicted to narcotics, there was even a possibility that it might be the pot of gold at the end of the rainbow: the nonaddictive painkiller—a narcotic-strength drug that was at the same time as safe as aspirin—that pharmaceutical company chemists had been seeking since the 1930s, the elusive treasure they had playfully dubbed the "bee without a sting." If so, its commercial potential was vast, in the hundreds of millions of dollars—which was not to discount the purely scientific value of Substance X. If, as Hughes suspected, Substance X was part of a fundamental mechanism in the brain regulating the perception of pain, it was possible that it might capture the attention of the Nobel prize committee, and probable that competing researchers were going to be very, very interested as well.

The opiate field had not yet become glamorous in 1973, but the brain was one of the last great unexplored frontiers of science. How the three-pound mass of tissue, composed of some one hundred billion nerve cells—the same number as stars in the Milky Way—worked to coordinate not only the basic machinery of creatures as complex as humans, but memory, learning, and perception was still largely a mysterious puzzle which scientists were eager to solve.

Some pieces of the puzzle had been in place since earlier in the century, when the discovery that nerve cells exchange messages in the form of chemical transmitters created the basis of modern neuroscience. By the early 1960s, four primary neurotransmitters, linked to diverse behaviors—acetylcholine, norepinephrine, dopamine, and serotonin—had been identified. Although the precise way that neurotransmitters worked was not yet fully understood, researchers believed that these tiny pieces of protein were fired across the synapse, the microscopic gap between nerve cells; and that like molecular "keys" they fit into protein "keyholes"—called "receptors"—which, in turn, triggered the next cell to fire. Tiny shifts in the balances of these molecular human components governed not only how we feel physically, but also our mental state—who we are—at any given moment.

An additional array of chemicals called "neuromodulators" were thought to work at synapses arranged along the nerve before it reached the main synaptic junction at its terminal. These chemicals had a fine-tuning effect, altering primary transmitter chemical levels to speed up or slow down nerve impulses as they flashed down the fiber. Only a few neuromodulators had been positively identified. One of them, angiotensin, an important regulator of the heart, had been John Hughes's specialty while he was a postdoctoral researcher at Yale, and he, like many scientists, assumed that there were others. Substance X might possibly be one of them. Its precise role in pain perception was something Hughes was still trying to figure out.

Pain signals, in the form of nerve impulses, traveled along neural pathways from the surface of the body to the brain. There, pain centers—clusters of nerve cells which, when electrically stimulated, produced painful responses in laboratory animals—had been identified. However, scientists also suspected that the nervous system contained other "descending" pain pathways, which enabled the brain itself to modulate, and in some cases deaden, the perception of pain. The existence of such "descending" pathways might help to explain a number of medical anomalies, ranging from Henry Beecher's famous case studies of severely wounded soldiers in World War II who were completely anesthetized to their serious injuries, to firewalkers who felt no pain and sustained no injury while dancing on red hot coals.

So far, scientists had made little progress in mapping these pain pathways and identifying the chemical transmitters involved with them. Was John Hughes's Substance X the pain-modulating chemical key that would unlock a deeper understanding of the nature of physical and, perhaps, emotional pain? And, since narcotics also produced euphoria, could it also be linked to the brain's chemical code of pleasure? The prospects were tantalizing. For Hughes to claim any real success, though, and for the compound ever to be of use clinically, he not only would have to extract it but also purify it, and identify the protein substance's amino acid composition. The formula was the ultimate goal, but to begin to approach that objective, fresh animal brains were needed.

Hence, on cold and wet mornings in the fall of 1973, Hughes sat in the public slaughterhouse of Aberdeen amongst a pile of pig's heads, packing away what was left of their brains into the crate on the front of his bicycle, far from scientific glory and, indeed, very much alone. Even his boss, Hans Kosterlitz, was not entirely convinced that Hughes would be able to succeed at his ambitious task, and Kosterlitz had originated the idea of the "morphine within." Kosterlitz was the source.

BRAIN SOUP

Hans Kosterlitz's battered Ford Anglia was parked in its usual spot near the archway in the courtyard of Marishal College when Hughes rolled in. Kosterlitz was seventy-one years old, short, gnome-like, and nearly blind in one eye as the result of a childhood shooting accident. His thick-lensed glasses exaggerated the owlish expression that contributed to his reputation at Aberdeen as a patriarchal sage. Unfortunately for pedestrians, despite his poor eyesight he still drove his car with the same enthusiasm that he showed in pursuing his research.

The Anglia always had a few new dents in it and when people from the Unit went out for dinner or drinks to Muldrum House or the Old Mill, there was a lot of jockeying over who would have to drive with Kosterlitz. John Hughes half-jokingly claimed that he had acquired his own Cortina so as not to keep having to refuse Kosterlitz's offers of a lift.

Kosterlitz was amazingly energetic for a septuagenarian. Alan North, an electrophysiologist in the Unit—who was a mountain-climbing enthusiast—would often meet him on the way to work and the two would race up the spiraling staircase to the third-floor labs. Somehow, Kosterlitz always managed to keep up with the younger, more athletic man, even though he took several minutes in the privacy of his office to recover from the workout. "Work hard, play hard" was one of his pet expressions. "A day not spent in the lab is a wasted day" was his other familiar motto.

Hans Kosterlitz arrived at work promptly at nine each morning, rarely left before six-thirty in the evening, and seemed to spend most of that time zealously spying on his staff. Once, a staff member kept a tally of the number of times Kosterlitz barged into the lab: In the course of a single day, he made thirty-eight appearances.

Kosterlitz's assistant for ten years was Angela Waterfield— whom he spent the first part of each morning contentedly pestering in her circular turret lab. A reserved, heavyset woman who eventually married a petroleum engineer and moved to the United Arab Emirates, she usually endured Kosterlitz's nagging and tantrums when his instructions were not followed to the letter, although everyone could remember the occasions when she rushed into the hall in tears with Kosterlitz storming and fuming behind her, shouting "This data is no good!"

He had a temper and, while he may not have subscribed to the teutonic tradition of his own university days at Heidelberg, Germany, where one bowed obsequiously to "Herr Professor," he was still hard on his people, and he knew it.

"I won't be kind to you," he remembered telling one former associate when they started working together—he was not. That was the way he got his people "not to be stupid."

For those who possessed the curiosity, courage, and patience to join Kosterlitz's small band of researchers, however, "the Prof," as he was fondly called, usually managed to endear himself even as he tyrannized them. "He was formal, precise, domineering, but he inspired a sense of loyalty," one ex-Unit staffer remarked. "There might be trials and tribulations, but in the end you were a Kosterlitz person."

No one who knew him questioned his wisdom. He was a trained physician, versed in physiology, neurology, and pharmacology, who had studied at both Heidelberg and the University of Berlin before leaving Germany in 1933, the year Hitler consolidated power. Kosterlitz, a Jew, had been fired from his post at the Charity Hospital in Berlin. Foreseeing even more ominous events ahead he left for England, then Scotland, followed by his mother, brother, and his fiancée, Hanna. "I had to begin completely over," he once remarked. "The affair struck me so deeply, it took ten years just to feel safe again, to feel I had a home."

His work in the 1930s on the body's chemical breakdown of carbohydrates and its relation to diabetes provided a key contribution to the 1947 Nobel prize-winning research by the Argentinian, Bernardo Houssay. The work also earned Kosterlitz a Ph.D. from Aberdeen University and enough of a reputation to enable him to marry Hanna, who by then had been resettled in Glasgow by the immigration authorities. She had spent the next thirty-five years putting up with his obsessions.

A small, wispish woman, Hanna's attitudes and opinions were for the most part old-fashioned. The subject of serious scientists, however, provoked an outspoken feminist response. "Never marry a dedicated scientist," she advised girls who came to their parties. "A dedicated scientist is married to his work—if I'm ever born again, I'll never marry a scientist. In fact, I'll never marry at all!"

In the early 1940s Kosterlitz's research had shifted to the influence of dietary protein on the composition of the liver, in the hope that this work would help provide a solution to the serious food shortages during the war; but it had finally proven less than successful. Now it was his research into the effects of opiates on the peristaltic reflex of the intestine that consumed him.

In particular, Kosterlitz was an expert on the *myenteric plexus* of the guinea pig *ileum,* the ileum being that portion of the large intestine which spurts waste matter into the colon. When dissected and rigged in a beaker the isolated tissue resembles a worm on a fishhook. Stimulated with an electric current, the ileum twitches and those twitches can be counted by recording devices.

Kosterlitz found that morphine and similar drugs would quell this spasm to a degree directly corresponding to their painkilling potency in humans. As a result, Kosterlitz's guinea pig ileum had become widely used in the research community as a tool to predict how effective new narcotic drugs would be in clinical practice.

It was not, however, the sort of work that made one famous. In fact, to all but a small circle of serious drug researchers in Great Britain and America, his twenty-year romance with the guinea pig ileum was something of a joke, a throwback to turn-of-the-century methods. Medical students at the University had nicknamed him "Mr. Guinea Pig," and in the eyes of the scientific world generally, circa 1973, Hans Kosterlitz remained, as one scientist bluntly summed it up, "an almost unknown pharmacologist doing pedestrian research in an obscure medical school in Scotland." The typical response to his work, Kosterlitz would often reflect, was "Well, it's all very nice but what does it mean?"

What it meant was so startling that even Kosterlitz still distrusted his conclusion, which remained known only to his closest colleagues. In the early 1960s—ten years before Hughes's trips to the slaughterhouse began—Kosterlitz had predicted that morphine worked by imitating a chemical already in the body, an endogenous opiate.

He had observed that opiates seemed to produce their twitch-quelling effects in a unique way. Their depressant action, he suggested, was "presynaptic" and "neuromodulating" —the drugs acted before the nerve impulse reached its terminus at the end of the cell, slowing it down, and reducing the release of acetylcholine, the transmitter he found to be primarily responsible for passing the twitch response along the nerve fiber. The data supported another farfetched idea, proposed by other scientists, that specific opiate receptors, where morphine and similar drugs combined, existed on nerve cells. Kosterlitz, himself, felt strongly that this was the case though he could not prove it.

He was certain that opiates were activating some sort of receptor, though, and tested all the known neurotransmitters to see if they would stop the ileum twitch in the same manner as morphine. None of them would. "That was the decisive point," Kosterlitz recalled, "where you had to look for another transmitter."

Despite the rather unsalubrious atmosphere of the "frog" room—Kosterlitz's dank, dingy lab in the Marishal College basement, where the frogs had once been stored for student dissections—David Wallis, a senior research fellow at the time, recalls that work was proceeding in a good-natured fashion in 1963, when Kosterlitz first began to talk about the possibility that the body might contain its own opiates, which worked to slow down the digestive spasms in living animals, the same way morphine did on the ileum. "I had a feeling," Wallis said, "he had been thinking of this for some time."

Given the source it did not seem so very unusual to Wallis that there could be such a thing as an endogenous opiate. At any time—in a pub, at his home in Cults, or in the frog room—Kosterlitz might begin talking, out of the blue, about a new scientific problem.

When, however, during the summer of 1963, he sprang the same idea on Andrew Wyllie, a medical student who was struggling without success in the frog room to measure the electrical effects of opiates on the rabbit vagus nerve, Wyllie found it quite nonsensical. "I was not big enough to take it," he recalls, "and remember going home thinking, 'what an odd man he must be!'"

Discussions about endogenous opiates took place in a fragmented fashion, in the frog room and elsewhere, over the next several years; but they never extended beyond Kosterlitz's small Aberdeen circle. It was certainly a logical deduction but there was absolutely no way to prove it. "If you say such things in public," Kosterlitz avers, "you risk making yourself foolish. It could cost grants." He wrote nothing down and he discouraged his coworkers from making any notes about such unproven theories, lest someone see them.

Gordon Lees, who is currently a reader in the Aberdeen University Department of Pharmacology, also began his association with Hans Kosterlitz in the frog room. "The idea was so highly speculative that Hans was not at all keen to speak about it, except privately," Lees recalls. "Not because he was formulating a secret plan to look for such a substance, but because he was dead set against public speculation. While the idea of an endogenous compound might be true, there was no idea of how to go about looking for it, not enough evidence to even start. Until there was firmer evidence, the idea was to be enjoyed . . . and forgotten." John Hughes had not only refused to forget about it, he had begun doggedly mashing brains in search of literal proof.

Kosterlitz had gone through the formality, at least, of retiring from his post as professor of clinical pharmacology in 1972 before opening his independent Unit for the Study of Addictive Drugs at Marishal. Now, a year later, there were half a dozen people working under his supervision in the small set of labs on the third floor of the college's south tower, with John Hughes acting as the Unit's deputy director.

Hughes was a young man and Kosterlitz an old man, and their working relationship was often characterized by emotional storms common between sons and fathers—which is to say that they argued a lot about everything. Hughes thought Kosterlitz overly cautious; Kosterlitz thought Hughes impetuous, and each thought the other eccentric. "They would never have chosen each other for friends," a close colleague remarks;

and yet, they were friends, Hughes recalls, "though it may not have been obvious to the casual observer."

They were an odd couple right from the start of their work together four years earlier, when Hughes had joined the Aberdeen pharmacology faculty. Hans Kosterlitz was an Old World patrician intellectual, cautious in his approach to both science and university politics, and decorous to other faculty members even when they snubbed him. He had not openly complained when in the 1960s, despite his outstanding qualifications, he had been passed up for the Chair of Pharmacology. Aberdeen University was not yet ready to award professorships to foreigners and Jews. As a result, Kosterlitz had served many of the intervening years in the middle level position of "reader" in the pharmacology department. John Hughes on the other hand was, well, John Hughes.

There was nothing complex about him, nothing hidden, no secrets. He was up-front: abrasive, always convinced he was right—and more than willing to make his opinions known to one and all. Although no traces of a South London accent remained, Hughes was a true-born Elephant and Castle cockney—a "cheeky cock sparrow," who had done extremely well for himself.

Hughes's mother was still alive while he was in Aberdeen but his father—a "sanitary inspector" who ran a "cleansing station" to delouse bedding, belongings, and people—had died when Hughes was fifteen years old, which might account for some of the extremes—good and bad—in his relationship with Kosterlitz. Undoubtedly, some of his precociousness stemmed from the fact that he was the youngest by ten years of two brothers and three sisters who had also done well for themselves. One sister, for instance, was head mistress of a girls' school in Finchley and a brother, David, sold medical equipment; but John Hughes's talents were exceptional.

Everyone in the lab respected his scientific capabilities and to a certain degree his lofty self-image was appropriate to his accomplishments as a postgraduate at Yale, where he had coauthored two impressive papers on the manufacture and release of angiotensin, in the heart. There was even something undeniably refreshing about his youthful ebullience and ambitious self-assertion; so perfectly normal by American standards but so heretical in Aberdeen, where people tended to think it better to put oneself down.

He might have seemed more charming if only he could have kept a lid on it. "To put it nicely," one coworker said, "he was brusque. To put it not so nicely, he was contemptuous of people he did not consider his equals."

Aberdeen University was by no means a place renowned for successful scientists. The faculty members were solid and respectable but—to Hughes's way of thinking—they did not work very hard; in many cases, they did no original research at all and were in some ways as archaic as the academic gowns many still wore to their lectures. More than once—and in no uncertain terms—he had told some distinguished senior faculty member simply to "stuff it" and Kosterlitz, although he could be almost as temperamental in the privacy of the lab, often found himself publicly in the long-suffering father role, making excuses for his younger colleague.

Arguments between the two often erupted over morning coffee to the amusement of the rest of the staff, and frequently continued after the break—with the older man chasing him up and down the third floor corridor, while haranguing Hughes.

"John would argue with anybody," Alan North remembers, "but Hans was just as intransigent." The outcome was usually the same: Hughes, with a gesture of futility, would walk out of the fray, muttering in frustration, "I don't know how your wife puts up with you" and retreat into his lab.

They had been arguing about brain-produced opiates for eighteen months, long before the Unit for the Study of Addictive Drugs had opened. Although the idea of an endogenous opiate had surfaced in his own mind first, Kosterlitz still wondered how Hughes—given the complexity of the brain and the rather limited techniques at his disposal—would be able to isolate such a chemical. He would listen and, typically, dismiss Hughes's ideas—as he did most ideas forwarded by his younger associates—saying, "Oh, I thought of that years ago," shooting them down with a long list of tough objections. "You know, John, the chances of isolating something are pretty slim. . . . You must be very careful, John . . ."

Kosterlitz had only reluctantly given him the go-ahead on the project several months earlier and then because Hughes made it a condition of accepting the job as the Unit's deputy director.

Aware of the risks involved, and given what he saw as Kosterlitz's reluctance to do new things, Hughes was surprised that in the end Hans Kosterlitz went along with the project at all. The funds were approved later that winter; space at Marishal was allotted to Kosterlitz, and Hughes began some preliminary experiments. Kosterlitz had provided an idea, Hughes was going to provide the muscle, and as far as Hughes was concerned, it had now become *his* project.

John Hughes's laboratory—a small, dilapidated room—fit perfectly into his horror-film vision of Marishal College. The walls were lined with old wooden cabinets and the floors, stained with burn scars from thousands of past experiments, were covered by a snake pit of wires.

When the once-derelict wing had been taken over the previous summer by the Unit, they were unaware of the building's antique electrical wiring system, which required plugs made in Aberdeen and designed sometime before the turn of the century by the Northern Electrical Company. The entire third floor became precariously connected by circles of extension cords. If one fuse blew, they all went—a constant reminder to Hughes of the limitations of his facilities there compared with the proper resources and equipment he had used in American labs.

The room was sparsely furnished with a used red carpet, Hughes's big oak desk and chair, and another chair for visitors next to the door alongside the refrigerator. The ceilings were twenty feet high and the four tall windows offered an excellent view of the city: one could see the turrets of Provost Skene's House, as well as the green copper domes of the library, St. Mark's Church and His Majesty's Theatre—a trio of buildings known locally as "Education, Salvation, and Damnation."

Hughes also shared a larger lab down the hall with Frances Leslie, whose workbench frowns could not completely obscure the fact that she was a petite, attractive woman; and Graeme Henderson, a young Scotsman from Glasgow completing his Ph.D. in the Unit, who had spent the past two years working under Hughes in the department of pharmacology, and who had the longest hair and was the most left-wing of any of Kosterlitz's young protégés. Henderson had his own horror-film vision of the situation as he attempted to cope with what he saw as Hughes's "Jekyll and Hyde" personality. The smaller room—and the view—were Hughes's exclusively, and the door was usually shut.

Hughes was working by himself, with the Unit's only technician, Helen Anderson, who—apart from being generally helpful in the lab—claimed the added distinction of having a brother-in-law who tossed the telephone pole-sized log called a caber in the Highland games. After one visit to the George Street slaughterhouse, she refused to go back, and her principal tasks became the preparation of solutions and washing up—jobs Hughes hated but which, with Anderson assigned to them, left him little in the way of skilled assistance for the major work. Graduate students like Henderson and Leslie could not be assigned to his project, for if it failed, it might endanger their Ph.D.'s.

Hughes's equipment, in the initial stages, was hardly the last word in technological sophistication: a steel rod, a large glass jar, funnels, paper filters, and assorted test tubes. Even

the Joblin rotary evaporators—the most advanced of his tools—
had a basic, arcane appearance: the pear-shaped glass vials,
connected by coils, looked like pieces of alchemical appara-
tuses that Paracelsus might have used—or, more aptly like
something from the Glenfiddich distillery a few miles away,
near the ruins of Balvenie Castle in Dufftown.

Hughes liked what scientists since the days of alchemy
had fondly dubbed the "bangs and stinks" of their profession,
but eleven o'clock in the morning was an hour dreaded by
those in the south wing of Marishal who thrived on peace and
quiet. During the next two hours, between eleven and one,
Hughes would pulverize frozen pig brains into an icy mush
with his steel rod. It was hard, physical labor, something
Hughes respected, and he performed the task with such relish
that, one colleague recalled, "the whole floor would shake."
This noise particularly disturbed a professor of petroleum
geology in the room directly below Hughes, who eventually
registered a formal complaint that permanently banished
Hughes's brain-mashing operation to the "gents" room in the
basement.

Having mashed the brains, Hughes had to dissolve and
filter them to obtain a fraction of brain chemicals containing,
he hoped, the one he wanted. He made a "soup" of pulverized
brains using liters of Acetone, an organic solvent which destroyed fats but left proteins and salts—the most likely constit-
uents of a brain-produced opiatelike neurotransmitter—intact.
These "bucket extractions" did nothing to enhance Hughes's
popularity; the smell of pig brains and Acetone that drifted
from his lab (a reek of rendered fat and airplane glue) was
remembered as "extraordinary" even by one seasoned colleague.

Having lived on coffee and a bowl of cornflakes since
four in the morning, by one o'clock Hughes was usually
famished and left his "brain soup" to have lunch in the
Michael Hall commissary, where a motherly old woman cooked
and served hot meals for very little money.

By midafternoon he had converted his supply of brains into about five liters of "soup" and began to filter it until all that remained was a small, moist, gray mound of brain substance which Hughes then redissolved in Acetone and dripped bit by bit into his rotary evaporators. The glass coils and vials of the evaporators were pressurized to create a partial vacuum, so that—at the very low temperatures necessary to avoid the risk of ruining his mixture—he could "flash evaporate" any unwanted materials as well as the excess Acetone. Hughes sat for hours on a stool, with two or three evaporators going at once, gazing intently at the equipment, his unlit pipe in his mouth, as the material from the bottom of the pear-shaped vials bubbled into the coils.

"The process was tricky," he says. "You couldn't leave it cooking and go out for a pint." If it boiled too violently, he would lose it; if it had not heated sufficiently, pressure in the apparatus would force contaminants back into the mixture. The Joblin evaporators—typical of Aberdeen parsimony—were the cheapest one could buy and they were always breaking, and sometimes exploding.

Quite often during this delicate and crucial juncture of the day's operations, Kosterlitz would dash into the lab and sit down in the chair by the fridge, offering some idea or suggestion that had sprung to mind since morning coffee. Hughes would suffer these interruptions in absolute silence, gazing fixedly at his rotary evaporators as if Kosterlitz were not even there. Over four years, Hughes had fought his way to a measure of independence while working under Kosterlitz's scrutiny; he was grateful, at least, that Kosterlitz did not tinker with his equipment or hover over his shoulder and nag, as he did with others in the Unit.

Hughes dissolved the remaining residue in ether, filtered it again, then dried and collected it. The final product was a tiny amount of yellow, waxy material that smelled like rancid butter. This was crude Substance X. It would take two days to convert the full five liters of "brain soup" into a few grams of the unwholesome-smelling substance, which Hughes stored in a flask in the freezer. Then back again to the slaughterhouse.

Sunsets from John Hughes's lab were particularly vibrant in autumn, when frost in the air put a sharper edge on the light and the granite city gleamed silver. Hughes continued working and, as the city darkened, one by one the others drifted off to their homes or to the KGB, as the nearby Kirkgate Bar was called by its third-floor regulars.

At the end of the day it was Kosterlitz, often as not, who initiated the pub sessions. This surprised newcomers to the lab who were unused to people of his age and stature popping in to ask, "Do you think you'll be thirsty in half an hour?" At the pub, he held court over his usual two half-pints of McEwan's dark ale, then drove home to Cults, his car swerving slightly in synchronization with the to-and-fro motion of his head, as the Anglia sped into the dark, misted Aberdeenshire countryside.

It was usually seven-thirty when Hughes again pulled on his balaclava, mounted his push-crate bicycle, and jolted over the cold, damp route back to his house near Duthie Park. These were the slaughterhouse days, exciting days, when Hughes felt certain he was the only one in the world seriously trying to isolate the brain's own morphine—at least for now. Major advances reported from laboratories in the U.S. indicated that other scientists were already on to the idea. Hughes was not sure how advanced they were, but anything this important was bound to stir competition and some of it would be coming from people who could accomplish in months what might take him years to do.

Hughes pedaled harder. He knew he would not be the only one for long. The race was on.

LOCKS AND KEYS

In the early 1970s, before Hans Kosterlitz had opened his drug research unit at Marishal College or John Hughes had begun his pig-brain collection, scientists in the U.S. had been converging from quite different directions on what would become an international competition to isolate endorphins. Work on lab rats at UCLA hinted that an internal chemical mechanism might be involved in modifying pain, but the approach which was generating the most excitement stemmed from research at Stanford and Johns Hopkins on "opiate receptors," the molecular keyholes on nerve cells which were activated by narcotics.

The idea that such "opiate receptors" exist at all was first proposed by Arnold Beckett, a professor of pharmacology at Chelsea College, London, in the 1950s, when drug houses were turning out thousands of variations on the morphine molecule, trying to develop the "stingless bee." Some slight alterations in the molecular structure of morphine had no effect, while others could alter activity drastically. Beckett had reasoned that how well opiates worked varied with their ability to "fit" into his conjectural opiate receptors. One variation, etorphine, which was ten thousand times stronger than morphine and useful only as a wild game tranquilizer, seemed to fit the receptor lock more precisely than any other opiate. Another variation, nalorphine, was found to be a "morphine antagonist." While nalorphine was also a good fit, it would block, without activating, those same target sites, thereby reversing some of the physical and emotional effects of opiates in addicts.

If receptors for opiates could be found, the feat would enable researchers to begin to comprehend the whole sequence of events involved in the action of narcotics—including, perhaps, the reasons why people became addicted to them. It might also aid scientists in designing drugs that would fit these keyholes without producing addiction. As a result, the search for opiate receptors was an intriguing project in its own right, and the scientists working in this direction were not initially concerned with or did not grasp, as did Kosterlitz and Hughes, the even more theoretical possibility that a naturally occurring chemical in the body might trigger those same target sites under normal circumstances. Besides, demonstrating that opiate receptors were actually present on nerve cells had proven difficult enough. It was impossible, given the technology in the 1950s when Beckett formulated his theory, and it would remain so for the next twenty years, until Avram Goldstein, at Stanford University in Palo Alto, California, finally pioneered the techniques that proved Beckett right.

Goldstein ran one of the most technically up-to-date labs and was perhaps the most intelligent of the American scientists working on discovering the basic neuromechanisms of opiates in the body—"maybe *too* intelligent," some close colleagues have been quick to add. Compared with Avram Goldstein, someone like Hans Kosterlitz, who studied the action of drugs on isolated tissues like the guinea pig ileum, really was "old school." Goldstein believed in high technology and was familiar with the battery of new methods, employing radioactive tracers and supersensitive detection procedures, which were enabling researchers for the first time to determine how drugs worked in the body on the molecular level. He was hardly shy about evaluating the impact of his work on the field: "I thought, from the beginning, that pharmacology was a discipline in transition," he once said, "that it was moving away from tissue preparations like the ileum to a biochemical footing. It has; I did it."

Goldstein not only believed that opiate receptors existed but at that time he was the only other scientist besides Kosterlitz and Hughes who believed in the existence of endogenous opiates. He had even attempted to find them in a series of unsuccessful experiments in 1972, at about the same time as Kosterlitz and Hughes finalized plans for their own research project. Goldstein's analytical mind worried the Aberdeen scientists.

A striking figure, tall and lanky with a Lincolnesque beard, Goldstein was, in one colleague's assessment, "a kind of Renaissance man," who flew his own plane and, in addition to his classic textbook *Principles of Drug Action,* had authored a definitive pamphlet on instrument flying. His father was Rabbi Israel Goldstein, a founder of Brandeis University, the religious leader of Manhattan's largest conservative Jewish congregation, and a man who headed virtually every major Jewish organization at one time or another during his long career. Sharing his father's charisma but rebelling against his traditional beliefs, Avram Goldstein preferred the hard realities of science to spiritual vagaries. The towering stature and beard, which added to an impression of sepulchral severity, became Goldstein's scientific trademark, along with his competitiveness. The two things he admired most were "irrefutable fact and winning." "Science is always a race," Goldstein professed, "and scientists are competitive people. Because the monetary rewards are minimal, they go for the ego rewards. . . ."

By any standards, Avram Goldstein had had a highly

successful career. His M.D. and Ph.D. degrees had been earned at Harvard Medical School. He was currently earning nearly $70,000 a year as chairman of the Stanford University Pharmacology Department. He and his wife, Dora (herself a respected scientist), were living in one of the expensive outlying red-wooded communities of Palo Alto. But Goldstein had come to feel that his work lacked relevance and that he had become a "high-priced errand boy." He had chosen to devote his talents to battling an epidemic which had l the West Coast and was spreading across the nation in the form of a massive influx of potent "China White" heroin from Southeast Asia's Golden Triangle.

Addicts nodding out on street corners and in the doorways of Palo Alto's small Hispanic ghetto, across El Camino Real from the Stanford Campus, provided Goldstein with ample evidence that the problem of addictive drugs did not confine itself to university lecture halls. He had also read the government reports, in which concerned U.S. public health officials were estimating a leap in the addict population from 125,000 to nearly three quarters of a million. Effective treatment was urgently needed.

In 1968, Avram Goldstein himself had been instrumental in setting up the first methadone clinic in California. Now he wanted to go one step further and establish his own Addiction Research Foundation, which would combine laboratory investigation with experimental treatment programs for addicts. He hoped quickly to establish a reputation in the opiates field that would bring recognition—and money—to his endeavors. He therefore went at it, a former associate recalls, "with the enthusiasm of a religious convert." Receptor theory was his first priority target.

Goldstein's basis for hope in an area where he was very much a newcomer rested on a technically exquisite method he had developed in the summer of 1971—a technique for testing

brain soup called "grind and bind," which became the foundation for all the future work on receptors in the field.

"Grinding" consisted of decapitating about a hundred
male mice and homogenizing their brains into a "soup" of
cells with the consistency of a milk shake, in a machine which
resembled a cake-mixer. By spinning his crude mouse brain
soup in a centrifuge at varying speeds, Goldstein and his lab
workers could break the soup down into separate and concentrated mouse brain-cell components which might contain receptor sites.

Typical of Goldstein's high-tech approach, one high-speed
centrifugation yielded brain fractions containing only the nerve
endings, while another yielded "pink jellylike" pellets containing only brain-cell nuclei and a parchmentlike layer of "floated"
cell membranes.

"Binding," the next step in Goldstein's strategy, consisted
of washing a radioactively labeled opiate through each of these
brain-cell fractions and then measuring the levels of radioactiv-
ity. Goldstein reasoned that any radioactive traces stuck to the
samples indicated that some of the opiate was tightly bound to
cell fragments which would, in turn, prove the existence of
opiate receptor sites. However, there was a problem, for which
Goldstein devised a brilliant solution.

Since opiates were easily trapped in fatty tissues and in
the spaces between cells; radioactive "noise" from labeled
drugs caught at these places could mask any signals from
actual receptor-sites. In order to compensate for this difficulty,
Goldstein used two uniquely different drugs, levorphanol and
dextrorphan, classified as stereoisomers. Like a pair of gloves,
these chemicals were mirror opposites that could be distinguished from each other as right- or left-handed. Only one,
levorphanol, fit receptors; dextrorphan could not.

Goldstein saturated his "mouse-brain soup" with nonradioactive dextrorphan, knowing that it would combine with
the nerve cells in all the sorts of nonspecific ways that might

have otherwise been confusing. But, of vital importance, dextrorphan would be "as ineffective as a misshapen key" in binding to the opiate receptor sites, which would remain unoccupied. Then he added radioactive levorphanol and spun the mixture in a centrifuge. Since all the other possibilities had been accounted for by the dextrorphan, any radioactive levorphanol remaining in the soup would indicate binding to receptors, and only receptors.

Despite the cleverness of Goldstein's grind-and-bind technique, his own results had been disappointing so far: Only about 2 percent of the radioactive material remained in the beakers. "It was like picking up a very weak signal on a short-wave radio during a static storm," he recalls. While that was not nearly good enough to prove the existence of opiate receptors, "stereospecificity" became the litmus test for detecting them and a number of other researchers in the field began struggling to make Goldstein's technique work.

Goldstein, meanwhile, had taken his experiments a step further. Reasoning that there must also be a chemical trigger in the nervous system for opiate receptors, he had already taken a stab at locating endorphins in the brains of mice. It was, admittedly, a shot in the dark—using antibodies Goldstein had developed to hunt down and identify morphine in the urine of drug addicts. "Our position," Goldstein concedes, "was that of a child who enters a barn full of manure and, based on the overwhelming evidence of his senses, says, 'There must be a pony in here someplace. . . .' "

"What does this . . ." Huda Akil hesitated, searching for the right word, ". . . *mess* mean?" The question concluded her brief lecture at the International Congress of Pharmacology in July 1972, in San Francisco, broadly titled "Pharmacology and the Future of Man."

Syrian-born, her heavily accented English still somewhat

fitful, Akil was understandably nervous; it was her first presentation at any scientific gathering, much less one whose audience included some of her own heroes—like Hans Kosterlitz and Avram Goldstein, whose names dotted the footnotes of her just-completed doctoral dissertation.

She was one of the few women at the nearly all-male gathering—an unusually attractive presence, twenty-three years old and vivacious, with dark hair and flashing, dark eyes. The "mess" she was describing was going to become one of the most intriguing puzzles presented to that Congress. In her ten-minute talk, she detailed a series of experiments, conducted by John Liebeskind's pain research group at the University of California in Los Angeles, on *stimulation-produced analgesia,* or *SPA,* as they were calling it. When parts of the central gray matter in the brains of rats were stimulated with a low-voltage current, the animals became impervious to pain, and this electrically produced pain relief was remarkably similar to the relief brought by morphine.

Huda Akil's teacher, John Liebeskind, an untenured psychology instructor in his early forties, had written a few papers of no great note during a decade at UCLA and, in the publish-or-perish world of big time academia, was perilously close to perishing when in 1969 the series of events that ultimately led to the puzzle Akil described began to unfold.

Liebeskind's work was originally directed toward *producing* pain, not relieving it. By stimulating centers in the pariaqueductal gray matter (PAG) of rats' brains, he was hoping to demonstrate that aversive brain stimulation could be as effective in conditioning animals to perform varied tasks as Skinnerian "foot shock." He was assisted in this early effort by David Mayer, the senior graduate student in the group, and by Thomas Wolfle, who was also completing his Ph.D.

Wolfle was trying to train rats to jump over a low barrier to avoid PAG stimulation. The technique was proving frustratingly ineffective for reasons which only began to be apparent when, in December 1969, Mayer and Wolfle attended a meeting up at Stanford. David Reynolds, a scientist at NASA's Ames Research Center, showed a sixteen-minute film in which abdominal surgery was performed on rats anesthetized only by electrical stimulation in the PAG. The sites to deaden pain located by Reynolds in the rats' brains were located close by those the UCLA group was using to *produce* pain.

Mayer went back and took a closer look at Wolfle's stymied efforts to train PAG-stimulated rats to high jump. "The animals had a tendency to violently turn in one direction when the current was applied," Mayer recounts. "They were turning and banging their heads against the wall of the cage, bloodying up their faces, but they didn't seem to mind. That was strange, so I started poking and prodding and . . . they didn't respond to pain at all."

During the spring and early summer of 1970, Mayer and Huda Akil, who had arrived in Liebeskind's lab eight months earlier, set out to detail this stimulation-produced analgesia. By placing their electrodes more carefully, pain immunity in the rats would develop without the "head-turning" side effects. In fact, the animals seemed perfectly normal and would respond to all the sights and sounds in their environment— except for the pinches, prods, shocks and heat-lamp torments devised by the researchers.

"The animals were not 'zonked,'" Liebeskind explains. "We demonstrated that we hadn't destroyed their brains. They weren't paralyzed, asleep or dead. They were normal in all general appearances, except one: *They felt no pain.*"

Mayer and Akil carefully mapped the active sites and in the fall of 1970 submitted a paper to *Science* magazine. "It came back with a tepid, 'yes,'" Huda Akil recalls. "Liebeskind thought that if they didn't get the point, it wasn't clear enough." A revised draft of the paper, published in *Science* in 1971, eliminated any ambiguities.

"We thought this meant there was something whose job it

was to block pain," Akil explains, "that electrical stimulation was not just jamming the system, screwing up a known pain pathway—it was *turning on* a natural, active pain-blocking system."

A publication in a back issue of *Scientia Sinica,* the "obscure" scientific annals of the People's Republic of China, had provided Liebeskind's group their next clue. In 1964, two Beijing biologists—Tsou and Jang—reported on new microinjection techniques which enabled them to administer minute quantities of morphine (a million times smaller than the therapeutic dose) directly to individual nerve cells. They discovered that the drug was active only on a small locus of nerve cells in the brain, and that these morphine-sensitive sites were, curiously, also located in the PAG—in exactly the same regions which later became associated with stimulation-produced analgesia. "That clinched it," Akil said. "I read that paper—it was a very good experiment—and it started me thinking, 'How far can you take the morphine analogy?' "

During the fall of 1971, she decided to investigate the narcotizing action of brain stimulation as if it *were* a narcotic, seeing if she could reverse the SPA effect with nalorphine, an "antagonist" drug known to effectively block the effects of opiates.

Akil chose the *tail-flick* test, using five rats, freshly implanted with electrodes in their PAG, to study the problem. Each rat's tail was placed over a small light bulb and usually it took about three seconds for the animal, feeling the heat, to flick its tail away. When SPA was switched on, however, it took six seconds or longer for the tail-flick: often the tests had to be terminated before the animals burnt themselves severely.

Would nalorphine stop the pain-killing effect of electrical stimulation in the same way it blocked morphine? If so, morphine- and stimulation-produced analgesia must be working on the same system of nerve cells. She injected one animal with nalorphine late one night before its brain stimulation, and found that its pain responses were no longer affected by SPA. "I thought, 'Oh, I don't believe it, it's not true,' " Akil recalls. "So I did another animal and it was the same, then another animal, and I ended up doing the whole study that evening. It was a memorable night. I was very thrilled."

Yet the implications of her evidence remained so murky in her own mind, that during a private conversation with Liebeskind a few weeks before Christmas, when he inquired if she thought her work would make sense someday, Huda Akil replied, "Yes, but certainly not in my lifetime."

In January 1972, Liebeskind went to Paris on a one-year sabbatical, leaving Akil working to complete a more extensive study with naloxone, an even purer opiate antagonist than nalorphine. He sent her final results to the journal of the French Academy of Science, *Contes Rendus,* where an article on SPA coauthored by Akil and Liebeskind had appeared just one month before Akil gave her talk in San Francisco.

In San Francisco, Hans Kosterlitz and Avram Goldstein, in their individual ways, contemplated the meaning of new information that naloxone would reverse the amazingly morphinelike effects of SPA. When the discussion period began, a hand in the first row went up. Akil did not recognize her questioner.

"How can you talk about stopping pain?" the man asked her.

"Well, you're right, I should have said 'pain response,' " she replied, thinking the problem was a matter of semantics. After all, how can you say precisely what a rat is feeling?

Again the questioner asked, "How can you talk about stopping pain?"

Flustered by this, Akil stammered out an answer. Then the questioner jumped to his feet and began to scream at her: "How can you talk about stopping pain?! Only God can stop pain!" Security guards quickly hustled the man out of the room, kicking and shouting, "Burn in Hell! Burn in Hell!" as the other participants stared in disbelieving silence. She was relieved to find her initial nervousness had disappeared when Hans Kosterlitz asked her the first real question.

Declaring her work interesting, he wondered why the effect was reversed with naloxone; afraid of saying something stupid, she gave him a general answer that the morphine antagonist and stimulation-produced analgesia must both be working on the same system of nerve cells. The idea that the electrical stimulation might be triggering the release of an opiate chemical that was being blocked by naloxone had not occurred to her, although it had, certainly, to Kosterlitz. Kosterlitz, in fact, had been discussing ways of isolating such chemicals with John Hughes only weeks earlier, when he came across the article by Akil and Liebeskind on SPA in *Contes Rendus*. According to one account, Kosterlitz expressed his concern to Hughes that, if the Liebeskind group knew their biochemistry, they would soon be giving them a run for their money.

Without making his own thoughts known, Kosterlitz grilled Akil in San Francisco to determine how much she actually knew. To his relief, he quickly realized that the UCLA researchers were not going to be their competitors—at least not right away.

Avram Goldstein also closely cross-examined Akil, and she began to feel confused. The anxious reactions of the esteemed scientists in the audience impressed her with a sense of the immediate importance of her work, work for which until then she had had only a very long-term expectation. But as they began to express excitement with what she was saying, she only registered tension: Where had she gone wrong, she wondered. What was going on in their minds?

In the bustling lab of Johns Hopkins University's Department of Pharmacology and Experimental Therapeutics in downtown Baltimore, Solomon Snyder did no hands-on lab work of his own. Instead, in his dual role as professor of pharmacology and professor of psychiatry, he depended on the "amplification effect," as he called it. He directed a staff of bright, ambitious, whiz kids like himself—who even Snyder's enemies had to admit turned out a voluminous amount of work for him—albeit work occasionally marred by "errors of commission caused by speed, slop, and carelessness," as one critic saw it.

Comic book exclamations like "whoosh," "fsssssst," and "bam" dotted Snyder's vocabulary. Along with his success, his hyperactivity was part of his mystique. Thirty-five years old, he only seemed at ease either when he was at home, playing with his two young daughters, or when he played the guitar—he was an accomplished classical musician, who had taught guitar to help meet expenses while in medical school. Otherwise, Solomon Snyder was a picture of pent-up energy: a slim, sallow man, who could not sit in a chair for two minutes without crossing and recrossing his arms and legs until they were so tightly bound around him that he looked like a coiled spring. He liked to get things done, and done fast.

Unlike Avram Goldstein, whose intelligence at times diverted him into complex problems and away from the simpler roads to discovery, Snyder's feelings were always: "Bang! Let's do something real simple, take advantage of what's going on." Snyder was not initially keen, however, about mounting an assault on the opiate receptor.

From Snyder's neuropsychiatric point of view, opiate pharmacologists were "second-class scientists" and opiates themselves held no real fascination. His bibliography of over one hundred articles was primarily devoted to the biochemical origins of mental illness and, particularly, to the messenger chemical dopamine. Because antipsychotic drugs like Thorazine had been shown to lower levels of dopamine, Snyder and many other scientists believed it to be a chemical key to schizophrenia.

He readily admits that he probably would never have decided to follow up Avram Goldstein's receptor work if not for the federal government's "war on heroin." A windfall for opiate research, the quarter-of-a-billion-dollar addiction treatment program was initiated in June 1971, in the wake of reports from Vietnam that up to 30 percent of American soldiers there had become addicted to heroin—a far higher percentage than the battlefield casualty rate.

The report heightened concern at the highest levels of government. In the U.S., the Nixon administration's ongoing but ineffective "law-and-order" approach to the drug problem gave way to waging a "war on heroin" as the President called it, and a "national offensive" was mounted to battle narcotics addiction by supporting methadone maintenance programs and funding basic research that related to narcotics addiction.

Jerome Jaffe, a prominent Chicago psychiatrist, was recruited to administer the White House Special Action Office of Drug Abuse Prevention (SAODAP) and to serve as Richard Nixon's "drug czar." Six million dollars was made available immediately, including grants of $400,000 to establish national centers for addiction research. Jaffe was a close friend of Solomon Snyder and had had long associations with both Avram Goldstein and Hans Kosterlitz. "I encouraged them all to apply," he says.

Snyder and Goldstein each received center grants of $400,000. Goldstein's grant enabled him to get his Addiction Research Foundation off the ground. A less generous but still substantial amount of the "war on heroin" money found its way into Kosterlitz's Unit for the Study of Addictive Drugs and helped to defray the costs of Hughes's work on the project there.

"I heard Avram Goldstein give a talk on receptors at Gordon Conference in 1971," Snyder recalls. "Some of the work presented there was really sophisticated. By comparison, Avram's work was primitive, but it impressed me enough so that, after Jerry Jaffe approached me, I tacked a proposal about 'opiate receptors' onto an otherwise foolproof grant application.

"It was still a far-out idea and I wasn't sure I could do anything with it, especially given Goldstein's poor results. But once the money was approved I felt obliged, at least, to think about it."

The grant was approved in the winter of 1972, and by then Solomon Snyder had Candace Pert to think about. For six months she had been working in his lab on acetylcholine, and by now she was getting bored.

When Candace Pert arrived at Johns Hopkins in the fall of 1971, she began painting rainbows everywhere. Rainbows, she believed, meant good fortune; pictures of rainbows eventually swathed her lab bench and even occasionally decorated her toes in swirls of red, yellow, black, and white polish. Though she was only twenty-four years old when she arrived, the signs were already apparent—as surely as her rainbows— that there had never been anyone quite like Candace Pert in the sciences before.

She was dark-haired, full-figured, self-assured, and flamboyant, launching herself into a world in which such uninhibited behavior was unexpected and threatening. "A real beatnik gal," Pert recalled one older male colleague bristling. Even among the close circle of ambitious youngsters led by Snyder, she radiated an unnerving amount of energy.

She had graduated with honors from Bryn Mawr, where she had studied biology and then married her psychology instructor, Agu Pert. A rugged-looking man with sheepdog blond hair and a moustache, he was a quiet contrast to his wife. He was doing research at the National Institutes of Health in Bethesda, Maryland, while she worked on her Ph.D. at Hopkins in nearby Baltimore. Their first child, Evan, was one year old.

Snyder had assigned her to the opiate receptor project in the spring of 1972, but her introduction to the subject of receptors had been Avram Goldstein's book, *Principles of Drug Action*. She had read it the summer before coming to Hopkins while recuperating from a horseback riding accident. At that time she was dosed with enough Demerol, she says, to know firsthand "what it feels like to have your opiate receptors plugged up."

Highly imaginative, Pert wondered about the science fiction possibilities of understanding the chemistry of emotions and so was breathless about working with Snyder right from the start. "Sol knew about brain chemistry; he has a labyrinthine mind," she said, and she idolized him. To the annoyance of some of her coworkers, Pert seemed to be Snyder's pet, even when she made mistakes.

In the wake of Huda Akil's exciting results with SPA during the winter of 1972, John Hughes stepped up his preparations for the brain chemical project in Aberdeen, and Avram Goldstein's lab assistants struggled to get up to speed on his endogenous opiate project. Unbeknownst to them, plans for experiments that would conclusively show that opiate receptors existed had been laid at Hopkins with the help of Pedro Cuatrecasas—Snyder's next-door neighbor on the third floor of the neurosciences building. A Mexican-born biochemist, Cuatrecasas was one of the codiscoverers in the late 1960s of insulin-binding sites, which made him one of the few scientists in the world who had actually been able to demonstrate that receptors of any kind existed. He was as close as you could come to a receptor specialist.

The key to his success was the "Multiple Manifold Machine," a simple device that Cuatrecasas had helped to build in 1968, while working at the National Institutes of Health. It consisted of a shallow steel trough attached to a vacuum pump and was covered by a lid that contained forty-five small filters, each one about the size of a quarter. A second lid—containing forty-five small reservoirs for test tissues—formed an airtight seal when placed on top of the filter lid. The machine was a study in efficiency: Cuatrecasas could test more samples in one hour than other scientists, like Avram Goldstein, could do in a day, even using the fastest centrifuges.

Cuatrecasas had been asked to discuss the application of his "rapid filtration" procedure to insulin receptors at one of the monthly Department of Pharmacology staff meetings. "That was the first discussion," he remembers. "I made my presentation and Sol asked, 'Can this be applied to opiates?' My reply was probably, 'Why not?' That winter, Candace spent six weeks in my lab learning the rapid filtration technique, and there were several troubleshooting sessions to discuss the project with Sol and Candace in the conference room, next to our lab. Sol was the driving force. He was clever. He was not putting it down on paper, but the 'opiate receptor' was just a first step. Sol had a master plan." If Cuatrecasas's technique could be applied to opiates, Snyder felt, it could be used to gain a precise understanding of where and how drugs and neurotransmitters worked, including those linked to mental illness.

The result was the Hopkins method. As it evolved between the spring and fall of 1972, this technique to locate opiate receptors was a simplified version of Goldstein's 1971 experiment: rat, mice, or guinea pig brains were homogenized—Snyder believed it was unnecessary and inefficient to begin by separating the brains into cell fractions—so whole brain soup would do nicely. Samples were placed in the reservoirs of the Multiple Manifold Machine and a radioactive opiate was washed through it, under high pressure. Candace Pert called this combination her "magic cocktail."

The first tests were run with radioactivity-labeled dihydromorphine, which was available, ready-made, from New England Nuclear, a Boston-based supply house for radioactive isotopes. As a result of improved labeling procedures, the drug was much "hotter" and therefore more easily detectable than Goldstein's radioactive levorphanol. However, for three months, throughout the summer of 1972, results were negative. Pert dealt with her daily frustrations by imaging herself "a zen archer," aspiring to that effortless state of mastery when nature would suddenly yield to her. But prolonged failure was not Solomon Snyder's style, and in August he called her to his office. "We discussed whether to drop it," he says.

Instead, they decided to try again, this time with naloxone, the powerful antagonist which counteracted morphine. Years earlier, Hans Kosterlitz had demonstrated on the guinea pig ileum that naloxone, although without narcotic effect, binds more tenaciously than do most active opiates to what Kosterlitz supposed were receptors. (This was also thought to be the reason naloxone produced its powerful effects in hospitals when tiny doses of the drug would bring overdose victims out of heroin comas almost instantaneously.) In her lab at UCLA Huda Akil was also working with naloxone.

Radioactive naloxone was custom-made for the Snyder team by New England Nuclear, and Pert tested it. Again results were negative; the technology still did not seem up to the task and this time Snyder took her off the project. "Out of compassion," Pert remembers. "He thought I would never get my Ph.D."

She was reassigned to work on acetylcholine, and in early September, reluctantly, she attended a weekend meeting on that subject. Pert spent those three days brooding about receptors instead, and by Monday she had decided to try the experiment with naloxone again. Afraid to tell Snyder what she planned to do, she "borrowed" some of the nonradioactive drug from her husband, who had been using it in animal experiments of his own, and sent it to Boston to be tagged.

September 18 fell on a Friday, and Candace Pert loaded her scintillator with filtered samples of "hot" naloxone and "brain soup" for the last time that week, and left the machine on over the weekend. Pert never completed her experiments on a Friday anyway: if the results had been negative they would have spoiled her weekend.

"Monday morning I came in and got the counts," she recalls. "As I was copying the numbers down I couldn't believe that it was working so beautifully. My friend, Ann Young, sitting at the next desk said, 'What's the matter?' And I said, 'Do you know where the nearest bar is?' And she said, 'Is it that bad, is it that awful, do you need to get drunk?' I said, 'No, I want to buy a bottle of champagne.' " The results this time were unquestionably positive: 66 percent of the radioactive opiates remained stereospecifically bound in the "brain soup" complex, clear-cut proof that opiate receptors existed. Solomon Snyder and Candace Pert had scored a dramatic scientific success.

Being able to demonstrate the presence of any receptor was a breakthrough at the time, but unlike receptors for naturally occurring chemicals like insulin and the neurotransmitters, the discovery of opiate receptors was odd and, despite the growing evidence pointing to their existence, largely unexpected, raising a host of challenging short-term and intriguing long-term questions. Subsequent follow-up experiments performed at a frantic pace with a variety of drugs in the Hopkins lab indicated that cellular soups rich in opiate receptors could be used like Kosterlitz's guinea pig ileum to predict the strength and other characteristics of narcotic drugs. The important difference was that now, for the first time, opiates could be screened directly on brain cells without using animal or human test subjects. Moreover, once the distinct molecular reactions triggering the opiate receptor were known, it might even be possible to develop drugs that would activate the opiate keyhole to produce strong pain relief but not dependence. Snyder and Pert made national news.

They submitted a paper titled "Opiate Receptor: Evidence in Nervous Tissue" to *Science* on December 1, 1972, and held a press conference on March 5, 1973, four days before the paper appeared. The White House had first been considered as the proper location to announce the discovery of the sites in the brain where morphine acted, since Jerome Jaffe—the President's drug czar—had his office there and everyone involved felt that Snyder's success would be a valuable aid in understanding addiction and developing long-lasting counteractants to narcotics. Richard Nixon, however, was mired in Watergate problems, and in the end it was decided to have the ceremony in the labs at Johns Hopkins.

Jaffe together with William Bunney, the director of the National Institutes of Health and a proponent of funding basic research on drug addiction together with Snyder, helped to organize the event. Reporters and photographers from the *Baltimore Sun,* the *Washington Post,* and *Newsweek* were invited.

Bunney made the introductions and hailed the discovery of receptors as a "major advance" which would increase the scientific understanding of brain neurochemistry and aid in the development of new treatments for heroin addicts. He went on at some length about the impact of science in the battle against addiction and then Snyder and Pert fielded questions about how they had made the discovery and what it meant. "What would happen next," Snyder told the reporters, "was anybody's guess."

Headlines the next day announced, "Effect of Heroin on Brain Discovered ... Will Aid Search for Antidote." The publicity—though resented by some of Snyder's newfound competitors—abruptly made the "second-class" opiate field very sexy.

"Sol splashed his stuff," one colleague said, "and everyone's work went whoosh!" Confirmation of the receptor site discovery was almost immediate, as was the controversy over who was to receive credit for it.

"When the Pert-Snyder paper appeared," said Eric Simon, "I tore my hair out. I'd been scooped." A professor at New York University Medical School, Simon was fifty-four in 1973—hawk-nosed, balding, a steady but usually conservative worker. In 1965 he had collaborated on a bold, but ill-fated experiment to find opiate receptors using radioactive nalorphine. He had abandoned the project "in disgust," and spent the next five years investigating the effects of opiates on *E. coli* bacteria, hoping that the one-celled animals would respond to the drugs like nerve cells in more complicated creatures.

"There were some interesting results when we tried to addict *E. coli* to morphine," he recalls. "But I wasn't terribly successful."

After reading Avram Goldstein's article on receptors, Simon had resumed his own work on the subject, and by October 1972, Simon—along with his longtime associate Joseph Hiller—was getting "reasonably good" results in his own "grind and bind" experiments using radioactive etorphine, the narcotic drug ten thousand times stronger than morphine. He had not, as yet, published his results, but by the time the Pert-Snyder paper appeared, he had already been asked to present his data at the 1973 Federated Biological Societies meeting in April, in Atlantic City.

Simon found himself sharing the platform in Atlantic City with Solomon Snyder who, in the wake of his groundbreaking announcement the previous month, had drawn a capacity crowd to the ballroom of the Hotel Dennis where the Pharmacology Society was meeting. Relations between the two men became strained for the next several years. Simon felt that he was the simultaneous discoverer of opiate receptors and deserved equal credit for it; but Snyder, in subsequent papers on the subject, when he cited Simon at all, only credited him for having obtained evidence supporting the Pert-Snyder discovery.

Avram Goldstein complained to colleagues that Snyder was a publicity hound, but some months later he called a press conference of his own in Palo Alto, to announce *his* discovery of the opiate receptor some two years earlier, citing both Snyder and Simon as supportive evidence. Still, in private he was forced to concede "we are behind in the race."

The real prize of the race, however, was only now becoming apparent to all. Opiate receptors actually did exist—and not just in the brains of rodents. Further experimentation by the Snyder and Simon groups demonstrated the presence of opiate receptors in all vertebrates, from the primitive hagfish to human beings.

But what was their real purpose, what was their function in the body? The conclusion Kosterlitz had reached ten years earlier and kept secret was now being echoed in public by Avram Goldstein, who was lecturing about the "bizarre coincidence" that receptors should exist in animal and human nervous systems to receive the juice of the opium poppy. Solomon Snyder hinted to reporters at his press conference that the next step was to determine the "normal" function of opiate receptors, because "nature did not put opiate receptors in the body solely to interact with narcotics."

Clearly, some substance *already in the body* could produce the same effects and had the same chemical "key" as morphine to the relief of pain. There had to be such an endogenous chemical triggering these opiate receptor systems, as another researcher put it, "unless nature was insane." What was it, where was it, and what was it made of?

SUBSTANCE X

As the Americans haggled over credit for the discovery of opiate receptors during the spring of 1973, work in Aberdeen was proceeding at a business-as-usual pace. While Hans Kosterlitz directed an attempt to apply the techniques used to identify receptors by the Americans to his work on the guinea pig ileum, John Hughes was conducting preliminary experiments using various solvents on the brains of guinea pigs, trying to work out an extraction procedure that could upscale his search for the brain-produced opiate. Unperturbed by the news from abroad, Hughes shrugged off Avram Goldstein's stab at finding such a chemical with morphine antibodies as "too logical" and the Pert-Snyder demonstration of opiate receptors as a mere "technical advancement." Hughes was also in the middle of packing up his books and equipment preparatory to moving from the pharmacology department to the gothic surroundings of Marishal College, where Kosterlitz was setting up his Unit for the Study of Addictive Drugs. Soon Hughes would have the time and space necessary to begin his work in earnest.

As he waited for the labs to be installed, he enjoyed what

was to be some last relatively normal family time. Spring for Mandy and him meant getting their garden into shape. After the long winter, they both relished being able to muck around in the "blanket-sized" plot they planted behind their small house—when they were not arguing over the best way to make compost heaps. Hughes was much the same at home as he was in the lab, "like a blunt instrument," Mandy recalls. Their marriage was contentious, though their arguments usually ended in laughter.

As the weather got warmer, Hughes also dabbled in painting. He was a terrible painter, but there were certain things Hughes did badly yet simply savored doing. Golf was another: his aspirations far outstripped his abilities, although he played with a stalwart fanaticism. His strange splay-footed stance and awkward preparatory waggle were always good for a laugh at the Kirkgate Bar—when Hughes was not there. Dancing was still another: the fact that he had two left feet did not stop him any more than the fact that he was tone deaf deterred him from trying to sing. On family car trips later that summer he repeatedly roared a rendition of "Nine Green Bottles," vastly entertaining his little daughter Katherine, the only person in the world who could appreciate his performance.

Hughes was almost as much of an amateur when it came to the task of isolating and identifying chemical substances in brain tissue, relying mainly on gumption and dedication to complete a job that would have intimidated even the most experienced lab hands. His work on the brain chemical project, however, was one endeavor in which John Hughes would never settle for anything less than perfection.

The experimental design which had emerged after months of head-knocking sessions between Hughes and Kosterlitz was in the end a simple strategy. If a brain-produced opiate did exist, it had to satisfy two criteria: It had to depress twitches either in the guinea pig ileum (or in another tissue which Hughes had discovered reacted to morphine the same way— the vas deferens of the mouse, that tiny duct which in all male mammals carries spermatic fluid from the testicles to the sperm sac). The second crucial test was that the compound's effects must be reversed by a morphine antagonist—a drug that would block opiate effects—in this case, naloxone. Other organic compounds might depress the ileum or the vas, but only an opiate would also have naloxone-reversible effects.

That August, John Hughes had begun working on a small scale with the organic solvent Acetone to extract material from guinea pig brains that would be active on the vas deferens. He had stored a number of unsuccessful samples from these early experiments in his refrigerator. Near the end of October, Helen Anderson, his assistant, was cleaning out the fridge and before she threw out the frozen guinea pig extracts, Hughes rechecked them. A couple of the bottles that had been negative before this time produced a small but positive result.

Hughes rushed into the big lab shouting at Graeme Henderson, "Come and see this! Come and see this!" Then he rounded up Hans Kosterlitz, and they all stood on top of the pile of electric wires in the small lab and watched the vas deferens twitch and gurgle over the hum and scratch of a recording machine that printed out a graph of its activity.

Slowly, John Hughes added a few drops of his guinea pig brain extract to the bath. The twitching subsided. He added a few more drops and the twitching stopped altogether. Then he added naloxone, and the twitch came back, weakly—but it still could be seen as a small set of peaks on the graph. "It was next to nothing," Henderson recalls, "but John was tremendously excited."

Hughes later attributed the magical reaction to the refrigerator, which had acted as a preliminary purification step. Compounds that ordinarily masked the effect he sought had degraded during storage, while the active substance he was after remained stable.

After the Pert-Snyder success, Kosterlitz turned most of his efforts to receptors, but in his spare time he had been making hypothetical predictions as to what the size, charge, and composition of a brain-produced opiate just might be. At the same time, he remained openly doubtful that Hughes would actually be able to decipher the compound's actual structure, even if he did find it.

In fact, a few weeks after the Unit opened, Kosterlitz told Graeme Henderson, "I hope John doesn't get too caught up in this. There are more important things to do." The miracle of the deep freeze had really not changed his opinion; Kosterlitz's natural response was always one of extreme suspicion.

Contamination was one constant concern. From the inception of his research, Kosterlitz had been deluged with narcotics, which he kept safely stored in a large black Milner's fire-resistant safe in his office. But there were a dozen different varieties of sample opiate drugs in use on the third floor on any given day and a one-part-per-millionth trace of morphine on Hughes's equipment (or in the Acetone) could throw his results completely off. That fall Hughes started taking the precaution of wearing surgical gloves when he worked, and the word went out in the Unit, "No narcotics in John's lab." Indeed, it would have been a disaster if the compound which Hughes now called Naloxone Reversible Activity (NRA) and which his coworkers dubbed "Substance X"—turned out to be nothing more than some fancy narcotic from Kosterlitz's safe.

Hughes, too, could not help but be aware of the potential difficulties that still lay ahead. That night when Hughes got his first positive results there were no toasts made at the KGB. "There was no glory in that it was only a start," Hughes says. "It might have been an observation on the road to mediocrity."

That same fall, Hughes's slaughterhouse days began, and before long he was able to duplicate the same weak activity with pig brains that he had stumbled across with guinea pig brains. Stubbornly, he clung to the belief that the chemical he was after was there, in his waxy, yellow, crude fraction, somewhere. But Substance X showed only a partial naloxone reverse, hardly constituting a scientific proof, let alone the sort of precise chemical profile which would be required to achieve any future clinical promise from his work. Hughes needed to purify the active essence of Substance X, so he began the complex, frustrating process of panning for scientific gold.

As winter approached, space in the big lab which John Hughes shared with Graeme Henderson and Frances Leslie began to take on a decidedly more high-tech appearance than it had during the earlier "bangs-and-stinks" stage of Hughes's operation. A series of different-sized glass columns—ranging from three centimeters to over a meter in height—crowded his lab bench, surrounded by piles of instruction manuals. Everything was labeled with John Hughes's name.

The taller columns were filled with Sephadex polymer granules, a sandy substance that when swollen with water, formed overnight a slurry gray goo consisting of billions of tiny granules—each approximately the same size. In the late 1950s, a Swedish scientist named Jerker Porath had discovered that these granules could be used as a "molecular sieve" that would separate out mixtures of unknown chemicals. Heavier molecules forced their way through and around the tiny granules, while lighter ones were either trapped in the spaces between the granules, or moved down through the goo more slowly.

As Hughes dripped Substance X through the Sephadex column, the fluid emerging from the bottom was collected by a moving rack of test tubes with the heaviest molecules collected first. Samples were then carried back to the small lab and each tested on the vas. Only a few of them worked at all.

Kosterlitz had predicted that since morphine was a small molecule, the essential ingredient of Substance X would be too and Sephadex filtration confirmed this suspicion. Given the size of the Sephadex granules Hughes was using, and the arrival time of the active fractions at the bottom of the columns, Hughes guessed that what he was looking at had a low molecular weight (750 daltons or less), but his finding was far from conclusive; all known neurotransmitters had similar weights. It would require another step to narrow down the possibilities.

Hughes began using smaller, Amberlite ion-exchange columns, filled with specially prepared resins to separate his crude extract more finely, according to the electrical charges of its chemical components. A movable rack of test tubes collected samples from these columns as well and, during the next several weeks, as Hughes tested them on the vas, he was able to add an important dimension to the emerging profile: Substance X ions had a smaller negative charge than any of the known neurotransmitters and more importantly, smaller than any pharmaceutical opiates.

After six anxious weeks, Hughes and Kosterlitz felt assured that Substance X was not a contaminant; still, Hughes could not be totally certain that its activity was a biological fact. A very real possibility persisted that the results he was seeing were caused by a substance not "naturally" present in brain tissue, an artifact, resulting from a chemical breakdown in the brain after death, or a reaction in combination with the Acetone that Hughes was using—in other words, a fluke.

This next phase of the project became, like most scientific work, tedious, exacting and dull; but by December, Hughes felt he was getting closer to pure Substance X. Unfortunately, after a typical Sephadex or ion-exchange run, half of his precious material was lost in the high-tech apparatus. The following days—which grew darker, colder, and more miserable—again found him grimly bicycling through the weather to the "killin' house," pulverizing brains in the basement again, and trying not to listen to the voice, nagging in the back of his head, "You're dealing with an artifact, John. What are you doing?"

It was during this tenuous first flush of success that Hans Kosterlitz committed a series of unusual and, to Hughes, almost unforgivable indiscretions. He began with Solomon Snyder. The newcomer to the opiate field had asked the veteran Kosterlitz to help plan the program of a conference Snyder was organizing the coming May 1974, in Boston. Unaware of what was happening in Aberdeen, Snyder had conceived of the meeting as a showcase for work by the Hopkins group on the subject of the opiate receptor. Kosterlitz, however, had decided—without consulting Hughes—to ask Snyder to include the Substance X findings on the Boston program. Although he was extremely reticent about unproven theories, once a discovery was made Kosterlitz was not in the least inclined to be wary of potential rivals. In his opinion attempts to conceal new information were "silly and stupid."

The two men had never met before Kosterlitz and Hanna spent several days with the Snyders in Baltimore that December. For all his nervous energy, Snyder was struck by the vigor of the much older man who, he marveled, "flew without jet lag and seemed to have no interest in rest." In a convivial mood on the evening of their arrival—as he often did with visitors—Snyder served sweet drinks which, he boasted, "taste as if there's no alcohol in them." Kosterlitz, mercifully, had brought along his own bottle of unblended Glenmorangie.

Neither man remembers the exact moment when Kosterlitz told Snyder about the project but several times during his stay he intimated to Snyder that it was a "new area," and that his young fellow—John Hughes—was getting some interesting results. "We have a compound under strict discretion," he told

Snyder at one point, as Snyder, listening quizzically, filed the information away for later use. Snyder impressed Hanna as "an understanding man, a psychiatrist," and she never quite forgave him later for trying, in her view, to "pinch" the discovery.

Upon his return to Aberdeen, Kosterlitz told John Hughes about the upcoming conference, but at first Hughes was reluctant to attend. He felt it would be a mistake to participate before the results were more definitive, given the reputation of some of the American labs. But Kosterlitz would not keep quiet.

A second leak about the Aberdeen findings came three months later in March 1974 at a tropical paradise called the Hacienda de Cocoyoc, an expensive resort built on a seventeenth-century sugar cane estate about fifty miles south of Mexico City. The occasion was the fifth meeting of the International Narcotics Research Club, a group of serious opiate researchers, which Kosterlitz, together with his friend Harry Collier, research chief of the Parke-Davis Pharmaceutical Company in London, had been instrumental in founding.

The Club's first unofficial meeting, in 1969, in Basel, had been attended by a dozen scientists who had arrived for the annual International Pharmacology Congress. That initial meeting of the Club was recollected by Collier as the "Conference of the Cigar." A carefully budgeted luncheon for the twelve speakers at the Hotel Euler, Basel's only four-star restaurant, had been paid for by Collier's British employers. After lunch, the hotel management had sent around brandy and cigars which nearly everyone, naturally, helped themselves to, thinking them part of the menu. These refreshments, however, had not been ordered by Kosterlitz and Collier, who had to foot the extra bill—hence Collier's ironic title.

Cigars notwithstanding, no new discoveries were announced, and it was not until the group's second meeting two years later, in Aberdeen in 1971, that Goldstein's receptor experiment provided the first signal of important developments to come. Goldstein himself coined the Club's name the following year, in San Francisco, during the same Pharmacology Congress at which Huda Akil announced her results with SPA. Goldstein wanted to lend an "informal formality" to the small contingent of opiate scientists who comprised the International Narcotics Research Club's rather exclusive membership. He also elected himself as the Club's first secretary and drew up a set of bylaws, which he promptly lost on a bus.

When the group met at Research Triangle Park, North Carolina, in 1973, the membership had grown to fifty, and had doubled again by 1974, when the conference in Cocoyoc opened in March. John Hughes remained behind, working in Aberdeen, but Kosterlitz, along with almost a hundred other Club members, was present.

The Mexican meeting was plagued by the usual annoying catastrophes that beset large meetings. Electrical failure blacked out several of the sessions and the Hacienda's management demanded payment for bills which many Club members had settled in advance. Several of them ended up paying twice.

Sydney Archer, the portly Associate Director of Research at the Sterling Drug company in Rensselaer, New York, was pleased to find nine different restaurants to choose from in Cocoyoc. Archer had befriended Kosterlitz at the Conference of the Cigar; they both fancied themselves gourmets and they had been tablemates at all the meetings since.

Archer held over one hundred patents, but his reputation rested principally on one: 2-dimethyl-allyl-5, 9-dimethyl-12-hydroxy-6, 7-benzomorphan—which, Archer joked, "even I can't pronounce." The drug's generic name was pentazocine: its tradename was Talwin, and it had been touted in the late 1960s as the long-sought "bee without a sting." Sterling, which also manufactured Bayer aspirin, had hailed Talwin as a "nonnarcotic" analgesic—until it was found that drug addicts were using it as a heroin substitute, and that it produced hallucinatory side effects.

Archer was expecting no surprises from the meeting—which centered on opiate receptors—until after lunch on the second day, Kosterlitz, swearing Archer to secrecy, confided to him that John Hughes had found an opiate substance in pig brains that not only worked but was naloxone-reversible. "Who else have you told?" was Archer's choked response to the news.

Kosterlitz told David Mayer next. Mayer, since collaborating on the original stimulation-produced analgesia experiments with Huda Akil and John Liebeskind at UCLA, had moved to the Medical College of Virginia, where he was now working with Donald Price, Amir Rafi, and a group of intrepid students willing to undergo "experimental pain" in the interests of science. By applying an electrical charge to their teeth, Mayer was able to establish a pain threshold for each of his human test subjects.

Rafi, an anesthesiologist who was also a trained acupuncturist, then twirled acupuncture needles into what is called the *Hoko point*—located between the thumb and forefinger—where, according to the traditional Chinese medical practice, tooth pain is controlled. Mayer again measured the students' pain thresholds. In almost every case, response to his electrical torture device was quelled. When he injected his subjects with naloxone, their pain returned consistently. During his talk at the conference, Mayer made several suggestions closing in on the idea that endogenous opiates must somehow be involved in the pain-deadening effects of acupuncture.

At the conclusion of his talk, another power failure blacked out the lights in the auditorium. "After they came back on," Mayer recalls, "Kosterlitz came over and said, 'You can't tell anybody, but we've found an opiatelike material!' "

Then, as the final session drew to a close and the participants, half brain-dead from the tropical sun and the previous night's room parties, struggled to concentrate on the discussion that followed the last paper, Kosterlitz calmly took the microphone and announced the discovery of Substance X to one and all. It was his *pièce de résistance.*

"He got up quietly," Avram Goldstein remembers. "He said, 'I would like to make an announcement. I have something interesting to tell you. John Hughes has stayed in Aberdeen because we have preliminary evidence of a natural substance from pig brains that has morphinelike activities on the mouse vas deferens and I don't want to say anything more.' "

Sydney Archer could not believe that Kosterlitz was giving the game away. "What are you doing?" he questioned him in private. Kosterlitz smiled at Archer's dismay, but when John Hughes found out about it, he was not amused.

Hughes was more prone to paranoia than Kosterlitz—he was, after all, staking his whole reputation on the Substance X project—and his fears were partly justified by the hard realities of competition against Americans. The abundant resources and equipment at the disposal of the Goldstein and Snyder labs—or those of any U.S. drug company—would make it easy to duplicate and even eclipse Hughes's discovery, once they found out about it.

American and British styles of science were also markedly different. British research grants were smaller, though longer-term, and ideas there tended to be nurtured over the years, like fine wine. Kosterlitz's guinea pig ileum research was just the sort of meticulous, low-budget, ongoing project that was the typical delight of British science—original and, to the enlightened, brilliant. Had it not been successful, it would still not have mattered that much, for the scientific community in the U.K. was a cozy, supportive clan; all the important people knew each other, and a seemingly eccentric passion, like

Kosterlitz's work with the ileum, was not just tolerated, but encouraged.

There was nothing cozy about the Americans; even the best of scientific friends in the States might become fiercely competitive antagonists. It was part of the way of life; while plentiful, grants were short-term—usually two years. Researchers were therefore compelled to produce results or see their money whisked away. Publish or perish. No tolerance of failure, no safety net. Big Science, Big Money.

Given the situation, Hughes was furious about the Cocoyoc announcement. It was a very bad thing to have done; it was giving something away. "Kosterlitz," he felt like saying, "you silly old bugger . . ."

After Kosterlitz's announcement, Hughes became more guarded and possessive of the work. At times, Kosterlitz might be in the dark about the details of the project, but if Hughes could help it, there would be no more Cocoyocs.

By March 1974, Hughes had eighty-one micrograms of Substance X purified to a powdery white solid—barely enough to see in a test tube and not nearly enough to begin the extensive experiments needed to determine its amino acid formula. The only consolation was Hughes's knowledge that they were still alone, out in front of the pack—or so he and Kosterlitz thought.

It was Lars Terenius's work on opiate receptor sites that had first brought him to Hans Kosterlitz's attention. An original proof of the existence of opiate receptors from Terenius's own "grind and bind" experiment had been submitted to the "Letters" section of a Scandinavian journal on November 6, 1972, about a month before the Pert-Snyder paper arrived at the offices of *Science*.

Technically, he was the first to establish the existence of opiate receptors—although his results, which appeared six months later than the Hopkins group's, were neither as persuasive nor as fully documented. Terenius had also made a pioneering search to find binding sites for estrogen, the female sex hormone that causes ovulation.

Frances Leslie, Kosterlitz's postdoc, was having trouble duplicating the Pert-Snyder procedure, and so Kosterlitz had invited Terenius—geographically the closest of the successful "binders"—to come to Aberdeen and demonstrate his receptor analysis techniques. Terenius, conveniently, was on sabbatical in London throughout the winter of 1974 when the invitation arrived and he traveled up to Aberdeen for what was to become a two-month detour.

At thirty-two, Terenius was already a full professor of pharmacology at the University of Uppsala—a remarkable feat in the Swedish academic community, where such prestigious positions are few in number and highly sought after. He was a handsome man with deep-set dark eyes, whose most striking physical feature was his prematurely gray, almost white hair. Quietly sensitive, he impressed John Hughes when he arrived in Aberdeen near the end of April as "a real northern European depressive," but he was Kosterlitz's idea of a gentleman.

In a small lab a few doors down the hall from Hughes, Terenius began setting up a "receptor binding" experiment. The sight of Hughes going about the messy, smelly business of extracting pig brains "in the back corners of the lab," was one of Terenius's first recollections of the Unit, but he was not told anything about the nature of Hughes's extraordinary activities. Hughes, in turn, knew nothing about Terenius but, learning of his arrival, he had warned Graeme Henderson and the others in the lab, "Don't say anything. Keep it quiet."

Terenius, meanwhile, had his own reasons for reticence. For almost six months, together with his assistant, Agneta Wahlström, in Uppsala, Lars Terenius had been trying to isolate an endogenous opiate from the brains of rats. His methods were essentially similar to those Hughes was employing—except that they were testing their extracts directly on rat brain concentrate, rich in opiate receptors, rather than on the ileum or the vas. By the time Terenius arrived in Aberdeen, he and Wahlström had extracted two crude opiatelike substances which they were calling "Fraction A" and "Fraction B." "Fraction A" appeared to be a low molecular weight compound. "Fraction B" was too complex to profile in any detail but, like "Fraction A," competed for receptor sites with radioactive opiates; and the action of both could be reversed by naloxone. Terenius hoped to be able to check his results using Kosterlitz's guinea pig ileum technique.

Two weeks after his arrival, Terenius and Kosterlitz drove from Marishal College to the Foresterhill Hospital on the outskirts of the city where the university's only scintillator was housed. Driving with Kosterlitz being the adventure it always was, Terenius found himself anxiously watching the road. It was one of the first warm days of the year, the sun was shining and the granite of Aberdeen's buildings sparkled.

The warmer weather drew Terenius out of his winter funk and he began to explain to Kosterlitz his reasons for wanting to learn the guinea pig ileum assay. As he started to describe his two morphinelike fractions, the car suddenly jolted forward and Kosterlitz whirled toward him, struck uncharacteristically silent.

"Well," Kosterlitz announced slowly, "we are also working on this. . . ."

Later that afternoon, Terenius told John Hughes about his findings and, for the next several days, an uncomfortable distance separated Kosterlitz and Hughes from their Swedish guest. "It seemed like we couldn't discuss it," Terenius remembers, "that we had to keep the door closed."

"At first I was reluctant to tell him anything," Hughes says, "but over the following days we began cautiously feeling each other out, exchanging tidbits in the corridor, and that quickly led to a general sharing of information."

Hughes and Terenius were in basic agreement on the mystery substance's sketchy profile, but Terenius did introduce one important new piece of information. Hughes had speculated that the superstructure of Substance X was formed out of a ring of carbon atoms similar in shape to morphine. Terenius, however, was convinced that the compound was a peptide—a short chain of amino acids.

If Terenius was right, then peptidases, a group of digestive enzymes that break down proteins and peptides, would break down Substance X, too, causing it to lose its ability to quell the vas deferens twitches. When the theory was tested, Terenius explains, "the enzymes killed the activity," and that was strong although not incontrovertible evidence that Substance X was a peptide—even to John Hughes.

Kosterlitz, meanwhile, had begun drawing theoretical models of the structure of Substance X on the blackboard in his office, like a scientific locksmith trying to fashion a key out of some combination of amino acids and other organic chemicals which would fit into the receptor's "keyhole." His chalk work was interrupted in late May, however, when all three scientists—Kosterlitz, Hughes, and Terenius—went to Boston to report on their results.

Many of the scientists attending the Boston Neurosciences Research Program in May, 1974, had heard Kosterlitz's unexpected announcement at Cocoyoc and were excitedly awaiting Hughes's findings. Terenius, too, had prepared a paper on endogenous opiates, but prior to leaving Aberdeen, Kosterlitz had asked Terenius to wait with his results until after Hughes made his presentation. Terenius, out of respect for Kosterlitz— almost forty years his senior—quickly consented to take a back seat and "to be a commentator" on the Aberdeen research.

The site of the conference was an estate used as a retreat center by the Massachusetts Institute of Technology and located in the Boston suburb of Jamaica Plains. The ivy-covered mansion reminded Hughes of an "ambassador's house," surrounded by elegantly manicured lawns, dense woods and well-kept gardens. He noted with pleasure that the rhododendrons and azaleas were blooming.

Avram Goldstein, Candace Pert, Huda Akil, and David Mayer were all in attendance. The meeting's organizer, Solomon Snyder, treated the Aberdonians to dinner one night, after which he accidentally put his car into reverse, slamming it into one of the restaurant's walls. It was the sort of driving performance that made Hughes and Kosterlitz both feel right at home.

Kosterlitz was a familiar figure to most of the scientists present. John Hughes was a virtual unknown, but with the word out about his discovery, Hughes found himself pressured at the first morning session by strangers eager for hints about what he was going to say in his talk the next day. He refused any comment; expressions of interest were "antipathetic" to his nature, he said. He thought the Americans, in particular, too fulsome in their new relationships. He did not mind that one was immediately on a first name basis with them, but the accompanying pretense of instant, intimate friendship galled him.

Hughes was only attending the conference because he felt he had no choice. "I was on my guard . . . ," Hughes recalls, "suspicious. It was folly to go public with the discovery in Cocoyoc and I felt foolish to be elaborating on my findings, even sketchily, in Boston. Frankly, I would have preferred it if there had been no meeting at all. But once I was committed to give the talk I had to do it." Backing out after Kosterlitz had announced the results would have looked even more foolish, implying that the Aberdeen scientists were withdrawing the result.

The fact that Hughes knew that Solomon Snyder would be in charge of writing up the reports—the proceedings of Neuroscience Research Program meetings were *always* edited by the organizer—did nothing to allay his fears. He had an "uneasy feeling" about the whole affair.

The first day of the conference, in keeping with Snyder's original aim, was devoted to papers by, among others, Avram Goldstein, Eric Simon, and Lars Terenius on the subject of opiate receptors. "Maps" were the chief area of new progress covered in the day's discussion. With Michael Kuhar, another Snyder researcher, Candace Pert had developed a sophisticated new technique called autoradiography. Clusters of receptors, tagged with radioactive opiates and enlarged microscopically, would show up as grains of light on specially treated photographic film enabling researchers to see precisely where opiate receptors were located in brain tissues. It was a marvelous development. Here was graphic proof that the receptors were distributed in the areas of the brain that researchers had previously identified as "pain pathways," the same systems of nerve cells carrying and acting on pain messages as Huda Akil and the Liebeskind group had implicated in stimulation-produced analgesia.

Equally exciting was Pert's observation that high densities of opiate receptors were also found in the limbic system—the part of the brain where emotions like pleasure and anger were thought to be mediated as well as along nerve pathways associated with the transmitter dopamine, which had been implicated in schizophrenia.

It was fascinating data, but John Hughes was unquestionably the star of the show. As he introduced his talk during the second day's session, his offhand remark that he would be "adding to the confusion" by announcing the discovery of "morphinelike" transmitters in the nervous system drew an ironic laugh from almost everyone present, except Avram Goldstein. Even Kosterlitz noticed Goldstein's "shocked expression." Hadn't Goldstein believed him in Cocoyoc?

Hughes's talk was brief and purposely hazy. He outlined his reasons for believing that the morphine receptor did not exist by chance but interacted with a naturally occurring "morphinelike" compound, citing as supporting evidence the demonstration of opiate receptors in nervous tissue and the reversal of the effects of stimulation-produced analgesia by the morphine antagonist naloxone. Exhibiting as proof a slide of a recording of vas deferens activity, showing the powerful narcotic effect of his pig-brain substance and the reverse effect of a small dose of naloxone, he described his Acetone extraction procedure and subsequent attempts using a glass column filtration, to purify the compound. The evidence, he stressed, ruled out contamination—the extract was quite unlike any known narcotic, possibly a peptide, with an apparent molecular weight of between 300 and 700 daltons.

Goldstein interrupted twice with questions, but Hughes would not elaborate on the details of his extraction technique. He felt that no one on the American side would be prepared to give anything like that away.

Some years later, Huda Akil described Hughes's Boston announcement of the discovery of an endogenous opiate in terms of wonder. "I think it is very rare," she said, "that a scientist is privileged to watch the birth of a new era in his or her field. It was something like waiting for the sun to come out and—all of a sudden it does. It had that feeling about it. We knew it was there, we knew it was important but nobody could quite get hold of it and then, all of a sudden, there it was in your lap and I remember thinking I'm never going to forget these days, because I may never live through anything like that again."

During the formal and informal discussions following the announcement, David Mayer toyed aloud with the idea that Hughes's Substance X might be released during SPA and speculated that Chinese acupuncture might work the same way. "This new knowledge," he wrote in the conference proceedings, "may help to elucidate the neuroanatomical and physiological correlates of pain, thus providing new ways to relieve it."

Finding new ways to relieve pain was one obvious and exciting prospect and Candace Pert's "mapping" studies had raised the equally interesting possibility that Substance X might have effects on the emotional pain of mental illness as well.

There was, however, a less idealistic aspect to the Boston meeting—at least for the Aberdonians.

After John Hughes told everyone about the compound—a "dumb move" in Pert's view—competition became a real threat. "We knew what we had," Hughes says, "but we hadn't purified it completely yet, and—this is the problem in science; it's a pretty cutthroat business, like any other business. An awful lot of people got interested."

The situation was further complicated by the fact that John Hughes had not as yet laid official claim to his findings by writing a paper, and when he did so in the summer following that Boston conference, his article was rejected by the scientific journal *Brain Research*.

It was returned to Hughes with a fourteen-page, anonymous referee's report that began by deriding the conceptual soundness of this proposed Substance X from an evolutionary standpoint. The readers implied that pain was necessary, even good—so why should nature provide a built-in mechanism to relieve it? The critique went on to drub many of Hughes's methods and procedures. Rumors spread through the lab that Avram Goldstein (who, as it turned out, had nothing to do with the referee's report) was trying to sabotage its publication in order to get something of his own into print first. Satisfying the objections of *Brain Research* would delay Hughes's paper for months.

And during that time, credit for the discovery of Substance X was up for grabs.

Lars Terenius was the first potential rival to make his

intentions known. "I don't want to compete," he insisted emotionally to Hughes, a few weeks after the Boston meeting. Nor did he want to collaborate on the formidable task of determining the composition of Substance X. "I didn't want to go into the chemistry of it," Terenius would later say. "I was more interested in what it would do." In the months that followed, he switched his efforts in Uppsala to investigating the possible functions of the endogenous opiate which he believed could be studied in the body—without knowing precisely what it was made of. However, the responses of the American labs more than justified Hughes's fearful expectations.

It was only a matter of days, following the announcement in Boston, before Gavril Pasternak, a graduate student in Solomon Snyder's lab, was assigned to a brain-chemical project. Twenty-six years old, a stout man with a wispy moustache, Pasternak was a graduate of Johns Hopkins Medical School. He had been working with Snyder since 1969 and had been assigned to the opiate receptor project after Candace Pert's success with it the year before. Pasternak resented the impression that he was "Candace Pert's grad student," and a sibling rivalry quickly developed between the slow, methodical Pasternak and his flamboyant coworker. Snyder frequently found himself mediating the wars of silence between the two and hoped the new assignment would placate Pasternak.

Before the Boston meeting, Pasternak had been experimenting in an open-ended fashion with various enzymes, to see if they would break receptors down into their individual chemical components. It was his sort of "meticulous, possibly useless" project. After several painstaking months, he had reached the interesting conclusion that opiates activate more than one site on receptors, and might even trigger different activities. He called them "high- and low-affinity binding sites."

During his enzyme studies, Pasternak had also obtained

some circumstantial evidence of the existence of an endogenous opiate, so later, after Boston, he felt justified in thinking
that Substance X was not the exclusive property of Hughes
and Kosterlitz.

The week following Hughes's announcement, Pasternak
recalls, he met with Snyder, his enzyme work was shelved,
and he was assigned to the isolation project. Candace Pert
remembers Snyder telling people in the lab after the Boston
meeting, "Now we've really got to get them," but according
to Pasternak's account, the race with the Aberdonians got off
to a very slow start. For months after the Boston meeting,
Snyder left him alone to plod his way through the work as
best he could.

"Snyder was never a screamer, always very low-key,"
Pasternak recalls. "But if something did not work, you did not
talk to Sol. He was a master at manipulating silence. If you
didn't have results, there was nothing to talk about and since
talking with Sol was the best thing, you tried to get results."
Pasternak, at times, felt like a forgotten man. Snyder seemed
content to be simply in the running on the road to discovering
endogenous opiates.

The reason had mainly to do with Snyder's neuropsychiatric
research priorities. Using the same rapid filtration method her
friend Candace Pert had used on opiate receptors, Ann Young
was close to identifying receptors for the transmitter dopamine, an important breakthrough in the study of mental illness
since dopamine receptors were also binding sites for drugs like
Thorazine and Haldol that were being widely and successfully
used to treat schizophrenic patients. "Dopamine was much
more Sol's thing than opiates," Pasternak claims. "Dopamine
was Sol's first love, the plum, because it was supposed to be a
key to schizophrenia. So he didn't push me for a long time."

Pasternak started his extraction procedures on calves'
brains obtained a few at a time from the nearby staff slaughterhouse. Clues that Hughes had provided at the Boston meet-

ing as to the size and characteristics of Substance X allowed Pasternak to employ a simplified method of obtaining an endogenous opiate identical with Hughes's, which he eventually started calling a morphinelike factor: MLF. He simply boiled the calves' brains, causing the large proteins to disintegrate, then spun the remaining fluid in an ultracentrifuge to precipitate out intermediate-sized proteins. The remaining clear fluid contained only compounds of the same low molecular weight as Substance X.

He dried the liquid to a white powder and tested it, using Candace Pert's techniques to see if it would compete with radioactive opiates for receptors in concentrations of receptor-rich brain tissue. Receptor binding, the Hopkins specialty, did display a degree of originality, but it was not as immediate a way of checking opiate activity as Hughes's vas deferens technique.

In late July Pasternak finally obtained a fraction that worked, and spent the rest of the summer involved in mapping studies to see if MLF paralleled the receptors in the brains of various animals. He found that the "maps" overlapped so precisely that there could be no doubt that he, and all the other scientists working on the problem, were not dealing with isolated, if interesting, chemical entities: there was a *system* of opiatelike chemicals and opiate receptors in the body.

Pasternak started spending late nights in the lab, running columns and trying to step up the pace of his work. By Christmas 1974, he had made little progress toward getting the MLF into a pure state. "I was not a biochemist and didn't go about things very well," Pasternak admits. The results were positive, but not nearly good enough to begin to decipher its formula.

In Palo Alto, plans to set up Avram Goldstein's Addiction Research Foundation were close to complete by the time Hughes had made his announcement. Goldstein had raised

$500,000 from the Drug Abuse Council and an additional $400,000 grant from the federal government's Special Action Office of Drug Abuse Prevention. Plans to locate the Foundation on the Stanford Medical School campus had fallen through, and by that spring Goldstein was haggling for the use of a building off campus on Welch Road, where a methadone clinic was already in operation.

Brian Cox, a transplanted Londoner with a Van Dyke beard who had been working with Goldstein for a year and a half, was offered the job as the Foundation's lab director. When Hughes announced his discovery, Cox recounts, the "main thrust" in the lab involved a project which Goldstein quickly came to consider a "bad choice."

After his initial work on receptors in 1971, Goldstein had decided that the best way to amplify the receptor's signal and eliminate "background noise" would be to purify the material responsible for "stereospecific" binding—the SSB, as he called it—and he pressed his lab workers into service on the astonishing task of trying to chemically amputate naked receptors— the actual pieces of protein responsible for binding—from the brain cells.

Cox and Rudy Schultz, visiting from the Max Plank Institute in Germany, were, Cox remembers, "getting nowhere very fast on the problem," while Schultz's wife, Karin, continued the work begun in 1972 of identifying an endogenous opiate, using antibodies. "We were dabbling," said Cox, "but after Cocoyoc, that began to change." Goldstein had lost the race to the receptor, a race he helped initiate and consolidate with his doctrine of stereospecificity, and he did not like to lose.

He had returned from Cocoyoc angry with Kosterlitz for not giving him more details, but even angrier with himself for falling behind. He was surprised at how good Hughes's ideas on the endogenous opiate had looked to him at the Boston meeting.

Kent Orphein, a researcher in Goldstein's lab, had been doing bioassays on the guinea pig ileum. After Boston, Goldstein switched Orphein's assignment. Extraction of an endogenous opiate from brains was too cumbersome a process, Goldstein felt, so he instructed Orphein to look for opiate activity in existing peptides and brain extracts, particularly those from the pituitary gland. This pea-sized organ located in the brain just above the roof of the mouth controls so many vital bodily functions—respiration, heart beat, growth and reproductive behavior, to name a few—that it is commonly called the body's "master gland." In the eyes of a fellow researcher, it was "typical of Avram" to look in the pituitary gland, "just to be contrary," but Goldstein reasoned that even if Hughes and Kosterlitz identified their compound first, his group might find something similar in a different brain region. Orphein began the slow job of screening the first of thousands of crude extracts.

In October 1974, in a two-story building surrounded by shrubbery and eucalyptus trees on Welch Road, near the Stanford Medical Center, the Addiction Research Foundation opened. At Goldstein's whimsical suggestion the basement laboratories had been built without doors to promote the free exchange of information, and each was painted a color of the visible spectrum and numbered according to its color's wavelength. Burdened by his new set of administrative responsibilities, Goldstein frequently was absent, logging flying time in an effort to raise the additional funds necessary to keep his foundation afloat. In his absence, Brian Cox was left to oversee the various research fronts; Kent Orphein had, so far, turned up nothing.

Then, in early December, a sample of adrenocorticotrophic hormone (ACTH)—the pituitary gland secretion that triggers the release of adrenaline by the adrenal glands—produced positive results on the ileum. The material was crude, containing chemicals besides ACTH, and its activity was such a surprise that Orphein kept the discovery to himself for several days, until he could duplicate it. When he did tell Goldstein about it, the results caused a dramatic new emphasis in the lab, to identify swiftly the agent responsible for Orphein's observation.

When samples of pure ACTH failed to produce similar results, it was obvious to Goldstein and the others that another ingredient in the crude material was responsible for the action, and Cox set up filtration columns to try and separate out the active ingredient.

Hansjörg Teschemacher, another visitor from the Max Plank Institute, was assigned the job of trying to extract the material from fresh cattle pituitaries, obtained at a nearby San Jose slaughterhouse. Goldstein's group had at last mounted the chase after John Hughes's Substance X.

BREAKING THE CODE

That winter, in Aberdeen, Substance X was officially renamed enkephalin. Although the compound was decidedly opiatelike, Hans Kosterlitz did not want its name to imply that the brain-produced chemical was anything like a known narcotic, so he purposely selected the vague term meaning "in the head." Its composition also remained frustratingly elusive.

John Hughes had two basic problems: He had to get a pure sample of enkephalin and he had to get it in quantity. That done, his fate would depend on the laboratory skills of John and Linda Fothergill, who had labs across the Marishal College parking lot in the department of biochemistry. Decoding enkephalin's amino acid formula required a set of peptide analysis techniques with which neither he nor Hans Kosterlitz was familiar. The Fothergills were. They specialized in protein chemistry, a relatively new field which combined advanced chemistry with the sort of molecular model-building techniques that Francis Crick and James Watson had used to determine DNA's double helix structure.

John and Linda Fothergill were young faculty members, a jovial, hospitable couple. She was a fleshy, dimpled New Englander from Vermont who would eventually assume primary responsibility for the enkephalin analysis; he was a Scotsman, with thinning red hair and a full red beard. Their labs, though no less crowded and gloomy than Hughes's, were fairly well equipped with modern X-ray defraction and fluorescence detection instruments, as well as the more traditional tools of chemistry, used to provide clues to the composition of unknown substances. Stick and ball models of proteins that resembled tiny star systems were mounted on pedestals in their offices. Together they had already deciphered the formulas of a number of proteins and peptides, some of them containing up to one hundred amino acids.

It seemed to Linda Fothergill that Hughes's small peptide would be easy to sequence once he got enough of it in a reasonably pure state, but distilling a pure sample from Hughes's mashed pig brains, using filtration and glass column separation techniques, was, in fact, proving to be very difficult.

John Hughes was staking his hopes on a machine called a high-pressure liquid chromatography (hplc) unit which could rapidly purify and detect peptides, using only a fraction of the amount of material he had been using up until then. The machine separated samples of unknown compounds by heating them to a gaseous state, then pushing the gas through resin columns filled with a neutral liquid at pressures of up to three thousand pounds per square inch. The method was also called "high-performance" liquid chromatography, but Sidney Udenfriend, the Hoffman-La Roche company scientist who first applied the technique to peptides, joked that "high price" was an apter description. The cost of one of the new commercially available hplc units was then about $10,000—far beyond the means of the Unit—so the previous summer Hughes had set about building his own. He had ordered dampers, gas tanks, columns, pumps, and monitors piecemeal out of laboratory equipment catalogs and pored over books and papers on hplc. Finally he had assembled an ungainly piece of apparatus which eventually occupied one entire side of the large lab Hughes shared with Graeme Henderson and Frances Leslie.

"He was not a 'toy' man," Alan North notes, "or a high technology fanatic. If he had been, the work might have been done faster." It took three months to make the hplc machine work properly and, even then, tubes leaked, the pump always seemed on the verge of exploding, and Hughes was continually rebuilding broken parts. Despite Hughes's best efforts, his problem of purity had stymied any attempt throughout the fall at a full-scale analysis by the Fothergills.

As the days grew colder and began to darken by three in the afternoon, John Hughes's best guess was that by then the Americans were right behind them, and closing fast.

In the lab, the pressures began to show. The strain on Hughes was most apparent to his new assistant, Terry Smith, who bore the brunt of his already short temper. After a small windfall, a two-year National Research Council grant, which enabled Hughes to hire him, Smith had arrived in early January from London, where he had completed his Ph.D. at the Royal College of Surgeons, Hughes's alma mater. He was a quiet, bearded man who seemed perpetually bleary-eyed from lack of sleep.

Smith's introduction to the Unit for Research on Addictive Drugs took place at the annual Robert Burns Supper held each January 25. The party honoring Scotland's greatest poet was a grand affair sponsored by the University's Pharmacology Society. It included the traditional meal of Scotch broth and haggis—boiled sheep stomach stuffed with oatmeal, onions, and sheep entrails—along with copious amounts of wine and plenty of whisky for spirited after-dinner toasts to the loveliness of the ladies present and to the national poet's "immortal memory." Kosterlitz, Henderson, Hughes, and North almost anesthetized Terry Smith with toasts. Smith foggily recalls that there was dancing afterward, and that Hanna Kosterlitz had criticized his beard. The gaiety was certainly a pleasant contrast with the weeks and months that followed, when conviviality seemed as rare as sunshine.

"It was an unreal world for an outsider," Smith recalls. "I had never worked in an atmosphere of such tension." Days began when Hughes arrived storming that experiments were not being conducted according to his standards. He accused Smith of being lazy and untidy, and complained that he was not washing up properly; Hughes had to do no washing up at all.

Evening after evening in the Kirkgate Bar, Smith recited his litany of woes to Graeme Henderson. To insure that Hughes would not come along to put a damper on their conversation and worse, indulge his habit of mooching drinks, they had devised a code for evenings when they wanted to be alone. "Are you going to the 'seminar' tonight?" Henderson would ask Smith casually if Hughes was around.

Not all the pressure on Hughes was coming from American labs. "Some of it was coming from Kosterlitz," a coworker recalls. "He kept chiding John about the hplc unit eating up precious material and doubting his ability to compete successfully with the Americans." Since Kosterlitz was flying to the States periodically for scientific conferences, picking up tidbits of whatever was going on in rival labs, he was also often the bearer of bad news.

In February 1975, the news was particularly distressing. In a few months both Goldstein and Snyder were planning to present papers on their own versions of enkephalin at the International Narcotics Research Club's spring meeting at Airlie House, in Virginia. To make matters worse, the proceedings of the Neurosciences Research Program held the previous spring in Boston had just been published. Tacked onto Hughes's groundbreaking presentation was a description of Pasternak's morphinelike factor, and Hughes felt the entire piece was edited by Snyder to make it seem as if the Hopkins work had been announced at the same time as the results from Aber-

deen. Hughes's own paper, which established the primacy of
the Aberdeen findings, had been revised and accepted by
Brain Research, but was not yet scheduled for publication.

Furious, Hughes determined to have the formula cracked
by the Airlie House meeting, but, as he and Terry Smith
shuttled between the big lab where Hughes had his hplc and
the small lab where the vas deferens were set up, sending new
samples that looked promising to Fothergill, the samples were
invariably sent back: not pure enough. Days became weeks as
Hughes tried to finagle better results from his hplc machine,
but his frustration persisted.

Getting enough enkephalin to work with was the other
major problem facing Hughes that winter. Even with Terry
Smith assisting brain foraging efforts at the abattoir, their
supply consistently fell short of their needs. One alternative
was to ask for assistance from the commercial drug industry,
but Hughes had reason to be skeptical about such an arrangement. The previous summer he had reached an agreement
with the London-based Burroughs Wellcome Pharmaceutical
Company to exchange preferential access to information about
the Substance X formula for large supplies of pig brain extract.
The deal fell through, Hughes intimated, when he was asked
to delay the publication of his results so that Burroughs Wellcome could have time to work on the information exclusively.

Fortunately, Kosterlitz felt no such constraint. Early in
February he mentioned Hughes's peptide predicament to John
Lewis, research director at the Reckitt and Colman Drug
Company in Hull, England. As Barry Morgan, at that time, a
medicinal chemist at Reckitt with special expertise in peptides
recalls, Lewis was immediately captivated by the prospect of
collaborating with the Aberdonians. "Naturally, he was thinking that this might be a big painkilling breakthrough, that it
would be a quick inroad to a new therapy, a dramatic new
direction in pain control." As a result, one week later, Mor-

gan, a spare-time rock guitarist, was sleeping fitfully on the Nightrider from Hull to Aberdeen, where a morning meeting with John Hughes had been arranged.

"I could see right off," Morgan remembers, "that John was not a happy-go-lucky guy. He'd done a lot but he needed help and he was worried about the competition."

During that otherwise dismal winter, Morgan's attitude was refreshingly optimistic. He told Hughes that using the Reckitt facilities Morgan could easily supply ten times the amount of brain extract that Hughes could process on his own. Their combined efforts might be enough to carry the project through.

Over the next two weeks, the two men finalized an informal "pig-brains-for-information-sharing" arrangement. Hughes would be free to release his results as he saw fit, but if Hughes's compound was a nonaddictive painkiller, Reckitt and Colman would have a head start on other companies, and, if Hughes was successful as a result of Reckitt and Colman's help, they were to get a share of the patent. "Agreed in principle to make 100 kg brain extract in Hull," Morgan wrote in his log on February 27. "Note of urgency introduced by two possible competition groups publishing papers on 'the ligand' [the endogenous opiate] at conference in U.S. during May. Goldstein is going to describe 'isolation of ligand.' "

By mid-March, Hughes's efforts with hplc were finally yielding enkephalin samples of a purity which Linda Fothergill recalls as "just borderline." With supply now the most pressing issue, Hughes flew to Hull to inspect Morgan's operation.

The lab was small by drug company standards, but its fifty-gallon mixing drum for extractions and an equally gigantic rotary evaporator seemed Brobdingnagian, compared with Hughes's equipment in Aberdeen. The collaboration, however, got off to a shaky start. The first batch of extract did not work at all, and a second batch sent Hughes running around the third floor of Marishal, crowing that he found a new kind of enkephalin—which later turned out to be traces of buprinorphine, a powerful Reckitt and Colman narcotic, that had not been washed out of the giant mixing drum. "There was probably buprinorphine in the mustard in the Reckitt and Colman dining room," quipped one of Hughes's colleagues.

The work went satisfactorily after that, though, and by mid-April, the twenty-liter Winchester jugs of extract that Morgan sent up by train finally enabled Hughes and Smith to produce the first workable batches of enkephalin for Linda Fothergill.

To get a rough idea of the contents of Hughes's peptide, Fothergill was using a simple method called acid hydrolysis. The enkephalin is first boiled in hydrochloric acid—in the absence of oxygen—to break it down, then gel chromatography columns are used to separate its amino acid parts. Although the method would not disclose the order of the amino acids it would, at least, reveal those that were present in the compound and in what ratio.

"John sometimes came twice a day with samples," Fothergill recalls, "wanting me to do the analysis then and there, practically waiting on my doorstep until the results were completed."

Unfortunately, the process was slow and destructive; not all amino acids would survive it and by April the Snyder and Goldstein presentations at Airlie House were less than two months away.

Kosterlitz continued to be a source of pessimistic rumors about just how close the Americans actually were. In early May—around the time Hughes's long-delayed results finally appeared in *Brain Research*—Terry Smith recalls working with Hughes in the small lab one afternoon when Hans Kosterlitz walked in, sat down on the chair by the fridge, and announced darkly, "John, we might as well give up. Snyder's beaten us to it."

"You don't want to believe everything you hear, Hans," Hughes replied.

By the time Hughes, Kosterlitz, and Graeme Henderson left Aberdeen in late May for the Narcotics Club's meeting at Airlie House, Hughes's confidence began to have some real basis. Linda Fothergill was completing final tests to determine a partial amino acid formula for enkephalin. Hughes left careful instructions: Terry Smith was to collect the data, and Frances Leslie was to wire the results to him at Airlie House as soon as they were available.

While the mood was heady in Solomon Snyder's lab at Johns Hopkins, it was not the result of any new breakthrough on Pasternak's morphinelike factor. Snyder's own concentration remained focused on the chemical causes of mental illness, so the drive in the lab was to use the Pert-Snyder technique to discover other receptor systems in the brain where neurotransmitters associated with madness and the expanding family of antipsychotic drugs were thought to work. In the eyes of one colleague, the suite of rooms on the third floor of the neurosciences building had turned into a "receptor factory."

That winter, Ann Young had completed a series of experiments demonstrating that the antipsychotic drug Haldol worked by blocking dopamine receptors. Together with Suzanne Zukin and S.J. Enna, she was close to identifying receptors for a more-recently discovered chemical messenger called GABA (gamma-aminobutyric acid), thought to be essential to the action of Valium. Snyder himself had spent the winter completing a long article for *Science* on "Drugs, Neurotransmitters, and Schizophrenia."

"There was a constant sense of breaking through," comments Rabi Simantov, a biochemist newly arrived from the Weizman Institute in Israel. Simantov, owing to the peculiar demands of his own experiments, was coming into the lab at four in the morning to check his results, often to find one or two others still awake and working.

Gavril Pasternak, however, was plodding along on the morphinelike factor. He had tentatively identified one amino acid as tyrosine, but the work might have gotten completely lost in the excitement of other projects were it not for the timely intervention of Daniel Hauser, a chemist at the Sandoz Pharmaceutical Company in Basel, Switzerland—three thousand miles away.

The Pert-Snyder receptor paper had excited considerable attention at Sandoz, the international pharmaceutical and chemical giant. Scientists there had been working for years on derivatives of ergot, a parasitic mold that grows on grain. Albert Hofmann's accidental discovery in 1944 of the powerful hallucinogen LSD-25 (cornerstone of the psychedelic 1960s) evolved from Sandoz ergot research, as did a number of nonpsychoactive and clinically more useful compounds; for example, ergot progtomine, which was regarded as a wonder drug for migraine. Like opiates, though, the precise mechanisms of the ergot drugs were clouded in mystery and Hauser, together with other Sandoz researchers, was interested in applying the Hopkins opiate receptor strategy to ergot receptors, as a means of finding out where these compounds worked and why they varied so widely in their effects. So Snyder was retained as a consultant and Anna Marie Klaus, a promising Sandoz chemist-in-training, was sent to Baltimore to learn receptor binding in late 1974.

"When Anna Marie came back she told us that people in Snyder's lab were talking about an 'endogenous morphine' substance," recalled Daniel Hauser, in his early thirties at the time and head of a small chemistry unit at Sandoz. A memo, written by Hauser to his department chairman on April 17, 1975, discussed Snyder's work on the morphinelike factor and suggested that it might have important implications for pain relief. His memo was ignored. He wrote another, this time to Dietmar Römer, the chief of opiate and analgesics research at Sandoz. One of Römer's ultimate goals was to produce "a nonmorphine: something better and stronger than aspirin, to be sold over-the-counter for headache and common types of pain." The soft-spoken senior researcher coolly sized up the commercial possibilities of an endogenous painkiller and fired off his own memo, suggesting that management follow up on MLF. Römer's reputation was such that Snyder was contacted directly and Sandoz offered to throw the full weight of its support behind Snyder's project.

In Palo Alto, the weather was warm enough by April to permit Avram Goldstein to begin hosting poolside weekend gatherings for the Addiction Research Foundation's staff members. Endogenous opiates were the main topic of gossip. Ever since Goldstein's postdoc, Kent Orphein, after months of unsuccessful tests on pituitary extracts, had finally come up with a crude sample of adrenocorticotrophic hormone that was active on the guinea pig ileum, the Foundation's lab director, Brian Cox, along with their German visitor, Hansjörg Teschemacher, had been pulling out all the stops on the task of purification. Now, three months later, their work was yielding surprising results.

It appeared that Orphein's sample actually contained two substances which Goldstein began calling "pituitary opioid peptides" (POP-1 and POP-2); they differed from each other in their chemical characteristics and, markedly, from both Hughes's enkephalin and Snyder's nearly identical MLF. The POPs were larger peptides—with molecular weights of approximately 1,400 and 3,000 daltons, respectively. Cox had as yet no clue to their amino acid composition, but the raw data provided new and compelling hints that all the scientists in the field would soon be trying to cope not with a single chemical, but with a family of related endorphins.

Leaving lab procedures to Cox and Teschemacher—Goldstein was well aware that his attempts at bench work only worried his younger, more technically adept associates—he turned his attention to a bold theoretical exercise that he hoped might turn up some equally startling results. Like Hans

Kosterlitz, he had begun making theoretical models and in late May 1975, just before the scientists met at Airlie House, he was trying to invent on paper a peptide with a composition that would match the weight and charge of Hughes's still unidentified enkephalin. Working with his son Joshua—a Stanford science student who was spending several months in the lab that spring and summer—Goldstein was quickly able to devise six theoretical peptides that fit the enkephalin criteria; they were then synthesized in his lab and tested on the ileum. None of them worked, but with Goldstein continuing to apply the full weight of his intellect to the problem there was still a chance that he might, suddenly, leap to the correct conclusion.

The fifth meeting of the International Narcotics Research Club gave every indication of being a showdown between research groups working on brain-produced opiates. A few days earlier, rumors about the progress of the various competing labs had begun circulating at the Committee on Problems of Drug Dependence (CPDD), a conference held at the National Academy of Sciences in Washington, D.C., which most of the contenders also attended.

During the CPDD's morning session on May 21, tempers flared as Gavril Pasternak outlined the Hopkins group's latest data on MLF—their endogenous opiate. "It was not a good performance," one participant recalls. "Pasternak presented his material as though the work in Aberdeen hadn't been done."

At the conclusion of Pasternak's lecture, Kosterlitz jumped to his feet and barked, "Let's get this straight!" stating in no uncertain terms who the original discoverers of the endogenous opiate actually were. Stunned, Pasternak replied, "I've given you full credit in my paper." "Yes," Kosterlitz shot back, "but you didn't say so in your lecture!"

That afternoon when the scientists arrived by bus at Airlie House, feelings were still running strong, despite the pleasant setting—a rambling woodsy convention center about an hour's drive from Washington, D.C., in Virginia. Nearly two hundred scientists—an expansion in membership directly attributable to the mounting excitement over recent developments in the field—were attending the meeting.

Kosterlitz, Hughes and their colleagues from Aberdeen were very much at the center of events. "Airlie House was a great meeting, so exciting," recalls Graeme Henderson, who was visiting the U.S. for the first time. "The people from Aberdeen walked like gods." But the possibility lingered that John Hughes would turn out to have feet of clay.

Hughes spent the first night of the meeting anxiously awaiting a telegram from Aberdeen with Linda Fothergill's amino acid analysis of enkephalin. Lacking that, his data was sketchy—nothing which would indicate that he was truly ahead of Snyder and Goldstein. A telex arrived the next morning, and a joyful Hughes reported its contents a few hours later.

"The purification and study of the pure compound has now been achieved," he announced, boldly flourishing the telex, "and I have just received a partial composition." Glycine, phenylalanine, methionine, and tyrosine were the known amino acids in an estimated ratio of 3 Gly, 1 Phe, 1 Met, 1 Tyr—in organic chemistry shorthand. "With the probability," Hughes added, "of tryptophan or a tryptophan derivative of unknown amounts."

In the audience, as Hughes read his data, Avram Goldstein shook his head in dissent. It seemed to Goldstein that Hughes's amino acid composition was "all screwed up." He was both amazed and relieved that it was taking Hughes so long to get it right.

That same morning Brian Cox, Goldstein's lab director, delivered a detailed report on the "pituitary opioid peptides," which emphasized the differences between Goldstein's POPs and enkephalin. POP-1, the better understood of the two compounds, had an estimated molecular weight of 1,750 daltons (about twice the size of enkephalin); it was ten times stronger, and in low doses its twitch-quelling effect on the guinea pig ileum lasted for up to six hours.

By contrast, enkephalin's effect on the vas deferens lasted only about three minutes—a fact which Hughes attributed to its rapid breakdown by enzymes and Kosterlitz, later in the morning, cited as the reason why animals were not addicted to their endogenous opiates.

Gavril Pasternak then delivered a toned-down report on the morphinelike factor, carefully crediting Hughes and Kosterlitz, but mentioning nothing—beyond the obvious amino acid, tyrosine—about the sequence of MLF. John Hughes began to worry that Snyder and company were not telling all they really knew.

An exciting announcement from Lars Terenius's lab in Sweden capped the day. He and his assistant, Agneta Wahlström, were finding consistently lower-than-normal levels of an unidentified, morphinelike fraction in spinal tap samples taken from a group of *human* chronic pain patients. The results from Uppsala added a special urgency to the race to solve the chemical riddles of the "morphine within." Here, for the first time, was solid evidence which connected endorphins to human pain.

It was clear to all the researchers gathered at Airlie House in 1975 that they had stumbled onto something that was more complex and thrilling than any of them had ever anticipated. With the identification of enkephalin, POPs, and MLFs, scientists could now see they were dealing with a possible family of endogenous chemicals, which might cover a broad range of human pain syndromes.

On the third day of the meeting, the unexpected proliferation of endogenous opiates precipitated a lunchtime debate over nomenclature. "Scientists," said Harry Collier, the Club's cofounder, who was present at the debate, "would rather use each other's toothbrushes than each other's terminology." In this case, the conflict was settled by the New York University receptor researcher Eric Simon, who suggested that the word *endorphine,* meaning "the morphine within," be used generically as a name for all the brain-produced substances with opiate properties. The final "e" was dropped later. "It was a much sexier name than enkephalin or POP," says one Airlie House conferee, "and so it stuck."

Except among the scientists. Hughes and Kosterlitz continued to call their substance enkephalin while Goldstein continued to call his POP and Snyder continued to call his MLF. Until the race was won, the compound's name would be as much in dispute as its chemical composition.

After Airlie House, Linda Fothergill's work on the enkephalin project intensified. She had positively identified four amino acids—glycine, phenylalanine, methionine, and tyrosine. Glycine was found in quantities three times higher than the others, which suggested that it appeared repeatedly in the formula, but she suspected that the list was still incomplete and did not know the order in which the amino acids appeared.

Hughes had taken a few days off after Airlie House to tour the American South with Alan North. When Hughes returned to Aberdeen, Fothergill started work on a more detailed analysis of their peptide. Using the dansyl-Edman technique, a procedure for labeling each sequential amino acid of a peptide in turn, she hoped to discover the critically important order of amino acids in enkephalin's formula.

The method was a scientific version of "connect the dots." By comparing cards chemically treated to make each "dansylated" amino acid fluoresce under ultraviolet light with a standard map of all known amino acids, she was able to identify the first amino acid in the enkephalin chain within only a few days of beginning the procedure. The first amino acid was tyrosine.

"With dansyl-Edman you get one answer per day," Linda

Fothergill recalled. "John was counting the days." The second and third amino acids in the sequence were both glycine. Phenylalanine was in the fourth spot. Tyrosine-glycine-glycine-phenylalanine: Tyr-Gly-Gly-Phe.

They seemed to be finally closing in on the formula, but late that June, about a month after Airlie House and just after Hughes's thirty-third birthday, their progress stalled. "The fifth amino acid appeared to be methionine (Met), but in some of the samples, leucine (Leu) kept popping up instead," Linda Fothergill remembers.

At first, she thought the leucine was an impurity, and Hughes sweated over his hplc machine trying to get rid of it. He could not. "Results were always the same," she said. "Leucine was the niggle. It was there, but in quantities too small to know what to make of it." They felt sure there were other missing components as well.

Hughes hypothesized there might be as many as ten amino acids in the formula which he was, in private, predicting to be: Tyrosine-glycine-glycine-phenylalanine-methionine-glycine-phenylalanine-tryptophan—Tyr-Gly-Gly-Phe-Met-Gly-Phe-Tryp. Tryptophan was a good candidate to complete the composition but both Hughes and Fothergill toyed with the idea that enkephalin might contain something even more exotic. "It didn't seem possible that such a potent peptide could have a simple composition," she said. "We were looking for something, well, more interesting, possibly an amino acid no one had found before. A modified tryptophan was our guess."

However, since her procedures destroyed tryptophan, for all intents and purposes the missing amino acid remained invisible.

That June, Avram Goldstein arranged for deliveries of large quantities of crude ACTH from Joseph Fischer, who supervised collection of Armour & Company peptides from millions of pig pituitaries. Goldstein and his group, unlike

Hughes, were spared the tedious necessity of slaughterhouse days. At the same time, Goldstein wrote requesting samples from the discoverer of ACTH, C.H. Li, who directed the Hormone Research Laboratory at the University of California in San Francisco until his death in 1987.

One of the world's leading authorities on the chemistry of the pituitary gland, Li had made a number of notable discoveries (or "uncoveries," as he preferred to call them, since their existence had long been suspected), including four of the five other major pituitary gland hormones, among them those which controlled metabolic functions such as growth and reproduction. Since an extensive catalogue of the amino acid formulas of ACTH-related substances, compiled by Li and other scientists, already existed, there was a chance that by a simple process of elimination, Goldstein and his coworkers could be the first to identify a correct structure for their compound. They narrowly missed.

During C.H. Li's quest to uncover the inner workings of the pituitary and catalogue all the important byproducts of the body's "master gland," he had come upon another hormone called lipotrophin, which he had been touting for ten years as if it were one of his major achievements. His colleagues were less sure: the only suspected function of lipotrophin, which means "moves fat," was to dissolve and transport fat from adipose tissues to the liver, where it was burned up.

Unshaken by criticism—one American researcher called lipotrophin "evolutionary garbage!"—Li continued investigating the compound. By 1970, his group had learned how to synthesize the entire ninety-one-amino-acid chain of lipotrophin. Unfortunately, the process of making artificial quantities of the hormone was enormously costly, and yields from most animals were low.

In an effort to increase his stores of lipotrophin, C.H. Li turned to the pituitaries of camels. Camels were lean, hardy, low in fat, and Li wondered if the camel's leanness could result from an oversupply of lipotrophin. Conveniently, in 1972, a student of Li's, Waleed Ohan Danho, was returning for the summer to his home in Iraq. "He asked what he can get me," Li recalls. "I said, 'Bring me camel pituitaries.' " Danho returned to San Francisco the following fall with his pockets literally stuffed with five hundred camel glands.

The glands had not been properly frozen, however, and in transit from Iraq, chemical changes occurred. When Li tested them, he found no lipotrophin but, instead, a smaller fragment of the hormone, containing its last thirty-one amino acids.

Responding to Goldstein's requests, C.H. Li made a cursory check of his stock and then sent Goldstein several extracts related to ACTH—none of which worked. Since Goldstein had not asked for lipotrophin, Li overlooked the camel gland fragment which was completely identified and ready to be tested. Only months later did the two men learn that it matched Goldstein's POP-1 exactly.

Unaware of the near miss, late in the summer of 1975, Goldstein was concentrating instead on his efforts to construct a synthetic peptide identical to Aberdeen's enkephalin. Based on his own calculation and on the new information released by Hughes at Airlie House, Goldstein had come up with the formula tyrosine-glycine-glycine-glycine-lysine-methionine—Tyr-Gly-Gly-Gly-Lys-Met.

The peptide was synthesized and tested. It worked on the guinea pig ileum, but possessed only one hundredth the strength of enkephalin. "It was incorrect," Goldstein concedes, "but not by much."

At Hopkins in June, when Gavril Pasternak finished his Ph.D. and left for a research post at the Sloan-Kettering Institute in New York City, the MLF project was turned over to the balding, burly Israeli biochemist, Rabi Simantov, who spent the entire summer wrestling with its amino acid composition. He was faster, more skillful, and more optimistic than

Pasternak. With Sandoz offering to back him, and Hughes still faltering, Snyder's interest in the project had heightened, but they were far behind the Aberdonians and needed to push if they were going to catch up. "We knew we were racing," said Simantov.

In early September, he and Snyder flew to Basel for a meeting at Sandoz with Daniel Hauser and Dietmar Römer to discuss upscaling their operation. Simantov stayed on at Sandoz for an extra week to demonstrate his isolation procedure to a young company chemist named Francis Cardineux, who was to take over this preliminary operation. The only requirement was raw brains, and lots of them, to do the massive extractions required to get the formula quickly.

In Aberdeen, the turning point came that summer with the divine intervention of another outsider, Howard Morris, a Cambridge University researcher. Morris's first fateful meeting with John Hughes had taken place the previous February, when Hughes gave a lecture on enkephalin at Cambridge at the invitation of Leslie Iverson, director of the Medical School's Neurochemical Pharmacology Unit.

Howard Morris was then twenty-nine years old—a tall, bearded, outgoing man with a fondness for hiking around the English Lake District in his spare time. He had heard that Hughes had a new substance but was having a problem identifying its structure. Morris thought it might be a good subject for a mass spectrometry technique he had perfected that could analyze, atom by atom, minute quantities of proteins and peptides.

Mass spectrometry works by bombarding unknown substances with electrons until they disintegrate into charged atoms. Accelerated up to speeds of 200,000 miles per hour, these ionic bits stream through an "analyzer," a device which is essentially an electromagnetic prism that separates the bits according to their weight and charge. A beam of ultraviolet light etches a record of peaks and valleys on a moving graph of photographic paper as each fragment exits the machine. These patterns form a distinct signal, a spectrum of the mass of the substance, a "fingerprint," as Morris liked to say, of its atomic composition. Researchers like Morris could then translate the atomic data back into a chemical formula—or so they claimed. John Hughes was not so sure.

During his talk at Cambridge, Hughes mentioned that he thought enkephalin might contain a strange amino acid, perhaps a modified tryptophan. That suspicion especially interested Morris. Two years earlier he had used the mass spectrograph to discover a new amino acid, gamma-carboxyglytamic acid, the key ingredient in the blood-clotting agent prothrombin.

After the lecture Morris asked Hughes if he had considered using mass-spec on enkephalin. A few months earlier an attempt at mass-spec had been made in Aberdeen, which in Hughes's opinion had been "a disaster, a mess, a waste of precious material." His abrupt reply to Morris was typical Hughes. "Oh, yes, we've done that," he said, "and it doesn't work."

Hughes was not alone in his mistrust of mass spectrometry. Howard Morris himself once remarked that the extremely precise, yet profoundly tricky method might better be called "mass speculation." Unlike the more traditional techniques of protein analysis such as Linda Fothergill was using, there were no printed guidelines for mass-spec interpretation. It was all, so to speak, in the eye of the mass speculator.

Reliance on established reference maps, however, meant that unusual or unknown amino acids could not be matched or interpreted, and when classical chemists encounter such molecular freaks, Morris observes, "it gives the shits to everyone." From his vantage point, this is what seemed to be happening in Aberdeen.

It might take years to unravel the spectrum's meaning, but the spectrum would not lie; and Morris prided himself on being able to interpret most mass-spec signals in less than an hour. He was an unflappable apostle of the new technology, and believed in himself and in his machine, even if John Hughes did not.

On the way out of Hughes's lecture, Morris stopped to comment briefly to Leslie Iverson that success with mass-spec could vary depending on the procedures used; but since Hughes had curtly dismissed mass-spec, Morris did not pursue the issue. "Well," he smiled at Iverson, "back to the lab. . . ."

There matters rested for nearly six months, until another chance encounter—this time with Barry Morgan—brought Howard Morris squarely into the forefront of the enkephalin project.

On July 7, Howard Morris was giving a talk at a meeting of the British Chemical Society at Imperial College in London, and his topic was the application of mass spectrometry to protein structures which eluded classical methods. Barry Morgan was in the audience. Hughes had told him of his previous encounter with Morris, but unlike Hughes, Morgan thought Morris's method sounded good.

Morgan, who was processing some more material at Reckitt for another dansyl-Edman analysis, mentioned Morris to Hughes a few days later, and wondered if they should send the enkephalin batch to Morris instead.

Hughes estimated that at the current pace it would take at least six more months to solve the enkephalin sequence while Kosterlitz thought it might, perhaps, take as much as nine months. With the Snyder and Goldstein groups closing ground fast, and Linda Fothergill pregnant, and about to leave the project, Hughes gave in.

Morgan finished preparing a new sample of enkephalin and, in early August, Hughes placed an urgent phone call to Howard Morris. Hughes seemed to have forgotten their first encounter entirely. He sounded somewhat nervous to Morris, but he was friendly and uncharacteristically open about his findings, relating his suspicions that the substance was a peptide, containing perhaps ten amino acids. Morris, wanting to do the structure blind and free of any preconceptions, did not ask for any more details. "It's not foolproof, but there's a reasonable chance we'll get more information than you already know," he assured Hughes.

On August 11, Barry Morgan made the three-hour drive from Hull to Cambridge. Beside him on the front seat was a pear-shaped vial containing a few precious micrograms of purified enkephalin. He and Morris had pub fare, "a liquid lunch," as Morgan recollects, and that very afternoon Morris, with Morgan watching over his shoulder, ran the first tests.

By four o'clock, Morris had prepared the methyl-iodine derivative of enkephalin necessary for him to begin the analysis. Morris's mass spectrograph was an amazingly compact piece of technology, considering that part of it was a cyclotron, an atomic particle accelerator. The array of chrome chambers, plexiglass tubes, wires, and rods which composed the machine fit easily onto a single table in Morris's lab.

As the mass-spectrograph machine whirred softly, Morris inserted a thin hollow tube into the flask. The tiny amount of enkephalin inside was a barely distinguishable white ring on the bottom; the amount he drew out of the tube was invisible. He blew lightly through the tube, forcing the material onto the tip of a quartz-handled instrument resembling a screwdriver, then released it into the machine. A few minutes later, the graph began to move.

It was five o'clock when Morris removed the roll of pale purple photographic paper. He and Morgan drew the blinds in his office—ultraviolet charts blacken and fade in sunlight—and spread it out on his desk top, beaming with satisfaction. "We got a spectrum on the first experiment," he recalls. "It's unusual; we locked right onto it and I started to sequence it."

The case of the missing tryptophan was brought to an

abrupt conclusion: There was no tryptophan or a tryptophan derivative in the spectrum. Morris continued to scan the peaks on the graph.

"That looks like tyrosine," he said. "That's glycine."

"Oh, yes . . . yes," Morgan began to intone, his Welsh accent rising.

The first four amino acids in enkephalin were tyrosine, glycine, glycine, phenylalanine, exactly as Linda Fothergill had determined, but Morris now encountered similar difficulties assigning the fifth position. "There was this complex fragmentation of what seemed to be methionine and leucine," he remembers. "It was very odd. I had to hold fire."

At seven o'clock Morgan left for Hull and Morris went home to his Danish wife, Lene, and their small house outside Cambridge, carrying the enkephalin spectrum with him. It was unusual for Morris to bring work home with him, and Lene quietly began wondering if this was something unusually important.

During the following days and nights Morris tried to explain the chart in such a way as to agree with Hughes's prediction that enkephalin was a ten-amino-acid-chain peptide. Nothing was satisfactory. He had to be careful. The complex Met-Leu region, in position five, suggested several possibilities, each dramatically variant. Peaks in the spectrum that he had originally dismissed as impurities he reconsidered now as possible components.

Morris felt embarrassed and annoyed that the problem was taking him so long. Then one night after dinner, ten days after he had begun the analysis, the answer hit him. He was not 100 percent positive as he sat staring at the graph on his desk, but he had the giddy sense that the puzzle had suddenly fallen together. He and Lene had a drink, and the next morning he telephoned Hughes in Aberdeen.

Without detailing his suspicions, Morris said he wanted to run one more experiment and would need a new sample.

Hughes was keen to get on with the work and readily agreed. Hughes and Barry Morgan quickly prepared a fresh batch of enkephalin, which Morgan delivered to Cambridge on September 18. The following day, Morris began an additional procedure by adding cyanogen bromide, a reagent that would destroy the amino acid methionine, to part of the new sample.

Morris ran a few droplets of the solution through his machine. The results were exactly as he had anticipated: After the methionine-destroying reaction, his spectrum still revealed an intact five-amino-acid peptide with the formula tyrosine-glycine-glycine-phenylalanine-leucine. He had the answer.

He had been seeing two overlapping signals: there were two short, individual enkephalins, not one long one. Each had a nearly identical formula: Tyr-Gly-Gly-Phe-Met, and Tyr-Gly-Gly-Phe-Leu. "I telephoned John Hughes with the information," Morris remembers. "He didn't really believe me."

Conclusively proving Howard Morris's suspicions took another month but, except for one dramatic upset near the end of September, the work went smoothly. It was crucial that man-made versions of the substances be made up and checked to see if they would have the same naloxone-reversible effects upon the vas deferens as the natural compounds had had.

It took nearly two weeks for Barry Morgan, working with Jack Bower and Ken Guest at Reckitt and Colman, to synthesize the Tyr-Gly-Gly-Phe-Met sequence, and when the sample arrived in Aberdeen, Hughes's assistant Terry Smith says, "the damn stuff didn't work. There was no activity." What made matters still worse was the sudden appearance in the lab, that same week, of a synthetic compound sent by Sam Wilkenson, a friend of Hughes's at Burroughs Wellcome, that did work.

It was based on a Tyr-Gly-Gly-Phe-Met-Gly-Phe-Tryp stab at the sequence Hughes had taken the previous May, which he had casually mentioned during lunch at the drug company. Unbeknownst to Hughes, Wilkenson had gone ahead and synthesized the compound, as well as several others based on that preliminary data. When Hughes and Smith tested Wilkenson's compound on the vas in September, it was "Terrifying! Terrifying!" Hughes recalls. "It worked perfectly." But based on Morris's new information that there were two short enkephalin peptides, not one long one, Hughes was almost positive that the Wilkenson compound could not be correct and worked only because buried within it was the Met-enkephalin sequence. Hughes could not be sure, however, until he got a sample from Morgan that worked!

The second batch of synthetic Met-enkephalin was shipped by Morgan on October 5. Hughes spent his lunch hour impatiently waiting in the Aberdeen railroad station for the sample to arrive on the twelve-thirty train from Hull, then drove quickly back to Marishal with the small package. A familiar pear-shaped vial with a white powdery smudge at the bottom was enclosed in bubble wrap inside.

Looking more than usually beleaguered, Terry Smith had spent the morning preparing two fresh vas deferens that now bubbled and twitched on the lab bench beside a collection of half empty cups of cold gray coffee forgotten during the morning's preparation. All was ready for the final test by the time Hughes returned.

Kosterlitz joined them, stepping carefully over the extension cords and adapters on the floor. Aberdeen's cityscape gleamed in the afternoon sun outside Hughes's window, but none of the men noticed the view.

Puffing nervously on his pipe, Hughes stood on tiptoe, trying to look over Terry Smith's shoulder as Smith added the compound slowly to the organ baths. The electronically produced spasms diminished, almost coming to a halt.

"Give the naloxone! Give the naloxone!" Hughes commanded. Smith, holding off as long as he could, added the antagonist. The vas tissue started to twitch again nicely. This, at last, was the action of the brain's own morphine. The race was over. They had won.

Barry Morgan, slightly hung over from preliminary celebrations in Hull, arrived at Aberdeen airport on the morning of October 14, to complete final tests with Hughes on the synthetic methionine and leucine peptides using the vas and checking their results on the hplc.

It was eight o'clock that night by the time they were finished. Kosterlitz and the others had left for the day and Hughes and Morgan celebrated alone over beers at the KGB before they drove back to Hughes's house, near Duthie Park, to draft a paper on their results.

After six cold winters, John and Mandy Hughes were having central heating installed. The house had never been tidy, but now metal ducts, as well as the usual litter, cluttered the small living room. Hughes was positively jubilant, Morgan recalls, jumping up from the table at one point, and doing a little jig around the living room, singing in his monotone, at the top of his lungs, "We're going to be famous! We're going to be famous!"

Pressure to publish was enormous. Goldstein or Snyder could easily make a similar breakthrough; it was not a question of "if," but of "when." So Hans Kosterlitz contacted *Nature* magazine, asking them for priority treatment for an article from Aberdeen—"Identification of two related pentapeptides from the brain with potent opiate agonist activity," coauthored by John Hughes, Hans Kosterlitz, Linda Fothergill, Barry Morgan, Howard Morris, and Terry Smith—which arrived at the journal's offices on October 28. It was accepted for publication on November 13, and rushed into print on December 18, 1975.

That morning, John Hughes and Hans Kosterlitz woke up to find themselves celebrities. The *Times* of London carried a three-column article on its editorial page. Titled "Pharmacology: Brain drug like morphine," it gave the details of their discovery.

Solomon Snyder graciously sent a magnum of five star

brandy from Harrods to the Unit's offices in Marishal College with a congratulatory note once the race was over. Sampled appreciatively during morning and afternoon tea breaks, the bottle was consigned to a well-known secret hiding place for the comfort and encouragement of late-working Unit staffers in the tower on the third floor of Marishal College.

In April 1976, engraved invitations arrived, asking the six coauthors of the *Nature* paper—Hughes, Kosterlitz, Fothergill, Morgan, Morris, and Smith—to present their findings on May 6 before Great Britain's four-hundred-year-old scientific "academy," the Royal Society, at its biannual Conversazione, a fete honoring only the most outstanding scientific achievements.

Kosterlitz was in awe of the venerable "Royal" even though some of his colleagues felt that he had been unfairly excluded from its distinguished rank of fellows. "Chances for the Royal vary inversely with square miles from Cambridge," a friend of his comments cynically. Nevertheless, for Hans Kosterlitz this was true victory.

John Hughes and Terry Smith took the invitation somewhat more casually. They had already driven to London for the event before they realized that formal dress was required, and made a hurried trip to Moss Brothers, on Kings Row, to rent appropriate evening clothes and top hats.

Barry Morgan, walking spiffily down Shaftesbury Avenue in his tuxedo, stopped to have a quick beer before the Conversazione started. On route he passed a long line of teenagers, queued up to get into the studio where the weekly BBC rock 'n' roll program "Top of the Pops" was being taped. The bearded and long-haired Morgan was thrilled when two girls began shouting after him, "It's him. It's him." "It's the disc jockey."

In the foyer of the magnificent townhouse at Carlton House Terrace, an exhibit of rare orchids from the Solomon Islands and New Hebrides had been arranged by the Royal Botanic Gardens below a white marble staircase, where the

Royal Society's president, the Right Honorable Lord Todd, received each guest.

Twenty-nine exhibits were displayed on posters in six rooms. They ranged from "Form and Function in Bird Song" to "The Octopus Skin—A Window on the Brain"; but none attracted more attention than "The History of the Discovery of Enkephalin and Its Possible Physiological, Pharmacological, and Therapeutic Implications"—identified more succinctly as "The Brain's Own Morphine" on the Aberdeen group's poster board in the Wellcome lecture hall.

Kosterlitz, Hughes, and Morris spent most of the evening chatting up Great Britain's scientific elite. Linda Fothergill was in charge of explaining the exhibits to the less renowned scientific guests, leaving Morgan and Smith free to see just how much extra wine they could purloin from neighboring exhibitions.

It was a triumphant evening. "Aberdeen," as Terry Smith would later muse, "a minion on the backwater, a nonentity, a small fish, had taken on the big names and won." Simple science, hard work, and some great, good luck had prevailed.

It would all have been perfect were it not for the fact that the original draft of the now famous paper did not have Kosterlitz's name on the list of contributors. Even after Kosterlitz diplomatically lobbied to have the oversight rectified and he and Hughes resolved to include both their names on all subsequent papers on enkephalin, a sour note resonated.

Meanwhile, in the drug industry and among the other scientific investigators, a new race had already heated up: to see who would now dominate the fledgling endorphin field, who would be the first to exploit this brilliant discovery.

ALPHA, BETA, GAMMA

Curiously, the discovery of the most powerful of all the endorphins evolved from another chance encounter that same October, a few days after work on the enkephalins was completed. Serendipitous events began unfolding when Howard Morris attended a lecture that Derrick Smyth, a researcher at Great Britain's National Institute for Medical Research, was giving at Imperial College in London.

An annoying question had been troubling Morris in the weeks since he had used mass-spec to successfully analyze the amino acid code of the enkephalins. Morris doubted that two such nearly identical compounds could originate in the brain independently, but thought that the enkephalins, like other short peptides, might have broken off from a prohormone, a larger parent protein. Along with Kosterlitz and Hughes, he had spent hours in the Aberdeen library searching through the thick protein atlases, trying to spot their enkephalin sequences inside of known larger protein complexes. He had abandoned this tedious chore without success, until Derrick Smyth accidentally supplied the missing answer.

A small, dapper, talkative man in his early forties, Smyth

had been working at the National Institute for twelve years and was best known for his research on the prohormone which released insulin. Proinsulin itself was without effect, and Smyth had been investigating other puzzling cases of large inactive parent proteins which gave birth to smaller, active compounds. During this study he had come across lipotrophin (LPH), the pituitary gland hormone discovered by C.H. Li, which broke down fat for transport to the liver.

Smyth's talk at Imperial that afternoon was about how lipotrophin might be the prohormone for a smaller but even more powerful fat-moving pituitary secretion—Melanocyte stim- ulating hormone (MSH). MSH—which was also known to trigger color changes in the skins of frogs and chameleons— occupied the mid-portion of the lipotrophin molecule, and the previous year Smyth had initiated a series of experiments designed to prove that MSH was lipotrophin's "active core." Using various enzymes to duplicate the natural breakdown process of the ninety-one-amino-acid chain of lipotrophin, he found instead that an intact peptide, consisting of the last thirty-one amino acids of lipotrophin, LPH 61-91, was released more readily than MSH. Smyth called the peptide C-fragment and speculated that it might be the primary active ingredient of LPH. But active how? As far as he could detect, it had no fat-mobilizing properties. "It left severe question marks," Smyth recalls. "I didn't have the currant in the bun. I didn't know what it did."

Howard Morris, who had left Cambridge for Imperial College that fall, attended Smyth's lecture more out of polite- ness as a new faculty member than out of any particular interest in lipotrophin, but midway through the talk one of Smyth's slides caught his attention. It showed the MSH- containing mid-section of the lipotrophin molecule and a por- tion of the sequence of the mysterious C-fragment. Aspartic acid, lysine, and arginine came up as Morris scanned the slide, followed by the now familiar trio of tyrosine, glycine, and glycine.

"At a little sherry-do after the lecture," Morris remembers, "I asked Smyth what came after the Tyr-Gly-Gly. He didn't know offhand, but he said he did have another slide." Hustling Smyth over to his lab and grabbing a magnifying glass from atop his mass spectrograph, Morris squinted down at the slide and stammered, "I'm collaborating. . . . We can all collaborate. . . . Can't tell you until I report to my colleagues, but it's bloody important. . . ."

Smyth remembers that the effect of the slide on Morris "was like waving a red flag in front of a bull." The first five amino acids in Smyth's C-fragment were Tyr-Gly-Gly-Phe-Met—the Met-enkephalin formula.

Did Smyth have any samples of this C-fragment? Morris asked. Smyth replied that he had 30 milligrams of it—stored away in his freezer—and said he would send some to Morris straight away. That evening Morris telephoned Hans Kosterlitz, who excitedly suggested that Morris ignore the cost and messenger the compound directly to Aberdeen for immediate testing on the ileum and vas deferens.

The following day Morris called Smyth to follow up. Problems, Smyth reported: The C-fragment had spoiled in his freezer. He would have to make a new batch from fresh pituitaries. Ten days later, when it was supposed to be ready, Smyth had another excuse—this time, the preparation had not worked.

Morris's original misgivings about Smyth got stronger; he suspected that Smyth was stalling in order to buy time for his own experiments. Morris and John Hughes discussed whether to go ahead with their own preparation and study of C-fragment; but in the end, they decided to wait. Why bother if Smyth was already testing it? But Hughes, Morris, and Kosterlitz had added a new paragraph to the *Nature* paper, suggesting possible links between lipotrophin, Met-enkephalin, and larger pituitary opioid peptides which the authors credited Avram Goldstein with discovering. Derrick Smyth was not mentioned in the article.

A second fortuitous chain reaction of events was triggered on December 10, when Hans Kosterlitz mailed preview copies of the *Nature* article on enkephalins to several of his "friends and competitors," including Avram Goldstein, whose lab workers had been getting closer to purity on POP-1, but still could not identify its amino acid composition. The new information would lead to the discovery—just days before the Hughes-Kosterlitz findings were officially made public in the December 18, 1975, issue of *Nature*—that Goldstein's and Smyth's compounds (POP-1 and C-fragment) as well as C.H. Li's camel-gland fragment were the same final thirty-one-amino-acid fragment of lipotrophin, which upon testing proved to be a "super" endorphin—more powerful than Hughes and Kosterlitz's enkephalins, more powerful even than morphine.

Solomon Snyder was not on Kosterlitz's mailing list, but he received word of the discovery from Leslie Iverson, who was an editor at *Nature,* while Iverson was visiting Johns Hopkins. On December 11, Snyder called Daniel Hauser at Sandoz with the news. Hauser jotted down the enkephalin formulas. Now, at least three drug companies—Reckitt and Colman, Burroughs Wellcome, and Sandoz—possessed information on the potential painkilling breakthrough and were beginning the race to develop prototypes for a new, hopefully nonaddictive version of morphine based on the endorphins. Other investigators were already wondering about the possible application of endorphins to the treatment of mental illness.

That December, with the appearance of the enkephalin formulas in *Nature*, the pace and scope of endorphin research began exploding in often unexpected directions in laboratories throughout the world, as the solution to the mystery, itself, became the mystery. The brain definitely produced its own opiates, but why? At the same time however, the kind of innocent brilliance that had characterized the efforts of John Hughes and Hans Kosterlitz—the "small fish" who had taken on "big science" and won—was increasingly eclipsed by the efforts of high-level scientists like C.H. Li and Roger Guillemin and clinicians like Nathan Kline, who had done little or no work either on opiates or endorphins up to this point. Blood in the water attracts the big fish, or as Candace Pert once bluntly put it: "The discovery of the enkephalins was like waving filet mignon in front of a pack of hungry dogs."

A kind of fever was spreading: "Endorphinitis nobelitis," one researcher cynically called the syndrome—another dubbed it "endorphinomania"—and it would break only when the first trial experiments using the endorphins were conducted on humans.

Perhaps it was only a matter of "predestination," as C.H. Li likes to believe it was. In any case, fortune or "joss," the Chinese word for luck, had been extremely kind to Li. He was sixty-two years old, but seemed immune to the aging process; his face was unlined, he was slim, with dark golden-brown skin, in excellent health—a happy man.

Happiness, indeed, was his touchstone, his trademark, his credo. "If I am not happy, I'm not working," he once professed, though some of his colleagues, to whom this *tao* of indefatigable contentedness seemed a trifle overdone, joked that he took his own hormones.

Li had been expecting no surprises on the morning of December 14, 1975, when Bill Hain—his chauffeur, gardener, and personal technician—drove him to work from his home in Berkeley to the University of California in San Francisco, then accompanied him up the elevator and into the Animal Tower, where the lab animals were stored, through darkened corridors along a complicated route into the adjoining wing where the Hormone Research Laboratory was located. The research facility—created for Li in 1950 as an incentive to keep him at UCSF—occupied the entire sixth floor of the Medical Sciences building. His view took in the city, the Bay, and the Golden Gate bridge. There were easier ways to get up to his office, but Li had begun using this roundabout route during the 1950s, when his discovery of ACTH was being hailed as a major medical breakthrough—an effective treatment for rheumatism, arthritis, and even cancer.

"ACTH was like interferon," Li recalls. "People thought it was a wonder drug." For a while, the corridors outside his laboratory had turned into a scene resembling Lourdes, filled with ailing people clamoring for a cure. The experience had frightened Li and his almost obsessive shyness lasted years after the lines of heartbroken supplicants had disappeared.

That afternoon, Li was in his private office when a letter arrived from Avram Goldstein. The room was furnished with a desk set and chairs in blond wood and decorated with Li's favorite paintings—two original Dalis and several works by Japan's foremost modern artists. Off-limits even to his staff, this was Li's inner sanctum, reserved for private meditation and discussions with visiting scientists, and for entertaining his wealthy financial backers like the Laskers and the Geffens.

He read Goldstein's letter with a magnifying glass—his eyesight had been poor since childhood—mouthing the words and, as was his habit, unconsciously thumping the floor with his foot when he became interested or excited. The letter seemed to Li to be another of his "lucks."

Included was a Xerox of the forthcoming Hughes-Kosterlitz findings, which Goldstein had received from Hans Kosterlitz a few days earlier in the form of a preview copy. Here was a brief opportunity to move before the entire scientific community learned about the formula for enkephalins.

Goldstein's letter speculated that Li's lipotrophin might be the common precursor for Met-enkephalin and Goldstein's POPs. Had Li ever seen the Tyr-Gly-Gly-Phe-Met amino acid sequence before, perhaps in some smaller fragment of lipotrophin, Goldstein inquired? Could he supply samples of pituitary compounds containing this formula?

Indeed, Li recognized the Met-enkephalin sequence. It

was identical to the first five amino acids in the camel-gland extract which had lain in his freezer since Waleed Danho carted pockets of camel pituitary glands back from Iraq in 1972. It was the same thirty-one-amino-acid chain at the end of lipotrophin that Smyth called C-fragment and Goldstein called POP-1; and which Li would now name beta-endorphin.

"It was strange," recalls Goldstein, who had been the first to determine that the as then unidentified compound had opiate properties on tissues. "I discovered beta-endorphin, but I couldn't really 'discover' it because C.H. Li already had it. It was known, isolated, and on his shelf—without Li having any idea of what it was or what it did."

"Why didn't you ever send it to me?" Goldstein quizzed Li, in a telephone call a few days after Li got his letter.

"You asked only for ACTH fractions," Li replied, "not lipotrophin."

Disappointed, but anxious not to waste any more time, Goldstein asked Li to send him samples of lipotrophin and the camel-gland fragment for testing, as soon as possible. Li agreed to do so.

Two days later, on December 16, Li casually passed the news on to Roger Guillemin, who—without Li's knowledge—had been mounting his own secret drive for the past six months, trying to beat out Hughes and Kosterlitz in the endorphin race.

At fifty-seven, Roger Guillemin was as famous for his research into the important question of how the brain controls the pituitary gland as he was for an unusually rancorous feud that raged between himself and his rival, Andrew Schally, whose team in New Orleans was pursuing the same research goal. Their duel resulted in the discovery of the releasing factors—chemicals produced in the hypothalamus region of the brain, which then trigger the release of the pituitary hormones. But the ultimate, if unacknowledged, aim of both men was to win the Nobel prize and, in striving toward that objective—which they finally would share in 1977—they managed to ignore most of the rules of scientific etiquette. The relationship between the two research labs was typified by Schally's command to his group: "Don't talk to the enemy."

The intensity of this private war was fueled in part by constant frustration. The releasing factors existed in such minute quantities that Guillemin had required some 300,000 sheep brains—five tons of material, at a cost of $250,000—to isolate his first milligram of pure substance. Hughes's enkephalin isolation operation was, by comparison, a model of efficiency.

In 1969 Schally had beaten Guillemin, by a mere thirty-nine days, to the discovery of thyrotropin-releasing hormone, the first of the releasing factors. Since thyrotropin was the pituitary secretion governing the thyroid gland, TRF was of fundamental importance to the body's overall rate of metabolism, as well as holding clinical promise for the treatment of hyperthyroidism and other diseases of the thyroid gland. Schally also won a second round when, in 1971, he isolated leutinizing-hormone-releasing factor, a key command molecule in ovulation, of potential importance in developing new methods of birth control.

The following year the victory was Guillemin's. He announced his discovery of growth hormone inhibiting factor. Somatostatin, as he called it, turned off the release of growth hormone in late adolescence and maintained general metabolism in adults. In addition to providing a possible cure for giantism and other growth diseases, it was soon discovered that administration of somatostatin had a beneficial effect in cases of diabetes.

Under the auspices of a sumptuous National Institutes of Health grant, Guillemin began directing the search for growth-hormone-releasing factor, the chemical trigger that turned growth hormone on.

William Krivoy, a scientist at the Addiction Research

Center in Lexington, Kentucky, who Guillemin collaborated with briefly in the early 1960s, had discovered that, for reasons unknown, morphine would elevate levels of growth hormone in test animals. Guillemin's interest in endorphins stemmed from the possibility that an endogenous opiate might play a role similar to morphine in growth hormone release. It was, of course, also a way to score another victory over Schally. But there were other personal factors driving Guillemin.

He had been hospitalized the previous spring. Cancer was suspected, tests were positive, and part of his intestine had been removed. The illness seemed to affect both his personality and his approach to science. In years past he had left his workers at the Salk Institute in La Jolla, California, free to run the daily agenda of the lab, while he devoted most of his time to raising and managing the millions of dollars required to continue these efforts. Released from the hospital, he returned determined to direct lab operations himself and became a critical and overbearing taskmaster. Mounting tensions finally reached a breaking point during that summer, and his research team—which had been together for fourteen years—was about to break up, with Guillemin's tacit approval. He wanted to continue alone, but he was uncertain of the direction.

His research subjects began changing from week to week; he was behaving, according to science historian Nicholas Wade, "like a man desperate to make a big discovery in a hurry," when the endorphins attracted his attention.

"I read the Airlie House papers and I was flabbergasted," he recalls. "These people, Hughes and Kosterlitz, had a composition but no idea of the sequence. It was so obvious that here this was, on a silver platter. The work could be completed in just a couple of months."

Guillemin had an enormous ready supply of over 250,000 extracts from pig brains in his deep freeze. According to his own account, he returned to his lab in September 1975—while Howard Morris was finishing up his analysis of the enkephalins at Cambridge—and made a bet with his newly hired group of young staff members that he would have the structure figured out by Christmas. "I would do it alone," he boasted, "with half a technician."

Under cover of his growth-factor work, Guillemin, together with Scott Minick, his part-time assistant, began quickly screening frozen extracts for compounds with opiate activity on the guinea pig ileum. Three and a half months later, he had narrowed the field down to only three when, on December 16, he bumped into C.H. Li, glowing after his communications with Avram Goldstein, who told him about the upcoming Hughes-Kosterlitz publication in *Nature* and about his own expectations for lipotrophin.

That day, December 16th, Roger Guillemin had come to San Francisco to oversee work which was being done on the effects of his discovery somatostatin (the substance which turned off the release of growth hormone in the pituitary gland) in the treatment of diabetes. Clinical trials were just getting underway at the UCSF medical school, and that afternoon Guillemin was planning to meet with two drug company representatives and Peter Forsham, the director of the project, whose office was in the same building as Li's. "The meeting finished at four," Guillemin recalls, "and I thought I'd better go visit my old friend C.H. He showed me Goldstein's letter and told me about his compounds. It was an extraordinary thing. No one had taken lipotrophin seriously before."

But Guillemin's first concern was whether or not Li was going to supply the substance to Goldstein. "He is shrewd," Li remembers. "He said, 'Give it to me and no one else,' but I didn't think I could because Goldstein had showed me the paper and asked first."

Li did agree, however, to let Guillemin test the compound, too, and after measuring out a few thousandths of a gram of the camel-gland extraction with his microbalance, he scooped the tiny mound of powder into a small amber vial, and gave it to Guillemin just as he was leaving.

That same evening, at the San Francisco airport, before boarding the plane for his short flight back down to La Jolla, Guillemin called his technician, Scott Minick, from a pay phone. He read him the enkephalin formulas which Li had leaked to him from the *Nature* paper and asked Minick to call the lab's protein chemist, Nicholas Ling, at home. He wanted Ling to start synthesizing the compounds that very night.

Tests of Li's beta-endorphin were completed in the Goldstein and Guillemin labs during the same week as the Aberdonians' groundbreaking paper on the enkephalins was published in *Nature*. The results of the American tests were astounding.

When applied to the guinea pig ileum, beta-endorphin was over twenty times more powerful than morphine as a twitch-queller and far more stable than Hughes and Kosterlitz's short-acting enkephalins as Goldstein had predicted: its effect lasted up to six hours.

In Li's lab, one of his graduate students was working on the synthesis of lipotrophin. The "solid-phase" method of creating man-made synthetic peptides and proteins employs the same basic chemical reactions that nature uses to build them—with one important difference. In the synthetic product the amino acids are strung together backwards—from the last toward the first position in the sequence.

Li's student had started to build LPH, beginning with its ninety-first amino acid, and was slowly backing his way up the chain when Li suddenly interrupted him.

"Stop the procedure at position sixty-one. Go ahead, do it, don't ask questions," Li ordered.

By mid-January 1976, a synthetic version of beta-endorphin which was active on the ileum had been completed and, at Li's direction, his workers began to stockpile the material. Li's lab was particularly well suited to such labor-intensive operations; his "fellows," as Li called the team of about twenty-five mostly Oriental staff researchers, regarded Li with nearly ancestral reverence. They willingly slaved to do his bidding. Even so, the process of synthesizing beta-endorphin was so costly and time-consuming that if it had been on the open market, it would have sold for roughly $300,000 a gram.

Roger Guillemin, meanwhile, discovered a shorter, seventeen-amino-acid-length portion of lipotrophin—LPH 61-76—which also had opiate properties and which he named alphaendorphin. Another fragment—LPH 61-77—was characterized in his lab some months later as gamma-endorphin; both the alpha- and gamma-endorphins produced naloxone-reversible, twitch-quelling effects on the ileum, although neither was as potent as beta-endorphin, Li's "lucky" peptide.

Three weeks after the *Nature* paper appeared, on January 8, Guillemin announced the first of his "new" endorphins during a Harvey Lecture at the New York Academy of Medicine. He described endorphin isolation as a simple problem which he had easily solved in a few months.

His announcement was symptomatic of the rush for credit in the early days and weeks of 1976, after the Aberdeen *Nature* paper appeared. Solomon Snyder and Rabi Simantov, registering their claim to second place, hurried a paper into print that same January, based on research completed after their sneak preview of the *Nature* paper.

Derrick Smyth—who, as Morris and Hughes assumed, had been doing independent research on C-fragment—published an article on his results in February and that same month, C.H. Li published the first of hundreds of papers to come on beta-endorphin.

The scientists—Smyth, Goldstein, Li, and Guillemin—who had found these extended endorphins tended to glorify the alpha, beta, and gamma peptides in almost phallic terms: they each claimed that theirs was bigger, longer lasting, and more potent that the original enkephalins. All of which was true.

Derrick Smyth's particularly dogged insistence that since the enkephalins did not work very well they were probably only breakdown products of large peptides like C-fragment—and, therefore, of no real physiological importance—did little to enhance his reputation with the Aberdonians, especially since Hughes and Kosterlitz could not immediately disprove his claim. Hughes commenced a series of experiments to study other ways that the enkephalins could originate, hoping to refute Smyth and stay ahead of the field.

Kosterlitz had his own response to the increasingly strident chorus of claims and counterclaims which, he felt, was crowding out enkephalins and their original discoverers. Michael Kosterlitz, his son, who was studying physics in Birmingham, England, during the winter of 1976, recalls that it was around this time that he first fully became aware that his father was involved in a major discovery.

"Suddenly, when I called home, my father was never there," he says. "He was traveling all over, so I knew something big had happened. I once asked him, 'Why do you travel like this? You'll never get anything done.' He replied, 'I must, you see, to make sure the credit goes to the people it should.' "

The explosive pace of research during the next six months pushed back the boundaries of the new endorphin field. Not only were there many different kinds of endorphins, but by carefully comparing the potencies of the enkephalins with morphine and two synthetic opiates—which were distinctly different from morphine—Hans Kosterlitz (with Angela Waterfield and John Lord, an Aberdeen graduate who had returned to postdoc in the Unit) succeeded in demonstrating that there were also three different kinds of morphine receptors: delta, kappa, and mu. The field had suddenly taken on the complexity of particle physics.

Test-tube results, using the ileum and the vas, however, had their limitations. Since the final objective of medical research is, after all, the application of new findings to the treatment and prevention of disease, what the endorphins did in human beings was the crucial question. The first step was to test the endorphins on animals.

In January, on the heels of the publication of the *Nature* paper, Derrick Smyth—together with William Feldberg, one of the National Institute's notable pharmacologists—tested C-fragment on cats. The experiments were outstanding. When C-fragment was injected directly into the cats' brains, the animals became oblivious to pain. Based on the resultant data, C-fragment was judged to be a hundred times stronger than morphine—even more powerful than Goldstein and Guillemin had predicted on the ileum. Even Feldberg, a German Jewish refugee like Kosterlitz, who usually chided Smyth about bringing "ze muck" in for testing, was mildly impressed.

An amusing footnote to this story resulted after a February 1976 open house at the National Institute. During the session, Smyth described the work to a group of reporters, including one who was particularly persistent. Smyth, envisioning a fine, uplifting article (". . . brilliant scientists, wonderful new discovery . . .") was stunned the next day when one of London's most notorious tabloids featured a banner headline which read "Cats in Hell," over a picture of an adorable kitten.

The article went on to describe "animal-tester Smyth" and "former German-citizen Feldberg" in terms normally reserved for war criminals. Smyth, afterward, was besieged by threatening letters and phone calls, many suggesting that he apply his experimental procedures to various parts of his own anatomy.

Confirming Smyth's results, C.H. Li's beta-endorphin—

which was identical to C-fragment—was shown to produce profound analgesia, lasting for hours, in a series of tests on rats and mice. Unfortunately, the thirty-one-amino-acid-length beta-endorphin, as Li was finding out, was enormously expensive to make synthetically. The "short" enkephalins, on the other hand, broke down quickly but offered a significant cost advantage to drug company chemists who were beginning to step up research in the field.

A study of the analgesic effects of synthetic enkephalins appeared in the March 1976 issue of *Nature,* authored by Larry Stein and James Belluzi, two research scientists at the Wyeth Pharmaceutical Company in Philadelphia. A few weeks later, that same journal carried a similar article by the Sandoz team of Daniel Hauser and Dietmar Römer. Although the results were enigmatic, these articles were the first public signals that drug houses were developing their own endorphin programs.

When the International Narcotics Research Club met in Aberdeen in July 1976, Candace Pert announced her development of a redesigned, longer-lasting version of Met-enkephalin called a "protected analogue" because additional chemicals had been patched on to delay the enzyme breakdown which normally limited enkephalin's duration. Protected analogues were also being developed at several drug companies, but company scientists at the meeting in Aberdeen—among them, Römer and Hauser of Sandoz, and Robert Frederickson of Eli Lilly—were naturally more reluctant than Pert to reveal their results.

Roger Guillemin was not at the Narcotics Club's meeting in Aberdeen. He had, instead, attended a meeting in Strasbourg the week previous, where he conferred with David DeWied, the director of the Rudolph Magnus Institute of Utrecht, Holland.

DeWied had known Guillemin for twenty years, and had briefly competed with Schally and him to discover the releasing factors before turning his attention to a still-controversial research problem: the effects of pituitary peptides like ACTH, MSH, and vasopressin on learning and memory.

Guillemin had telephoned DeWied in late March, suggesting he test the endorphins and offering to supply him with samples. DeWied brought his results to Strasbourg with him: Rats dosed with minute quantities of alpha- and beta-endorphin seemed to learn faster and to retain learned responses longer.

The news only added to Guillemin's unabashed elation over the latest results from his own lab. Floyd Bloom, working with Guillemin at the Salk Institute, had come up with the contradictory but equally provocative result that rats given high doses of beta-endorphin became catatonic. This might mean, Guillemin announced in Strasbourg, that the endorphins played a role in some form of mental illness.

Before going on to the International Endocrine Conference in Hamburg, Guillemin sent a telegram to the Aberdeen meeting which was read aloud by Kosterlitz at the opening session. It congratulated Hughes and Kosterlitz on their achievement—the full importance of which was only now becoming clear, directly as a result of developments in Guillemin's own lab. In brief detail, he outlined Bloom's new and puzzling data, but it was the underlying message which was most important: Endorphins had been linked to madness, and Roger Guillemin wanted to be the first to tell the Narcotics Club about it.

THE MADNESS FACTOR

Throughout the spring of 1976, Floyd Bloom's colleagues at the Salk Institute in La Jolla, California, were treated to remarkable performances by his white rats. Taking a rodent out of its cage, Bloom would inject a minute amount of an experimental compound into the nape of its neck. For the first few minutes, the rat sat on Bloom's desk, placidly licking its paws, sniffing the air, and occasionally shaking like a tiny wet dog.

No unusual change in behavior was noticeable until Bloom jabbed it with a pin or squeezed its tail in a powerful clamp. The animal had no reaction—it seemed totally impervious to pain. A few minutes later, the rat lapsed into what Bloom termed a "waxy" condition: its eyes fixed in an unblinking stare, its body icy cold, it became malleable, like soft putty, and, much to the amusement and wonder of Bloom's coworkers, the rat could be twisted into all sorts of outlandish postures. Bloom, on occasion, would repeat the process until several lab rats were lined up on his desk in various comical, catatonic poses. The finale of his demonstration came when Bloom stretched out one of his "waxy" rats between two bookends—where it remained, rigid and unperturbed, for nearly three hours, as if in a trance.

The experimental chemical Bloom was dosing his animals with was beta-endorphin—at that time nearly as much of a mystery as the behavior it produced. In his mid-thirties, affable, and equipped, as one colleague notes, with a "mind like blotting paper," Bloom was a newcomer to the endorphin field. As the former chief of the neuropharmacology lab at the National Institutes of Health in Bethesda, Maryland, he had directed several projects mapping the body's known chemical messengers and determining how their signals altered behavior. The possibilities that the endorphins might modulate pain responses or have euphoric effects on mood—in some ways similar to morphine—were naturally of interest to him.

Bloom had moved to La Jolla in January 1976, a few weeks after the historic paper on enkephalins appeared in *Nature*. Financed by funds left over from the March of Dimes, La Jolla's Salk Institute looked like a temple of science. Parallel sets of monolithic Louis Kahn buildings, situated on a bluff above a thickly wooded escarpment overlooking the Pacific Ocean, exuded a kind of religious grandeur.

Bloom's own laboratories were not yet finished so he was sharing space in Roger Guillemin's lab where the alpha- and beta-endorphins and the enkephalins were, by then, being synthesized. "As long as I was working in the lab, we decided that I should test the behavioral effects of the peptides," Bloom remembers.

One of his specialized talents, his skill at giving intracisternal injections to rats (injections directly into the membrane of the brain) were particularly useful. The brain is protected by a thin membrane which, in turn, is covered by the skull—except at the nape of the neck where, in rodents and humans, there is a depression, easily felt with the fingertips. "The membrane is exposed there, there's a big hole," Bloom explains—a hole into which he could deftly pop a needle.

Alpha-endorphin and the enkephalins produced disappointing results, but in May the beta peptide was finished, and

Bloom set up his first experiment in Guillemin's lab. He had decided on doses of beta-endorphin ranging no higher than twenty millionths of a gram—an amount he now considers wildly excessive.

Guillemin and his assistant, Scott Minick, looked on as the first rat became "waxy." Bloom still recalls the incident with giddy astonishment. "It was a profound loss of everything. Within five minutes the animals developed extreme rigidity, there was an incredible drop in body temperature, they felt like icicles. I was amazed that they still lived."

The subject of waxy flexibility—or "flexy waxability," as Bloom soon took to calling the bizarre, endorphin-produced effects—became still more curious as spring turned into summer. Together with Steve Henrickson, he wired his rats to an electroencephalogram (EEG) machine. During the first moments after the injection—as the animal sniffed and groomed but otherwise exhibited no outward peculiarity—its inner life bordered on the supernatural. "The animal was doing absolutely nothing, but its head was generating an entire village worth of electricity," Bloom recounts. "The EEG pens were wrecking off the paper, ink spattering everywhere. We couldn't believe that so much was going on in its head."

Typically—after a run of such high amplitude discharges—the rat would go "waxy" and the EEG pattern would go flat. It was as if, Bloom says, "its hippocampus had short-circuited." Yet the animals' brain waves for sight, sound, and smell remained unaffected; even the rat's perception of the design on Henrickson's shirt registered clearly on the EEG. Bright lights and loud noises would arouse it, and so would naloxone, the morphine antagonist, which—Bloom discovered—gave a new twist to his animal act.

"It was a tremendous catatonia and you could cure it with a small injection of naloxone," says Bloom. "The animal went from being normal to being a zombie and back to being normal . . . just like that."

Bloom and Guillemin discussed the implications of what they had seen. Since endorphins had been discovered, scientists assumed that they had something to do with controlling pain in living creatures. But Bloom's "waxy" rats—sniffing and grooming while their heads exploded with electrical activity, or lying tranquilly stretched out between bookends—caused the two researchers to broaden this narrow perspective.

Clearly the animals felt no pain, but their strange behavior and the seizurelike activity in their brains were strong indications that the endorphins had other functions that went beyond pain relief, effects which were scarcely imaginable to scientists at the outset of research into the brain's own opiate.

Roger Guillemin took Bloom's early results—along with a slide of a "waxy" rat propped up by bookends—to Strasbourg in July, to publicly announce that the work suggested a link between endorphins and some forms of mental illness. Guillemin, along with others in the audience, appeared stunned when Lar Terenius, the Swedish biochemist who had already linked low endorphin levels to chronic pain syndromes in humans, disclosed for the first time that his group in Uppsala, Sweden, had found higher than normal endorphin levels in the cerebrospinal fluid of schizophrenics, and that they had begun limited testing with the antagonist naloxone to see if that would alleviate some of the patients' symptoms. After the seminar, Guillemin hurriedly left the room.

That schizophrenics experienced pain differently from normal individuals was a widely observed yet unexplained fact. Lars Lindström (who had known Terenius since 1964, when he had been his pharmacology student) began his psychiatric residency at the Uppsala Psychiatric Research Center in 1974. He recalls one striking example from his first year at the Research Center: "I saw a patient smoking, and there was this curious smell. He'd smoked the cigarette to the very end and his fingers were burning. When I told him, he said, 'Oh yeah,' and stubbed out the cigarette with his fingers."

The high endorphin levels which Terenius and Agneta Wahlström had observed might account for such numbness, but could they be producing the patients' symptoms as well? Lars Gunne, one of Lindström's senior colleagues at the Research Center, thought they might. Some years earlier he had conducted a series of experiments on pain patients and addicts using a new group of drugs called mixed agonist-antagonists. These powerful narcotic painkillers, less addictive than one would expect because they partly counteracted morphine, were found to be useless clinically because they produced a variety of bizarre unpleasant side effects. In early clinical trials one test patient experienced the waking nightmare that she was "blowing up and exploding"; another hallucinated that "people were chasing me and I was cornered." These responses were typical. Most test subjects concluded that the pain was preferable to the medication.

The fact that mixed agonist-antagonist drugs caused psychotic-like symptoms even as they blocked pain, coupled with observations by Candace Pert and others that opiate receptors and endorphins were concentrated in the limbic system—an area of the brain implicated in mood and emotional behavior—made the connection between endorphins and schizophrenia seem less farfetched. Perhaps naloxone, a morphine antagonist which also blocked the effects of endorphins, would reduce the mental patients' symptoms and if so, form the basis of a new therapy.

In May 1976, six subjects were chosen for the pilot study in Uppsala. Hallucinations were the "target symptom." Four subjects heard voices almost constantly; one of them heard bells; another had paranoid delusions about a girl named "Anna" who appeared regularly to frighten and torment her.

"We used about twice the amount of naloxone used to bring heroin addicts out of overdoses," Lindström recalls.

"The first patient, a young man, had heard voices all day, day after day. One minute after the naloxone injection, he was sitting in bed; he was staring at me. I asked, 'Did something happen?' I'd said nothing about what to expect. He said, 'Well, the voices disappeared!' There was complete silence inside his head."

Ninety minutes later, as the injection began to wear off, the patient told Lindström that the voices had begun to return but were "scarcely audible, like coming from a long distance." After six hours, the voices had regained their full intensity.

Over the next few days, Lindström tested the other patients with equally dramatic results. All four of the hallucinators reported, with various expressions of amazement, that the voices and bells had quieted. The young woman who was troubled by visual hallucinations told Lindström that "Anna" had left her—for the first time in several weeks. "It felt like we were sitting on something very important," Lars Terenius later related. "It made sense, but seemed too fantastic."

The results were also anecdotal, conducted without proper experimental controls and therefore subject to criticism. For that reason, Terenius only informally presented his results in Strasbourg—coincidentally upstaging Guillemin.

The following November, when an article about Floyd Bloom's "waxy rat" experiments appeared in *Science,* speculating that the beta-endorphin reaction of the animals was reminiscent of some aspects of schizophrenia, large scale follow-up tests of naloxone were underway in Uppsala. To insure that all possible biases and expectations were eliminated from the study, a double blind procedure was used; neither the experimenter nor the patient knew if naloxone or a saline placebo was being administered. This time, the results were disappointing. Naloxone was no more effective at stopping the hallucinations of patients than was saline.

At the same time, preparations for the ultimate test of C.H. Li's beta-endorphin secretly got underway in New York.

Performed without government approval, these experiments on mentally ill patients would be completed some months later, amid the controversial muddle of what others in the field began calling "Nathan Kline's Caper."

Nathan Kline was on an oatmeal kick. During the fall of 1977, he ate oatmeal every morning for breakfast with the same flamboyant enthusiasm he had used to convince a skeptical psychiatric community that drugs were often more effective than analysis in the treatment of mental disorders.

Kline was a short, spry man in his late fifties. His thick, curly white beard and modishly long white hair gave him a patriarchal appearance—a slight resemblance to Charlton Heston's Moses. As he rattled among the pots and pans in the kitchen, Kline spoke rapidly to Heinz Lehmann, who sat quietly at the dining table. Lehmann had learned long before that Kline's idea of conversation was an extended monologue.

Lehmann was several years older than Kline, polite, soft-spoken with thin, wispy, gray hair cut by a barber, not a stylist. Since leaving Europe during the war he had made his home in Montreal, where he was a Professor of Psychiatry at McGill University. For the past several years he had been giving a weekly seminar in Albany, New York, and frequently traveled from there to Manhattan for meetings with Kline.

They were old friends and, despite obvious personality differences, Lehmann and Kline had much in common. They both were psychiatrists deeply involved in the development of the first drug therapies for mental illness—fellow pioneers in a field that had made them internationally famous.

They first met at the Astor Hotel on Times Square in 1956, shortly after each had independently scored a major breakthrough for which, the following year, they shared the most prestigious American medical research award, the Lasker Prize—Kline for his introduction of a drug called reserpine, Lehmann for his introduction of chlorpromazine (Thorazine) into clinical psychiatry.

These drugs were not mere sedatives, but genuine anti-psychotic medicines that not only calmed hyperactive patients, but also made withdrawn patients more active. Despite some disturbing physical side effects, these drugs produced such dramatic improvement in severely disturbed patients that in the twenty years since they had been introduced the patient population in American mental institutions had been cut by two thirds. A million individuals had been restored to bearable, often productive lives. Nathan Kline and Heinz Lehmann had sparked a revolution in psychiatric medicine.

Kline won a second Lasker prize for iproniazid, the first of a group of compounds called monoamine oxidase inhibitors (MAOI) used to counteract depression. This award was marred, however, when one of his associates, Harry P. Loomer, sued Kline and the Lasker Foundation. Loomer alleged that Kline had been "false and fraudulent" in claiming complete credit for experiments that actually had been conducted by Loomer with another researcher. Kline later acknowledged Loomer's work and the suit was dropped.

Almost simultaneously, Lehmann had been quietly testing a second group of antidepressants—the tricyclics—which produced the same, near miraculous reversals of depression symptoms, with fewer side effects than MAOIs. (For unknown reasons, the MAOIs produced side effects ranging from mild headaches to cerebral hemorrhages if they were combined with foods like cheddar cheese, chicken livers, or pickled herring.)

In the early 1960s, Kline had championed the use of lithium against manic-depressive psychosis, and his enthusiastic arm twisting convinced several pharmaceutical companies to support research into the common, unpatentable, and therefore unprofitable, metallic salt. In the intervening period, Kline had been deeply involved in the introduction and evaluation of at least a dozen new psychiatric medications.

While Heinz Lehmann remained a fairly cautious, conservative clinician, Nathan Kline had been, from the start of his career, a promoter who liked to do things on a big scale. He had access to people in high places: the government, the drug companies, and the media. He openly enjoyed the trappings of his success—good food, fine wine, elegant parties, and a circle of friends that ranged far beyond the scientific and psychiatric communities to include celebrities like Dick Cavett, Bess Myerson, David Merrick, Leonard Bernstein, and David Susskind.

"He was a political creature," says his daughter Marna Anderson, and he relished organizing, mobilizing and pulling strings behind the scenes. Kline was "a man of action," recalls Lehmann; he moved quickly on new ideas with a wheeler-dealer's arrogance and a cavalier manner that at times even disturbed his good friend. For example, Kline, in typically unrestrained terms, once suggested, "Chlorination and fluoridation of water have been generally accepted as health measures. Why not lithium in the water supply?"

His critics called him a "wild man" which, in scientific jargon, has the specific connotation of one whose clinical studies, however demonstrative, are so consistently careless as to be all but useless.

During the autumn of 1976 Kline was Director of the Rockland Research Institute, a New York State–supported facility which he had founded in 1952 to explore new cures for mental illness. He also maintained a large private practice out of a suite of offices on the Upper East Side in Manhattan, a ten-minute walk from his home. His apartment, on the twelfth floor of a luxury high rise on East Sixty-sixth Street, was spacious and decorated with tasteful modern furniture and thick carpeting, dominated by a large color television set and an expensive sound system. A zebra-skin rug which hung on the wall was among the personal touches added by Kline after his divorce, a few years earlier. An extensive collection of African and Oceanic folk art filled several glass cases in the living room. Sliding glass doors opened onto a wide terrace with a fine view of Manhattan.

That fall, Lehmann's visits to Kline had become an almost weekly event. He usually stayed in the spare bedroom, at once avoiding expensive hotel bills and maximizing the amount of time dedicated to their increasingly animated discussions. Kline's daughter Marna recalls that during this period she would often find them talking until two o'clock in the morning, and then back at it again over breakfast at six. During that particular fall, their conversations had narrowed to a single topic: testing beta-endorphin on humans.

Although reserpine, Thorazine, the MAOIs, lithium, and the other therapeutic drugs discovered by Kline and Lehmann were unquestionably effective, at the time they were developed the two scientists had no idea why they worked. "A great deal was known about the brain and its diseases," Heinz Lehmann explains, "but there was very little data on the chemistry; we clinicians found that these drugs worked 'miracles.' Only then did the biochemists ask what they were doing. They found that they affected neurotransmitters."

The actions of the neurotransmitter dopamine had been singled out for study and speculation by researchers since 1963, when a Swedish scientific team had demonstrated that Lehmann's drug, Thorazine, blocked receptors for dopamine. Theories that Thorazine and similar antipsychotic drugs therefore worked by correcting an overabundance of dopamine were widespread, but by the 1970s it was clear that dopamine was not the only chemical agent involved in mental illness.

Despite the dramatic success of the drug therapies, a frustrating sizeable minority—330,000 patients in the U.S. alone—still remained institutionalized, apparently unresponsive to dopamine-blockade treatment.

"Our interest in beta-endorphin came about partially because—despite the effectiveness of these other drugs—a portion of the patient population didn't respond to them," recalled Heinz Lehmann. "So here were these new brain chemicals, the endorphins. Perhaps they were the missing link."

That November, as Lehmann's breakfasts with Kline became a steady affair, Floyd Bloom's "waxy rat" experiment appeared. It was accompanied in *Science* magazine by a second paper, received just a few days after Bloom's, reporting similar findings by Yasuko Jacquet—one of Kline's researchers at the Rockland Psychiatric Institute. Earlier that year, Jacquet had finagled a small sample of beta-endorphin from C.H. Li, which she administered in microgram doses, trying to produce pain relief in rats.

The rats exhibited the same "waxy flexibility" that Bloom had observed in his animals. But while this suggested to Bloom that elevated levels of endorphins might cause the signs and symptoms of mental illness, Jacquet drew just the opposite conclusion. She noted that the rats' behavior was similar to that of animals who had been injected with the antipsychotic drug Haldol. She speculated that a deficiency of endorphins might therefore be responsible for psychosis. Betaendorphin itself might have a beneficial effect on patients.

"Rats meant nothing to us vis-a-vis human patients," Heinz Lehmann recalls. "We simply thought, 'Here's a new substance that produces effects. Let's try it.' " Convinced that others were already contemplating a similar procedure, Kline and Lehmann hurriedly began gearing up for a test of beta-endorphin on schizophrenic patients.

"Scientists all have an adolescent sporting sense," Nathan Kline once said. "We all want to be first, and besides, it's fun to pioneer things. So we decided to jump the others in human experiments. We knew nobody would suspect us. We weren't members of the group we'd heard they called 'The Endorphin Club.' But we thought we were in a race with them, nevertheless, and were determined to win it."

To do so they would require help from C.H. Li.

Li had a virtual monopoly on beta-endorphin in America. The precious material was not for sale, but Li scrupulously controlled its distribution to other scientists in order to gain the maximum scientific and public impact for his "lucky" peptide. Among his colleagues this strategy was sarcastically dubbed "the Li principle." One of Li's stated goals was to be the first to test beta-endorphin in man. His primary interest was pain, however, not madness.

As a preliminary step in April 1976, Li had sent some of his manmade beta-endorphin for animal testing to Horace Loh, an opiate researcher and an acquaintance of Li's at the San Francisco Medical Center. The effects of beta-endorphin were strikingly positive: when injected directly into the brain, synthetic beta-endorphin was eighteen to thirty-three times more powerful than morphine.

Of even greater importance, Loh's follow-up experiments indicated that although the peptide lost much of its power when administered intravenously, it was still three to four times stronger than almost any known narcotic. This was a key consideration in any future human study of beta-endorphin since the intravenous method is considerably more practical than "spritzing" the compound directly into the brain.

Later that year, in September, shortly after the publication of Loh's animal studies, Donald Catlin—a pain specialist at the UCLA Medical School—entered the picture. Loh and Catlin were old friends; Loh was the godfather of one of Catlin's children and they had roomed together during the Airlie House meeting of the International Narcotics Research Club, where Catlin got his first exposure to endorphins.

Catlin had been following the field with excitement ever since. "Loh's paper demonstrating the effectiveness of intravenous doses of beta-endorphin really made me jump." He began making daily phone calls to Loh, asking to be put in touch with Li. Catlin wanted to offer Li a deal.

Since the tragic disaster of the fertility drug Thalidomide, strict regulations had been imposed on scientists planning to test new drugs on human beings in the U.S. A written protocol, stating why and how the tests would be conducted, and including evidence that the substance was safe in animals, first had to be submitted for approval to the Food and Drug Administration in Rockville, Maryland. This was the case even for natural products like the endorphins. If FDA permission was granted, an "investigative new drug" (IND) permit was issued, and only then were experimenters free to proceed with testing on humans.

Catlin told Loh that he would do all the paperwork for Li. "I said I would assemble all the literature to convince the FDA that beta-endorphin was safe enough to test in humans," Catlin recalls, "and I would get the privilege of being the first to work with it—in man."

Six months passed and Catlin heard nothing. Apparently he had not made himself clear enough, Loh told him; again Catlin explained his plan and asked Loh to pass it on to Li, and "that seemed to get his attention," Catlin recalls. In early 1977, Li told Catlin to begin work on an FDA protocol for human trials, but by then—on his own—Li had taken two other extraordinary steps in that same direction.

In December, Li had discussed plans for a human experiment with Kline and Lehmann; Kline had invited Li to come to New York and a dinner party had been arranged at Kline's apartment. All three men were fascinated by the idea of testing beta-endorphin on mentally ill patients, particularly on those who had been unresponsive to other drugs.

The FDA's rules for human testing had been laid down after Kline and Lehmann had done their most famous work, and Kline resented the new regulations, describing them as "the FDA's Catch-22"; but he seemed perplexed over just how to deal with them. Lehmann recalls that they discussed whether it was necessary to go to the FDA at all. After all, this was "treatment, not planned research. A physician is obliged, is he not, to use any means to help a patient?"

Li voiced no objections. He seemed to Lehmann to be as eager as the other two to get started on the testing, and he agreed to supply them with beta-endorphin.

Li's colleagues in San Francisco—familiar with Kline's "wild man" reputation—urged him to change his mind. "No," Li told them. "This Kline is very courageous."

As Kline and Lehmann waited for C.H. Li's crucial contribution, Li's technicians had been synthesizing a new supply of beta-endorphin. Work was necessarily slow and not all of the material was intended for the experiments in New York.

Later that winter, C.H. Li initiated a collaboration with Yoshio Hosobuchi, one of America's most prominent brain surgeons. Hosobuchi, in San Francisco, was following up experiments with stimulation-produced analgesia to relieve severe chronic pain in humans. He had already operated on the skulls of six terminal cancer patients—patients who no longer got pain relief even from high doses of narcotics—and he had implanted fine electrodes into the periventricular and pariaqueductal gray matter of the brains, through holes he had drilled in their skulls.

It was a delicate, eerie procedure. Since brain tissue does not register sensation or pain, only a local anesthetic was administered to the scalp; the patients, remaining fully awake during the operation, reported their sensations back to Hosobuchi—a necessity, since a slight misplacement of the electrodes would produce effects painfully opposed to the ones he sought. After the implantation, patients were allowed to administer their own brain stimulation by switching on a small bedside generator.

Hosobuchi's results had been extremely encouraging. Five of the six patients reported total relief from their pain, discontinuing their use of other medication. They felt better, their appetites improved, and they slept more soundly.

These patients presented a unique opportunity for C.H.

Li, and he discussed the possibilities with Hosobuchi repeatedly throughout the early months of 1977. "He [Hosobuchi] was working with fine electrodes. There was already a hole there, so why not put in a drop of beta-endorphin?"

Hosobuchi was reluctant to carry out Li's suggestion without permission from the University of California. "Don't be afraid, nothing will happen, I'll take care of them," Li counseled him. "If it works, you don't have to worry; if it doesn't, no one will know."

Still, Hosobuchi obtained permission from the University and the tests were carried out. The results were positive— although, Hosobuchi would later write, in addition to pain relief some of his patients also reported "dizziness," nausea, and a "hot sensation" prickling their bodies.

Donald Catlin—with no knowledge that any of this had taken place—was beginning to work on the application for the Investigational New Drug permit he would need to test Li's compound on humans. On April 30, 1977, Catlin mailed out the application and on May 5, he received a postcard from the FDA acknowledging its receipt.

According to the procedures outlined on the card, he was to wait one month; if by that time he received no further communication from the FDA, he could assume that his IND had been approved and he could then commence work. Catlin waited until June 6 (one month and a day) and, without having received any further notification from the FDA, began his own tests of beta-endorphin on three terminally ill cancer patients.

His procedure was different from Hosobuchi's. Catlin administered 30-milligram doses of the peptide to his patients by "intravenous infusion"—dripping the substance into a vein in their arms through a catheter, over a period of several hours. In this manner, one patient per day was tested for three days. All three reported moderate pain relief, at least, but the sample was too small and the results too indistinct to draw any firm conclusions.

Within days of finishing the first tests, Catlin received notification from the FDA to stop his work. The IND had not been approved after all; his animal studies had proven insufficient. He would have to test beta-endorphin on cats—as well as rats—to win final approval.

Catlin was still hunting down lab space, cats, and assistants when he heard the first rumors, from Horace Loh, about human tests of beta-endorphin already underway in New York.

By mid-April of 1977 Kline was telephoning Li—sometimes twice a day—urging him to hurry the synthesis process so that he could get on with the experiments. Kline sounded worried, recalls Li. Privately, Kline revealed his concern that Li had cooled on the project.

In June, a package finally arrived at Kline's office, containing a small amber vial labeled "Beta-endorphin 30 mg." The first secret tests were conducted over the next two months.

Six male patients, three schizophrenics, and three depressives who had been resistent to existing drug therapies, were selected as subjects from Kline's private practice. They and their families consented to allow treatment—without charge—with an "experimental compound" which, Kline emphasized, was something entirely new and extremely expensive, from $400 to $3,000 per treatment.

Kline felt this information was a necessity, Heinz Lehmann explains, "otherwise most people would not want to be a guinea pig." But, by heightening the expectations of the patients and their families, they immediately created enough potential biases possibly to invalidate their results.

One additional subject, named Edward Laski, was a friend and colleague of Kline's. Intense-looking, with bushy eyebrows and moustache, Laski, an Associate Professor at the Albert Einstein School of Medicine, was thirty-four years old and perfectly healthy. He was to serve as "control," becoming the first normal human to receive beta-endorphin.

The trials were conducted on June 29 and 30 in Kline's East Side offices. He had invested several thousand dollars of his own money in a sophisticated closed-circuit videotape system, in order to record the patients' reactions over several hours. The patient was displayed on a television monitor, in an adjoining room, so that his family could observe the proceedings.

Each patient was seated in a chair facing the camera. A catheter was inserted into a vein in one arm to deliver the compound. Another catheter, taking blood samples throughout the procedure, dangled from the patient's other arm. An inflatable rubber cuff—to measure blood pressure—was wrapped around his bicep. An oxygen tank and a table of syringes (loaded with adrenaline and the opiate antagonist, naloxone) were placed—off camera but nearby, in case of emergency.

"We didn't know what to expect," Lehmann says. "For all we knew, their blood might have turned green."

In each case, Kline first interviewed the patient during a troubled state, as the videotape rolled. A saline placebo was then administered for ten minutes, and a second psychiatric interview with the subject was recorded. Finally, a tiny dose—1.5 milligrams—of beta-endorphin was dripped into the subject's arm. A few minutes later, each was interviewed again.

Kline's videotape captured one of the depressives smiling. Otherwise, the results were inconclusive; if anything, the three schizophrenic patients seemed worse.

A second test was scheduled for July 12, one in which Kline hoped to repeat the experiment with much higher doses (3.9 milligrams), but their supply of beta-endorphin was almost exhausted. Kline telephoned Li, arguing that the results, however equivocal, merited a retrial; Li, convinced, sent Kline an additional 130 milligrams of beta-endorphin.

When the compound was retested, the most startling results involved a schizophrenic named Brian. "After about four milligrams of beta-endorphin his appearance changed,"

Kline and Lehmann later reported. "He looked more energetic, smiled frequently and talked volubly and at a much more rapid rate than was usual for him. He spoke of plans for the future, expressed an attitude of hopefulness and mentioned that he no longer was afraid that people were talking about him."

None of the other test patients responded. Edward Laski, the control, experienced only a "spaced-out, floating feeling. It was not a good feeling for me," he said, "not like alcohol, not like waking from a refreshing sleep."

In fact, as the substance took hold, Laski's strongest sensation was one of "perplexity." This strange altered state lasted for five hours and then, suddenly, went away "like flipping an on-off switch."

The schizophrenic, Brian, continued to get well. Several days later, in a follow-up videotaped interview, he told Kline that, while listening to the Beatles' song "Yesterday" on the radio, he had wept—for the first time in years—out of happiness: because he knew that "yesterday" was over. Over the next several weeks, as his improvement continued, his family reported that Brian had become "his old, salty self again."

Such sudden and seemingly miraculous improvements in schizophrenic patients do occasionally occur—sometimes simply as a result of their doctors paying attention to them—and Kline and Lehmann certainly could not prove that the beta-endorphin infusion caused it. In the months that followed, however, Brian became Kline's video star—in the press and before the scientific community—as Kline launched his "endorphin cure."

The New York City blackout occurred on July 13, 1977, at about 10:30 P.M. Lights dimmed, momentarily brightened, then went off completely—plunging all Manhattan into sudden darkness. Nathan Kline and Heinz Lehmann were in Kline's office on East Seventy-seventh Street. When the lights went out, Lehmann was at the typewriter—where he had spent the last six hours—writing and revising a paper on their results. Kline, on the telephone, was talking with Daniel X. Freedman, the editor of the *Archives of General Psychiatry,* in Chicago. It was the last of several telephone conversations he had had with Freedman that day.

Kline was in a near frenzy to get their results published quickly. For the past month he had been preparing Freedman for the big moment, but Freedman continued to be wary. The study, he said, lacked a good, systematic design, and he had suggested that they instead publish it in the "Letters" section of the British medical journal *Lancet*—where, he advised, there would be "fewer fences."

Over the telephone Kline had emphasized throughout the day the urgency of publishing the report. Testing was completed and, as he told Freedman, they had run out of beta-endorphin. No further work would even be possible for many months, and by then someone else might do the same thing—it might be too late for the "scoop" he was offering Freedman.

Freedman had known Kline for twenty years, and while he respected his notable achievements, he was used to Kline's momentous overstatements and self-aggrandizing crusades. "You had to be crazy like Nate or the experiment would have taken another five years," Freedman comments, "but I wasn't interested in helping him get publicity."

Freedman remained so skeptical of the findings, that, even after he had agreed to publish the article, he demanded that the scientists include what amounted almost to a disclaimer, detailing the shortcomings of the study. Kline agreed to do so, and he and Lehmann hurriedly wrote an additional paragraph explaining that the research was based on a limited sample; that some of the patients were receiving other medication; that doses of beta-endorphin used in the first series of tests were probably below the optimal level to evoke responses; and that, even at higher doses, not all of the patients had responded. Lehmann typed up the cautionary paragraph and, while Kline was going over it on the telephone with Freedman, the blackout dramatically capped the day.

A messenger from Purolator Courier arrived at the office at eleven o'clock that night and disappeared into the darkened city with a package bound for Chicago. It was a short walk back to Kline's apartment. The streets were uncanny, Lehmann recalls; it was the first time he had ever seen stars in the Manhattan sky. On the way, they met Dick Cavett, the television talk show host, a neighbor and friend of Nathan Kline's.

Lehmann had met Cavett before, when Cavett had gotten Kline to let him tape some interviews with schizophrenic patients. "It was not for his show, but out of curiosity," Lehmann says. "For the most part he did a tactful but not a clinical job. Afterwards, when I saw the patients again, they told me, 'Well, I talked to Dick Cavett and he said I should leave my mother's house' . . . that sort of well-intentioned but impossible advice. I had to undo some of his work."

As a protection against muggers, Cavett, who was walking a large dog, volunteered to accompany them as far as Kline's apartment building. Using a borrowed flashlight they got Kline's car out of the garage and drove to a restaurant in New Jersey, where the lights were still on. It was after midnight when they finally ate dinner and past two in the morning when they arrived back in the still pitch-black city.

Lighting some candles which they had bought on the way, Lehmann and Kline trudged up the twelve stories to Kline's apartment. The electricity still had not come back on the following morning, when they both climbed back down; but their research paper, they were later relieved to learn, had somehow made its way to Chicago.

A third batch of beta-endorphin, bringing the total to over 200 milligrams—about $80,000 worth of material and a

significant portion of the world's precious store of the peptide—
was supplied by C.H. Li to Kline and Lehmann that summer.
A total of fourteen patients tried the compound. The results
were occasionally interesting, but always questionable.

News stories arranged by Kline about the experiments
appeared in the press by August, only weeks after an investigative new drug permit—arranged for C.H. Li by Donald Catlin—
had finally been approved. A team of FDA investigators now
contacted Li; they wanted to know how Nathan Kline had
obtained the beta-endorphin he had been using.

Elsewhere, the Kline-Lehmann research, published in the
September 1977 *Archives of General Psychiatry,* was beginning
to provoke a vehement negative reaction among some members of the International Narcotics Research Club.

"The feeling on the part of the endorphin establishment
was 'how dare these barbarians diddle with our stuff,' " Daniel
X. Freedman recalls. "They had jumped the gun," another
researcher comments, "shot the stuff into patients without any
idea of what they were doing."

There were other signs of trouble ahead which Nathan
Kline chose to ignore. He was on the move, instead, making
telephone calls, writing letters, using his widespread contacts—
mounting a fresh campaign to get beta-endorphin testing underway in humans, on a large scale.

C.H. Li warned him to "wait, move slowly," but, Li adds,
Kline would not listen. "He liked the limelight too much.
He wanted to make a big noise. This is the problem with
clinical scientists. They want to belong, they want to be famous, they want more and more."

But Li's comments may not take into account his own
enthusiastic promotion of beta-endorphin throughout the fall
and winter of 1977, when he was described, by a colleague, as
"going around the world telling people that beta-endorphin was
practically a panacea, that it was good for everything." It was
early that December, in Puerto Rico, when the bottom fell out.

*   *   *

The "Endorphins in Mental Health Research" symposium—choreographed by a hopeful Kline to be a watershed event—took place at the Caribe Hilton in San Juan, Puerto Rico, on December 10 through 13, 1977, as part of the annual American College of Neuropharmacology Conference. Kline's plans, made before his beta-endorphin work had begun, originally included about 30 participants. Once the focus of the meeting became brain opiates and mental illness, that figure had ballooned to 150, including three reporters.

Kline had sent invitations to most of the prominent scientists in the endorphin field: Avram Goldstein, Agneta Wahlström, Candace Pert, and Floyd Bloom all agreed to be there. Hans Kosterlitz, although sure that the endorphins were involved in more than just pain relief, had turned down Kline's invitation, refusing to have anything to do with such "unscientific" proceedings. John Hughes had already received a thick sheaf of letters from one disturbed patient, pleading with him for treatment. Hughes, too, declined to attend.

Nor would Solomon Snyder be there. "I was skeptical," he says. "When you're dealing with the biochemical causes of schizophrenia, these are powerful ideas. When articles buried in the scientific literature come out in the media, you can raise false hopes."

Kline had also invited representatives from the National Institute of Mental Health, the Food and Drug Administration, and the pharmaceutical industry to the San Juan meeting. His grand objectives there were to gain approval and support from the scientific community, funding and cooperation from the drug industry, and to get enough room from the FDA to allow expanded beta-endorphin research—a house of cards based entirely on his and Lehmann's study of fourteen patients. "We were forcing the issue," says Lehmann.

There was a wedding going on in the ballroom next door

to the main conference room at the Caribe Hilton during the afternoon of December 10, so music and laughter could be heard through the walls. The conference room was completely full; C.H. Li, with his arms crossed, sat in the front row. Heinz Lehmann had taken a chair in the second row. Candace and Agu Pert sat behind him on the aisle, and in one of the back rows Avram Goldstein fidgeted in his seat, poised to pounce.

On the podium, dressed in a gray checked sport coat, a dapper Dr. Nathan Kline opened the proceedings with a key-note testimonial to the therapeutic wonders of beta-endorphin.

"Beta-endorphin appeared to act as an antipsychotic, to be disinhibiting, anxiolytic, and antidepressant," he confidently told the gathering. The substance, he added, had produced no adverse reactions or side effects and did not seem to be addictive. None of the patients, Kline quipped, had come back "for a treat instead of a treatment."

The videos were then displayed, but reviews were mixed. They looked convincing to Agneta Wahlström, yet, according to Floyd Bloom, "It was hard to tell just what the effect of the peptide was on the patients. It certainly was not the straight-forward 'magic bullet.' "

As soon as Kline finished his presentation, Avram Goldstein was on his feet. His ten-minute indictment began as an ironic attack on Kline's talk, becoming increasingly vehement as his anger mounted.

"A considerable supply of the rare and expensive synthetic beta-endorphin was committed to an experiment that could not, in principle, have yielded decisive results . . . a nonsense study," he declared. "We don't need tens of thousands of descriptions of encounters with UFOs; what's needed is one description in which it is clear there was an encounter."

He went on to dismiss the alleged positive effects. "It's known that if a psychiatrist talks to a hallucinating patient, that patient temporarily stops talking to those voices and starts talking to the psychiatrist." His angriest comments, though, concerned the midsummer publicity that surrounded the first trials of beta-endorphin on human patients. Goldstein charged that Kline was grabbing headlines "to raise public hopes without sound scientific evidence," a practice which, he concluded adamantly, "will serve science poorly in the long run." The study, he felt, should never have been published, let alone publicized.

Edward C. Tocus, one of the FDA representatives at the meeting, then joined the assault. He told the conferees that the Agency felt that since the Kline-Lehmann results were not based on a proper scientific approach, it "would not take cognizance" of the findings. "The patients had been taken out of their rooms, told this was a wonderful new drug," he later explained. "All of these things created biases."

Kline, cheerfully, tried to diffuse these criticisms. "Our justification remains the treatment of patients, rather than experimentation," he argued back. Rapid publication and publicity were necessary, "to communicate and to reassure others that they, too, can do human investigations."

But the position of Tocus and the FDA was that if large-scale testing of beta-endorphin was to begin, it must be preceded by large-scale animal testing; the work could not proceed simply on the basis of Kline's say-so.

This was disappointing news to others at the meeting besides Nathan Kline. A show of hands indicated that at least twenty other researchers were still interested in following up Kline's work—FDA permitting, of course.

That evening, after the meeting broke, Kline invited a dozen key people from the National Institute of Mental Health, the FDA, the pharmaceutical industry and the research community to a closed-door caucus. In retrospect, it amounted to a last-ditch effort to save the clinical testing of beta-endorphin. After several hours the session adjourned without a compromise.

Tocus and William Brown—a second FDA representative—

were willing to listen, but were not willing to be more flexible. The National Institute of Mental Health would not foot the bill for synthesizing the amount of compound needed for more animal and then large-scale human studies. The drug company representatives were noncommittal.

Sidney Udenfriend, Director of the Roche Institute of Molecular Biology—a research wing of Hoffman La Roche— was particularly cynical about the various research proposals at the time. Today, his opinion remains unchanged. "As soon as you find anything in the brain," Udenfriend claims, "you release a whole bunch of nuts who immediately want to find its role in schizophrenia and depression. It's always the same: they get huge amounts of money, test a few patients in uncontrolled studies and the only thing you can be sure they will say is, 'in a limited number of patients we have shown a statistically significant rise or fall of this or that. Now what we need is more money.' "

It would have taken an estimated $15 million worth of synthetic beta-endorphin alone to satisfy the FDA's preliminary demands. "We figured out what the work would cost, the minimum," Heinz Lehmann admits. "We asked for takers. There were no takers, and we were left hanging."

Despite the setback, work on the relationship between endorphins and mental illness had not been entirely without progress. Results, although inconclusive, "did take the field away from 'morphineness,' " says Floyd Bloom.

John Hughes agrees: "If someone has the courage to get up and say, 'Look, this is the cause of schizophrenia,' that has the effect of initiating research in that area. Maybe it's right, maybe it's wrong. Usually there's an element of truth there, but it doesn't really matter—as long as it provokes activity."

"Scientists like Lars Terenius take chances and risk embarrassment," comments Robert Lahti, an Upjohn Company researcher, "but if we're really going to help people, then these chances should be taken in research. We've got to get it out of the test tube."

But beta-endorphin, the most powerful of the body's own opiates, seemed to have leapt out of the test tube like a demon spirit out of an alchemist's cauldron. Results of experimentation with it in the winter of 1977 were, at best, controversial; at worst, they were overhyped, inconclusive, and unreliable—a discouraging outcome. Even after the FDA—at a conference in Bethesda, Maryland, a few weeks after San Juan—did agree to ease their restrictions on beta-endorphin testing, the damage had already been done.

"Kline's studies made it all look like crazy quackery," says one researcher. Testing the relationship between endorphins and mental illness was discontinued in all but a few labs. "Nobody wanted to touch this with a ten-foot pole," Heinz Lehmann remembers.

For Nathan Kline, there was worse news to come after the Puerto Rico conference. Within weeks, an FDA investigator arrived to audit his records. "It was the sort of thing," says Lehmann, "where they move in and put on their bedroom slippers. They make themselves at home. They are going to be there a long time."

The audit took three months, but Nathan Kline's troubles were to last for the next five years, culminating in a criminal prosecution which arose directly from his experimental testing of beta-endorphin on human beings.

THE ENDORPHIN BUSINESS

The Eli Lilly Pharmaceutical Company complex lacks the sanitized chrome-and-glass architecture that characterizes the drug industry. Lilly's buildings are hulking, stolid, and made of brick: structures that might just as well house the manufacture of auto parts or dog food. The modern skyline of Indianapolis, Indiana—a city that was built, in part, on Lilly's success—rises powerfully in the distance behind the Lilly campus and its four sprawling parking lots.

In the basement of the Biological Research building, Robert Frederickson worked in a small room that looked like a lavatory: green linoleum on the floor, tan tiles on the walls, no windows. Fluorescent lights in the ceiling buzzed continuously.

Until recently, Frederickson had shared Room S-19 with one of his technicians, a young black woman named Carolyn Harrell, and a bench of twitching, bubbling vas deferens preparations. By the summer of 1977, Carolyn Harrell had moved down the hall and was sharing space with Frederickson's other technician, Vigo Burgis, in an even smaller room where Burgis tested and housed rats and mice. For Frederickson, the move meant gaining some much-needed elbow room; for Harrell, it would take some getting used to. Procedures in the animal lab were often bloody, the room smelled, and it was hard for her to eat lunch there. Vigo Burgis's olfactory senses had long since gone dead.

Frederickson, a slim, slight man, looked even younger than twenty-eight, despite his neatly-trimmed beard. He was "a flick-jump specialist," he liked to say, "a student of rodents" who had joined Lilly in 1972 after finishing graduate school at the University of Winnipeg in Canada. He had climbed steadily up the company's research ladder to become chairman of the Central Nervous System committee, the group in charge of overseeing, among other things, all work on opiates. Antibiotics were Lilly's pharmaceutical mainstay, but narcotics research was an ongoing program in the giant company. Darvon, a mild, orally-active pain reliever, was the narcotic division's most successful product—bringing in nearly $100 million a year in sales.

By 1977, bonus and performance awards put Frederickson's salary over $50,000, but, recently divorced and making alimony payments, he had moved into a tiny apartment in a less-than-luxurious Indianapolis neighborhood. It was not a happy time for him personally, an especially bad time to face another hurdle on his endorphin project.

For nearly three years, Frederickson had been fighting an uphill battle against the skepticism of his superiors to develop an endorphin painkiller at Lilly.

He was among the first drug company scientists to begin such a program because he was one of the first drug company researchers to join the International Narcotics Research Club, having attended the Club's Chapel Hill meeting in 1973 and the Cocoyoc meeting the following year, where Hans Kosterlitz had made the out-of-the-blue announcement that a morphine-like substance had been discovered in Aberdeen. Returning from Cocoyoc, Frederickson had set up his own vas deferens preparations and had begun to distill human brains from the

Indianapolis morgue in search of the as yet unidentified compound.

He was making some progress by the Airlie House meeting, in 1975, when John Hughes had partly described the amino acid content of enkephalin and, by December 1975, when the paper on the enkephalins was published in *Nature,* Frederickson had successfully isolated human endorphins in a crude state, and had begun pressing ahead with plans to design a new drug based on the discovery. "I felt that by showing it in human brains, it might be more acceptable as a potential drug," he explains, but company opposition to his project had been stiff from the start. Even Danny Zimmerman, a Lilly chemist who was a close friend, thought Frederickson's "endorphin drug" idea was "pure fantasy."

Frederickson had been doggedly persistent, though, and the result was metkephamid, his baby. A compound fashioned after Met-enkephalin (code name: Ly 127623), metkephamid effectively produced pain relief in animals, was extremely safe, and it had fewer and less pronounced habit-forming side effects than did most standard narcotics.

For the past eighteen months, Frederickson had been nursing the compound along on a shoestring budget, and now it looked good, very good. In fact, it looked so good that, by August 1977, Frederickson was working frantically on a presentation requesting the go-ahead to form a project team and turn metkephamid into a commercial drug.

After the breakup with his wife, the hard work actually helped. Yet for all his effort, it was still a matter of considerable conjecture whether the powers-that-be at Lilly would go along with his idea. So far, the financial outlay for work on Frederickson's compound had been comparatively modest, a few million dollars. To fund a project team to do the work required to develop metkephamid into a "product" would push the company's financial commitment up toward the $30-million mark, and there was little reason to think that management would deem it worth the outlay.

Metkephamid was scientifically exciting, a glimpse into the way drugs might be designed in the future—even the most cantankerous of the research management staff at Lilly could not deny that. In addition, with the whole country on a "health" kick, it had the positive, new-age aura of being a "natural" product. "But 'new' was not enough," Frederickson remarks. "A big company like Lilly is not interested in anything that is going to make less than thirty million dollars a year—that was the bottom line."

Even were metkephamid to be marketed aggressively, it was unlikely to score that kind of profit. It was not yet effective in pill form, which took it out of the Darvon category and down into the less profitable ($50-million) market for injectable narcotics—dominated by Sterling Drugs' Demerol, a painkiller that had the advantage of being extremely cheap to manufacture. Making a peptide-type drug—like metkephamid—was, at its most efficient, a costly, cumbersome operation.

Frederickson was understandably nervous as the first Thursday in August approached.

Research Management Staff meetings were held every Thursday morning in a large conference room in the Analytical Chemistry building. Frederickson would be facing twenty people—representing Lilly's management, marketing, and research divisions—many of whom had voiced objections to his work since he had started his preliminary research on the endorphins in 1974. They were the ones who would have final approval over his project team proposal now. "The purpose of the whole thing was to make you feel like an insect," Frederickson recalls. "They have all the power and you're dancing for your supper."

The meeting, chaired by Earl Herr, president of Lilly Research Laboratories, the scientific arm of the company, started at nine o'clock. Herr was big and gruff, domineering, in his early fifties.

William Shedden was second in command, a stubborn

and opinionated senior vice president in his late forties. Shedden—who at that time boasted about being one of the youngest vice presidents at Lilly—would resign in 1982 after the "Oraflex" disaster, when the arthritis medicine for which he was responsible was tied to four deaths and several illnesses in the U.S. and Great Britain.

Herr had often sat in on discussions about the endorphin project at meetings of Frederickson's CNS committee. He was not openly critical, but both he and Shedden paid careful attention to the "advice" of the chemistry and clinical divisions, and they had been getting a lot of "advice" about Frederickson's work lately—that it was not likely to be commercially important.

The most vocal opposition to metkephamid came from Al Pollen, a plump man whose jovial look masked a stern disposition. Pollen was the inventor of Darvon; he was a traditional organic chemist who felt that drugs should be constructed from simple, cost-efficient chemicals, not amino acids. He also was developing a new drug called doxipicamine—a second generation Darvon—and, wary of any competing projects, had been down on the "endorphin drug" idea from the start.

The marketing people were equally negative. They had never been personalities to Frederickson, only faces and first names—Don, Randy, Mike, Rick—but their opinions were invariably the same: extremely conservative, concerned only with profits. "They did not want to be in the hot seat later," Frederickson recalls, "so they were automatically pessimistic about new projects."

When he left the conference room after the meeting that morning, Robert Frederickson was convinced his project was dead. So it came as a complete surprise, two weeks later, when he was notified by the Committee of their decision to move forward on his work—and of his appointment to chair the project team.

*   *   *

Eli Lilly's conservative reaction to the news that the brain produced its own opiates was not typical of the response to the discovery in the pharmaceutical industry.

Based on published reports in scientific journals, by May 1976—five months after the breakthrough on the enkephalins was published in *Nature*—at least six major drug houses (and, one researcher estimates, as many as twenty-five others) which would eventually invest a combined sum well over $100 million—had joined a new endorphin sweepstakes. This time the race was to turn the endorphins into what Dietmar Römer at Sandoz described as "the ultimate"—a nonmorphine morphine.

There was still considerable interest in finding a "bee without a sting," and if the stakes were high so were the potential gains. Americans spend $10 billion annually on pain relief medications, most of them popular over-the-counter preparations like aspirin and Tylenol, which work very well for minor aches and pains. But neither mild aspirin-type drugs nor conventional narcotics, which pose the risk of addiction, were useful in treating the more serious types of "chronic" pain resulting from arthritis, migraine, or nerve injury. The estimated number of people afflicted with chronic pain ranged as high as twenty million in America alone and they represented a sizeable untapped market worth hundreds of millions of dollars.

Two recent candidates for the lofty title of "stingless bee"—Lilly's Darvon and Sterling Drugs' Talwin—had not lived up to expectations. Darvon, although commercially successful, had become controversial amid contradictory claims, ranging from reports that it was completely inactive to warnings that it was potentially toxic. Talwin had slipped into pharmaceutical obscurity in the wake of reports of abuse and studies indicating that, despite its advances over earlier mixed-agonist drugs, it still occasionally produced bizarre, even nightmarish side effects.

"The field was open for new alternatives," explains

Sydney Archer, the developer of Talwin. "The next wave of interest in nonaddictive painkillers came with the endorphins. People thought 'how could our bodies produce an addicting substance?' It's unnatural, contrary to the interests of the organism. Naturally, industry went along with the scientists—the financial incentives were obvious."

Though beta-endorphin was quickly found to produce the most powerful effects on pain, the drug industry focused on the enkephalins because they were shorter peptides, therefore easier and cheaper to synthesize. Hundreds of variations on the enkephalin formulas were churned out by drug company chemists in a burst of activity following (and, in some cases, before) the publication of the Met- and Leu-enkephalin formulas in *Nature*. The speed with which drug companies jumped on the discovery was to be expected from a business standpoint. New discoveries, painstakingly pioneered in labs of pure researchers like Hughes and Kosterlitz, are handled very differently at the industrial level. Here the emphasis is on rapidly acquiring as many patents as possible related directly and indirectly to the new finding, in hopes that one of them will pay off. However, the process is never free of failure, and the competition in the drug industry for a quick success from endorphin research was fraught with expensive disappointments. By 1977, a year after the endorphin stampede, there already had been a number of dropouts.

Like Robert Frederickson, Larry Stein of the Department of Psychopharmacology at Wyeth Laboratories in Philadelphia, had also been a fast starter, and within weeks of the publication of John Hughes's much delayed *Brain Research* paper in May 1974, he had set up some extraordinary procedures which, he hoped, would break the code on enkephalin.

Stein was convinced that there was a link between Hughes's "endogenous opiate" and the work done by Huda Akil and David Mayer on stimulation-produced analgesia (SPA). Since he knew their teacher, John Liebeskind, slightly, Stein had telephoned Liebeskind at UCLA. "He was very cagey, asking specific questions about the work," Liebeskind recalls. "He wanted to duplicate the SPA procedure, so we decided to get together to shoot the breeze. We were both to attend a neuroscience meeting in New York two weeks later, and we had one of these swashbuckling scientific meetings—careening around New York, screaming around. Larry kept bringing things back to our experiment. The Hughes's report had just come out, and finally I understood why he was interested. I said, 'Okay, Stein, you're going to stimulate the area and suck up the brain fluids and be the first to sequence the stuff.' He said, 'You're right.' "

By December 1975, rows of lab rats were being electronically buzzed into an opiatelike oblivion in Stein's lab while he and his workers "vampirized" their brain chemicals through push-pull cannulas—tiny pumps in the animals' skulls which circulated saline solution over the stimulated areas, then scooped up and retrieved samples of the released chemicals. "Stein was a maniac about the work," recalls James Belluzi, the senior scientist on the team at Wyeth.

Gallons of rat brain "perfusate," as they called it, had been collected, but company biochemists, says Stein, "took our good stuff and pissed it away" on attempts at purification.

All was not lost, though. Near the end of that month, a few days before the enkephalin paper appeared in *Nature,* Stein received a telegram from Wyeth's British division, describing the structures of the two Aberdeen peptides. The enkephalin formulas had been leaked to their British colleagues, and although the leucine-enkephalin sequence turned out to be incorrect, animal testing had begun almost immediately. Conveniently, the rats in Stein's lab already had been fitted with electrodes and cannulas. "We were all geared-up to take a hypo of the compound and go squish," recalls Belluzi.

Belluzi completed the first animal experiments by Christmas. The effects, as Hans Kosterlitz had predicted, were short-lived; even at very high doses and injected directly into the brains of the animals, these peptides would produce pain relief lasting only about three minutes. "It didn't bother us," says Stein. "We were expecting a short-term effect, but we got roasted for our assertion that this was analgesia." In April 1976, Stein and Belluzi published their results in *Nature,* but interest at Wyeth had already been replaced by skepticism.

"I tried to encourage them to exploit the discovery," says Larry Stein. "I pushed the bastards to get deeper into it, I tried to bludgeon them into it." But, disappointed by the weak results of the first analgesia studies, drug development personnel at Wyeth remained cold and, by the summer of 1977, the number of synthetic versions of the enkephalins which the chemistry department was sending over to Stein and Belluzi had been reduced to a trickle.

Curiously, one of Wyeth's Met-enkephalin analogues (code: Wy 42,896) seemed to enhance the retention of long-term memory in laboratory animals. This, in turn, raised some new and interesting scientific possibilities which dubious drug company officials were quick to ignore. "A memory drug?" Stein says. "The guys at Wyeth never budged."

Reckitt and Colman and Burroughs Wellcome, the two British pharmaceutical firms with whom Hans Kosterlitz and John Hughes had direct dealings, benefited from their association as they mounted their own endorphin drug projects.

Work at Reckitt and Colman on a long-lasting, orally ingestible version of enkephalin had gotten underway a few weeks before the *Nature* paper by the Aberdeen team appeared. "There was a feeling that this was something for the future," recalls Colin Smith, a researcher at Reckitt in the winter of 1976. "The game was to devise, test, and patent as many synthetic variations of enkephalin as possible."

"The compounds were the rarest, the most important. The work was given top priority," remembers John Everett, a former Reckitt technician, who tested them on animals. "We had to be extremely careful. Syringes were washed out after use and the wash water collected to save the small amounts of enkephalin it might contain. Because these substances were from within the body and possibly nonaddictive, there was much more excitement than with ordinary drugs."

But the Reckitt and Colman program bottomed out. While their chemists had synthesized a number of variations on the enkephalins, some of which were potent, none of them had proven therapeutically interesting. John Lewis, the director of research at the company who had helped to initiate the collaboration with Hughes and Kosterlitz, had begun looking for buyers at other drug firms for Reckitt's line of synthetic enkephalins.

Burroughs Wellcome got off to an early, if shaky, start when, in the summer of 1975, Sam Wilkenson, a chemist at the company's East Bromley division on the outskirts of London, synthesized the close-to-correct Tyr-Gly-Gly-Phe-Met-Gly-Phe-Tryp peptide, which had caused John Hughes so much alarm. Although the eight-amino-acid sequence of the compound had been wrong, Wilkenson and his colleagues put together other experimental combinations of amino acids based on this model and, according to one company insider, had already synthesized the Met-enkephalin sequence by December 1975, when the *Nature* paper appeared containing the correct enkephalin formulas.

After that, however, the Burroughs Wellcome effort had veered away from painkillers. The bulk of their research was now taking place at their U.S. facility in Research Triangle Park, North Carolina, where Pedro Cuatrecasas—who had contributed the rapid filtration technique used by Solomon Snyder and Candace Pert to demonstrate opiate receptors—had been installed as research director.

"Our expectation was that enkephalin analogues would be effective pharmaceuticals," Cuatrecasas recalls, but instead of pursuing the difficult, expensive goal of producing a nonaddictive painkiller, Cuatrecasas had taken a clever and practical detour into antidiuretic drugs.

The most effective and widely used prescription drug for diarrhea, G.D. Searle's Lomotil, was a narcotic drug without narcotic effects; it did not enter the brain but it did bind, magnificently, to receptor sites in the intestine, where it counteracted spasms in a manner similar to the way other opiates worked on the guinea pig ileum. It was the only drug of its kind on the market and the field was open to competition from Cuatrecasas and his team.

Out of hundreds of Burroughs Wellcome compounds modeled on the enkephalins, one (code: BW 942) displayed similar, even superior, properties to Lomotil when tested in animals, so they decided to pursue it. It has since been tested successfully on four hundred humans.

"Once 942 is in use, an even better application may be found for it," Cuatrecasas explains. "In the meantime we learn technologies and gain expertise. The hope is, still, to make a nonaddictive painkiller."

That hope remained a distant prospect at Burroughs Wellcome, though, and with other companies' programs faltering by the summer of 1977, the serious competition to convert the endorphins into a "stingless bee" had narrowed down the Frederickson's lonesome effort at Lilly and to a Sandoz program which, by contrast, was the most intensive of any drug company campaign in the world.

Basel, Switzerland, is really three cities. From the Mittlere Brücke, the oldest and most picturesque of Basel's many bridges, the division is obvious. At Basel's approximate center, the Old City crowds the banks of the Rhine on both sides. On the right bank are the medieval white and tan buildings of the University under red tile roofs; on the left, the twin spires of the Münster, Basel's twelfth-century cathedral. Looking westward, toward the foothills of the Alps, a newer Basel is visible—quiet, residential areas of elegant townhouses and gardened boulevards. The chief reason for Basel's current prosperity is apparent when one looks to the west, toward the promontory that juts into the busy river port called Three Countries Corner— the place where Germany, France, and Switzerland all converge. A third Basel rises there—a gleaming mass of industrial parks and malls and buildings belonging to Ciba-Geigy, Hoffman La Roche, Sandoz, and sixty other pharmaceutical companies. This Basel is the capital of the international chemical-pharmaceutical industry.

At Sandoz, preliminary experiments were also underway by the time the enkephalin discovery had been officially proclaimed in *Nature*. Soon afterward, they escalated—with the enthusiastic backing of management—until a full-time chemistry lab, with three crews of chemists and eight other lab "units," each composed of a senior researcher and his or her technicians, had been assigned to the project.

Daniel Hauser, who had been instrumental in initiating the collaboration between Sandoz and Solomon Snyder in an attempt to beat Kosterlitz and Hughes to the formula, was in charge of the chemistry on the project.

With advance information about the enkephalin structures—communicated by Snyder early in December 1975— Hauser had consulted Janos Pless, a senior scientist in the chemical research division, who synthesized the peptides during the following week. Hauser had then sent a few milligrams to Snyder, allowing him and Rabi Simantov to complete their work in Baltimore, and had given the remaining material to Dietmar Römer, the director of the Sandoz analgesics division. Distinguished-looking and soft-spoken, the chain-smoking Römer was inclined neither to flamboyance nor hype; it was his highest recommendation that had convinced the previously indifferent Sandoz executives to support Hauser's initial collaboration with Snyder: they trusted Römer's enthusiasm for the continuing project.

Römer's laboratory specialty was animal testing. He directed "hot-plate" and "tail-pinch" trials with experimental painkillers on rats and mice and, for those compounds that looked most promising, he maintained a colony of twenty-five rhesus monkeys, ten of whom were narcotic addicts. Like Maurice Seevers, who fathered similar procedures at the University of Michigan, Römer felt that a clear-cut prediction of the effects of new narcotics on humans could only be obtained by first testing their painkilling potential and addictiveness on monkeys.

With enkephalins supplied by Hauser and Pless, he had started a series of tests with what turned out to be short-lived enkephalin analgesia. In February 1976, Römer and Hauser had submitted a paper describing the positive but transitory painkilling activity of enkephalins to *Nature*. It was published in June, a few weeks after that same journal carried a similar report from Stein and Belluzi at Wyeth.

Over the next three months, Hauser and Römer were to test more than two hundred analogues of the enkephalins before settling on one which, they felt, was the most likely to succeed as a drug. It was coded FK 33824.

"It was a heavy involvement," Hauser asserts, "but there was so much excitement to be doing this. In an industry it doesn't happen every day. Usually things take so many years, proceed in small steps, and people are never really excited. In this case everybody was making an exception. It was top priority everywhere. The enthusiasm went right to the top management. We felt it was important to be in the very front. If it was an endogenous opiate there should be no dependence. The first results pointed in that direction, that FK 33824 was not like morphine. We hoped we could show this clinically."

During that same spring of 1976 in Indianapolis, Robert Frederickson had made a similar breakthrough and was conducting his first tests on metkephamid. He had found an ally in Edward Smithwick, an experienced scientist in the Lilly Chemistry Division, who had agreed to supervise the chemical side of the work and to develop the hundreds of manmade variations on the enkephalins needed to begin to turn the breakthrough into a drug.

Smithwick faced two basic problems. First, the enkephalins which Hughes and Kosterlitz had discovered, while originating in the brain, would not cross from the bloodstream through the dense web of tissue under the skull called the blood-brain barrier. They were, therefore, only effective when injected directly into the brain. By fiddling with the structures of the peptides, Smithwick had to try to overcome that drawback and make a compound which was intravenously injectable or better yet orally ingestible. Smithwick's other challenge was to make the compound longer lasting than the enkephalins, which were only briefly active.

Using Met-enkephalin as his basic model, Smithwick had begun by leaving out one or more amino acids in its sequence in order to test which pieces of the compound were necessary for activity. The routine work had been completed quickly—after which, Smithwick started on the more considerable challenge of designing a peptide that could protect itself from enzyme breakdown, that could cross the blood-brain barrier, and that ultimately could be effective in pill form.

With only five people—Smithwick and his assistant Robert Shuman and Frederickson and his two technicians—dividing up the heavy labor, the less than $1-million price tag for the project at this early stage was low—at least compared to the amount Sandoz was spending. By March 1976, five hundred Met-enkephalin analogues had been synthesized in Smithwick's lab.

Frederickson carefully monitored the testing procedures, even though he was allergic to test rats and had to sniffle his way through the experiments. Smithwick visited the animal only once; he watched, appalled, as Vigo Burgis prepared to give an unanesthetized animal a brain injection by cutting the skin on its head and pulling it down around its ears. "I'd rather be a chemist," Smithwick muttered as he left, never to return. After that, he sent Shuman, his assistant, to deliver the daily samples.

By the end of March, Smithwick and Shuman had designed a compound—later named dalamid—which produced some pharmaceutically desirable effects. Dalamid was a Met-enkephalin with two basic modifications. The first position amino acid tyrosine, which was of importance for opiate activity, was also the first target of enzyme attack. When breakdown occurred at the chemical bond joining tyrosine to the second position glycine, the peptide lost its power. To overcome this obstacle Smithwick had replaced the glycine in position two with d-alanine, a mirror-image isomer of the amino acid alanine. The substitution had no effect on the peptide's activity, but the odd configuration of the right-handed amino acid essentially fooled enzymes, preventing rapid breakdown. By bonding nitrogen to the end of the peptide, he could further increase resistance.

Dalamid produced moderately good results on the vas deferens, and direct brain injections produced pain relief nearly equivalent to morphine, but despite its design it could not penetrate the blood-brain barrier effectively. Intravenous injections were barely active.

Then, in April 1976, about a month later, metkephamid had come out of Smithwick's lab. It involved one further modification: the addition of a methyl group to methionine, using a process that Smithwick and Shuman had only recently developed. This simple change produced an exponential improvement in its activity. When it was tested later that month, results on the vas deferens seemed to indicate that this compound was a thousand times more potent than morphine. When the initial results came off the pen recorder, Frederickson recalls, he signed and dated them—standard procedures for anything that might be patentable—and did a crazy little war dance around his lab bench.

Two days later the compound was being tested on Vigo Burgis's animals. It was remarkably more powerful than Met-enkephalin, dalamid, or morphine, and though it was not yet effective orally, it could be delivered subcutaneously.

If these results were not quite enough to make Frederickson's superiors on the central nervous system committee sit up and take notice, that same April, in *Nature,* the Wyeth team of Larry Stein and James Belluzi had published their article on the short-term pain-relieving effects of synthetic enkephalins and, the following month, a similar article appeared, in the same journal, by Daniel Hauser and Dietmar Römer, who were working along the same track at the Sandoz Pharmaceutical Company in Switzerland.

The implications were clear: Wyeth and Sandoz were going to be Lilly's competitors, Frederickson told the CNS committee, unaware that the Wyeth effort had already stalled. "That actually increased their interest," he recalls. "In the pharmaceutical industry, nothing justifies doing something more than if everybody else is doing it, too."

Progress at Sandoz was rapid. By January 1976—when Basel's traditional dancers appeared in the streets of the Old City to frighten away the spirits of winter—the Sandoz team had just finished testing their first synthetic enkephalins. By Carnival time, in March, with their craft and know-how being applied at maximum efficiency, and with the extraordinary backing of the parent company, they had produced the FK 33824 compound. It was distinguishable from Frederickson's metkephamid by a few slight chemical differences, but the two compounds were basically similar: they combined enormous potency and high resistance to breakdown.

It took several more months for Hauser and Römer to

complete preliminary testing. Then on August 4, 1976, they filed a "new substance" form for FK 33824 at Sandoz. It was the first step toward a clinical trial for the compound.

Animal tests, which Römer had started during the summer of 1976 and had completed by that winter, looked exceedingly promising. Hot-plate and tail-flick tests indicated that the FK compound was a strong, effective painkiller. On some of their tests it registered thirty thousand times stronger than Met-enkephalin and one thousand times stronger than morphine; and this was the case not only when it was injected, but also after oral administration.

Moreover, Römer's monkeys were extremely reluctant to self-administer the compound, as they gladly did with morphine. This behavior led Römer and Hauser to speculate that FK 33824 had no reinforcing properties, and that it therefore might have less abuse-potential than did conventional habit-forming narcotics. (The real reasons why the monkeys did not like the drug were only surmised later, after the human trials.)

Sandoz lawyers filed patent applications as soon as the drug's potency was discovered and Römer and Hauser submitted a paper describing their compound to *Nature*. In April 1977 they filed a proposal to test their enkephalin drug on humans. Laws regulating human testing are less stringent in Europe and trials were conducted during the summer of 1977 at Sandoz by Beat von Graffenried, Emilio del Pozo, and Jiri Roubicek, clinicians in the company's Department of Experimental Therapeutics. Physicians from the Psychiatric Clinic in Wil, Switzerland, and the Medical University Clinic in Freiburg, West Germany, witnessed the tests on forty paid male volunteers.

The trials were completed that autumn, and Hauser and Römer read the results with dismay. True, there were none of the classical morphine side effects such as nausea and changes in emotional behavior or mental alertness—but neither was any analgesia produced. And although pain relief was undetectable at the small dose levels used, a host of strange and frightening side effects were all too apparent. In several subjects the injection produced a welt on the skin, the size of a small saucer. Three to five minutes after the injection, every one of the volunteers complained of a sensation of heaviness in all their muscles, accompanied by throat constrictions so severe that many of them feared they were choking. This was followed in over half the cases by an impressive array of churning, gurgling sounds from their bowels, and two of the subjects flushed, turning beet red from head to foot.

"When the results were in, well, I didn't jump out a window," says Hauser, "but I did jump out of the project." A description of the test was submitted to *Nature,* where it was published in April 1978. In the intervening months, Janos Pless in the Chemical Research Division, had made a few attempts to redesign the compound, but the momentum was gone, and by the time the paper appeared, the Sandoz project had quietly come to a halt.

That left Eli Lilly.

With Robert Frederickson's "Project Team" in operation only eight months, the failure of the Sandoz compound was hardly cause for jubilation. Frederickson's detractors on the research management staff committee had a field day with the bad news, and he almost had to beg the Committee to let him go ahead with his own human trials of metkephamid. Reluctantly, they agreed.

He submitted an investigational new-drug application to the Food and Drug Administration the following November, and waited the requisite month. The FDA did not R.S.V.P., which registered as no objection.

Four male subjects for the study were selected and injected with increasingly higher doses of metkephamid. In his tiny office in the basement of the Biological Research building, Robert Frederickson received the results with an audible sigh of relief. Although metkephamid did produce some side effects—nasal congestion, "cotton" mouth, and heaviness in the limbs—they were innocuous compared with those produced by the Sandoz FK compound.

Remaining questions about how effectively the drug relieved pain were answered by studies on metkephamid at the University of Rochester and the University of Cincinnati, which reported that it was as powerful as Sterling's widely used drug Demerol in postoperative patients.

But would metkephamid ever really be turned into the prototype for a new generation of pain medications?

The compound still showed no particular advantage over Demerol and it was far more expensive per dose. Extensive human testing would be required before the FDA would approve a New Drug Application—the next tough regulatory obstacle blocking its way to the marketplace. These tests would be costly and would have to be approved by the research management staff committee at Lilly.

In the afterglow of his victory over Sandoz, Robert Frederickson found himself, once again, sitting beneath the buzzing fluorescent light in room S-19, steeling his nerves for a new test of wills with his incredulous critics on the committee over the future of his baby.

His predicament was characteristic of the endorphin research field by the late 1970s. Three years had passed since John Hughes, Hans Kosterlitz, and their coworkers had announced their discovery of morphinelike chemicals in the brain. Now, amid the controversy and accusations stemming from the testing of beta-endorphin on schizophrenics, and the pharmaceutical industry's overall lack of success at turning out an endorphin drug, some of the luster of the original breakthrough had dulled. The promise of the work remained undiminished, but at the moment the direction of scientists in the field was unclear.

FAMILIES

The changes in John Hughes's life and personality were not an overnight reaction to success. Rather, they had taken place over several years following the discovery of enkephalins. Celebrity appealed to him. He grew a moustache, replaced his horn-rimmed glasses with contact lenses, began to dress well (something he had never done before) and to act, in general, like a star.

Kosterlitz put up with Hughes's chest-beating at scientific meetings. Others who had been close to him were less patient. His normal aggressiveness, which could be charming, had taken on an unpleasant edge. "His attitude seemed to be, 'I'm better than you,' " one colleague recalls. " 'I came from nothing and look what I accomplished.' "

But newfound fame was only one reason for his metamorphosis. Hughes was reacting to personal and career pressures as well. His marriage to Mandy was breaking up. Playful banter at home had turned into real arguments, the aftershocks of which could be felt on the job. Fed up with one affront after another, Graeme Henderson finally threw a cup of tea in Hughes's face.

Work was going through a tough phase, too, despite the publicity generated by a bevy of reporters and television crews who visited the lab, inquiring about the discovery and whether it was going to be a wonderful new nonaddictive treatment for pain. There was no more room for advancement in the Unit. Kosterlitz, at seventy-five, showed no signs of retiring, and Hughes was so frustrated that at one point he grumbled to another researcher, in an oblique reference to Kosterlitz, "the authorities have been in too long."

The alternative was to leave Aberdeen and, by the summer of 1977, Hughes had made plans to join the faculty of the Imperial College of Science and Technology in London as a full professor. The scientific community's high regard for the enkephalin discovery virtually assured his appointment and Kosterlitz, recognizing that his younger collaborator's prospects were limited at Aberdeen, encouraged his decision to accept the new post. For Hughes it was a chance to expand his research in top-notch facilities. In particular, he was looking forward to collaborating with Howard Morris, who had moved his mass spectroscopy lab to Imperial two years earlier. Yet, for all his bluster, John Hughes had become attached to Aberdeen and was sad that summer when the time came to leave. He would miss being part of what he described as the "group of originals" led by Kosterlitz; and even with all its obvious advantages, he knew that Imperial College and London could never offer the kind of esprit de corps in which he had flourished at Marishal.

A farewell party was organized at the Bankary, a beautifully forested estate on the River Dee, near the Queen's summer residence at Balmoral. It was a sentimental afternoon as Hughes prowled the grounds with Kosterlitz and the other staff members, reminiscing about the past.

Mandy Hughes attended. Although she was afraid that the already shaky marriage would not stand the strain of the move, she had reluctantly agreed to go south with John, but their final breakup a few months later came as no surprise, especially to Hanna Kosterlitz. She had, after all, always warned girls against marrying dedicated scientists.

Hans Kosterlitz, meanwhile, had been globe-trotting between scientific meetings at a pace that would frazzle a thirty year old. Airline schedules and the *Good Hotel Guide* began to take a prominent place on his bookshelf, next to his collection of scientific journals. He was teaching himself high-pressure liquid chromatography on the machine Hughes had constructed, he was consulting for several drug firms, and, although he missed John Hughes, he had a new group of young people in the Unit to tyrannize and inspire. One of the new postdocs, Roger Snokum, won the Prof's heart by discovering the Yardarm, a restaurant near the docks which featured a lunchtime menu of Stilton cheese and real English beer.

Kosterlitz unabashedly enjoyed every opportunity to travel, talk, argue with people, eat good meals, and drink fine wine as well as savor the long-delayed recognition, and awards: The Schmiedeberg Plakette of the German Pharmacological Society in 1976, and the National Institute of Drug Abuse "Pacesetter" award—which he shared with John Hughes, Avram Goldstein, Lars Terenius, Solomon Snyder, and Eric Simon. He packed the hall at the 1977 Federated Biological Societies meeting—in distinct contrast to his lectures on the guinea pig ileum just a few years earlier, which had provided an excuse for other scientists to take a coffee break. There was even talk of a Nobel prize. Jockeying for a share of it had already started, when Roger Guillemin—who won the Nobel in 1977 for his work on the hypothalamic releasing factors—infuriated the prize committee by devoting much of his laureate's lecture to a description of his current endorphin research, instead of addressing the subject for which the award had been given.

Guillemin seemed to some to be staking out his claim to the Nobel prize for endorphins.

The competition for recognition also led to a rift between Candace Pert and Solomon Snyder the following fall, when the Lasker affair erupted.

The Albert and Mary Lasker Award is given annually in recognition of outstanding achievements in the field of basic medical research. It is considered a stepping stone to the Nobel prize (by the late 1970s, twenty-eight Lasker awardees had gone on to win the Nobel), so the announcement of the winners on November 20, 1978, was particularly dramatic.

The recipients were: John Hughes for his "discovery and isolation of two polypeptides now termed enkephalins"; Hans Kosterlitz, for his "early and pioneering contributions" that "triggered the search for the enkephalins and then made possible efficient monitoring of progress in their isolation and purification"; and Solomon Snyder, who "not only identified the receptor system," the citation read, "but, with his co-workers, went on to develop precise techniques for localizing these opiate receptors and, then, mapped their regional distribution in the brain." Missing was the name of Candace Pert, who had collaborated with Snyder on the receptor research before moving from Johns Hopkins to the National Institute of Mental Health in Bethesda, Maryland, where she was struggling to establish herself as an independent investigator. A number of people thought that she was being treated unfairly; none of them more than Candace Pert, herself.

"I was angry and upset to be excluded from this year's award," she wrote in a blunt letter to Mary Lasker. "As Dr. Snyder's graduate student, I played a key role in initiating this research and following it up." Hadn't she taken the same active part in the work being done in Snyder's lab as Hughes had performed for Kosterlitz? Why was Hughes included and she omitted? Refusing to attend the presentation luncheon,

Pert became a *cause célèbre* when Jean L. Marx broke the story in a long article in *Science* magazine.

Pert's contribution was indisputable; she had "first author" status on the original receptor paper and on many subsequently published papers concerning receptor localization and mapping. Unfortunately, throughout most of that period, Pert had been a graduate student—not an independent investigator, like Hughes—and graduate students did not, as a rule, share major awards with their chiefs.

The controversy brought out another underlying issue. Ellen Silbergeld of the National Institute for Neurological and Communicative Disorders wrote, in a letter to *Science:* "When the excluded scientist is young and a woman, I am discouraged to think that the scientific world has not become sensitive to such practices which, however inadvertent, have the effect of being systematically discriminatory." In *Science News,* Joan Arehart-Treichel labeled the scientific establishment an "old boys club," and charged that "sexism was a major reason" why Pert did not share the award. A letter by six female science writers was published in a following issue, supporting this view and asserting that the oversight was part of a "discriminatory pattern" against women scientists.

No one would argue that this was not the general case; women in science did face insults, indignities, low intellectual expectation (especially if they were pretty), and sexist labor practices, in addition to the enormous strain—if they had families—posed by the normal ninety-hour work week required for success in any research field. In the 1950s such situations may have been tolerated but—if the outbreak of tenure-denial lawsuits brought by women in the 1970s was any indication—Pert was not alone in actively demanding equal status.

Pert told people that she was not going to be another Rosalind Franklin, who had contributed immeasurably to Francis Crick's and James Watson's solution of DNA's structure only to have her work insulted in Watson's book *The Double*

Helix. The deal, as Pert saw it, was that if she would go to the awards ceremony, Snyder would say marvelous things about her contribution—which amounted, she thought, to a "pat on the ass."

It was a difficult situation for both Snyder and Pert. Pert found herself challenging and resenting a mentor of whom she was "in awe"; Snyder was caught between a former student who he thought "outstanding" and an angry Lasker committee. He called the members of the jury to ask them to reconsider her inclusion in the award. They flatly refused.

A few months later, a well-known scientist at the National Institute of Mental Health called Pert into his office. He had to make Nobel prize nominations, he said, and she thought he wanted her help in drafting her own nomination. Instead, he asked her to assist him in writing up Solomon Snyder's. She refused.

"Don't you love Sol?" her senior implored. "What are you trying to do to him? You have to help Sol. This is the way scientific recognition works. Then he'll help you, later. How old are you anyway? You're a nice girl . . ."

"Let's face it, Candace, you don't look or act like a Nobel laureate," a friend of hers joked later on. "Nobel laureates aren't supposed to have three-year-old children."

William Pollen, the director of the National Institute of Drug Abuse, felt strongly enough about the situation to write a letter to *Science News* regretting Pert's exclusion from the NIDA's 1977 "Pacesetter" award (which had gone to Kosterlitz, Hughes, Goldstein, Snyder, Terenius, and Simon). Other letters in both *Science* and *Science News* pointed out that she was not the only one omitted from the Lasker prize, either. "Why then was [Goldstein] excluded, as were Terenius of Uppsala and Simon of New York?" one writer asked. None of these three scientists expressed dissatisfaction over the Lasker award publicly, but the letters echoed feelings they expressed candidly in private.

If a Nobel prize for endorphin research was in the offing—and there is reason to believe this was the case—the public bickering over the Lasker affair muddied the waters. The Nobel prize is restricted to three scientists. Kosterlitz and Hughes were clear choices, but the third was obviously in dispute, and the sages of the Swedish academy tend to steer clear of such messy situations—no matter how prizeworthy the discovery.

If a practical application for the endorphins had been found, that might have swayed the judges in Stockholm to make a choice, but Nathan Kline's extravagances had stalled further research on schizophrenia, and the drug industry had yet to turn up a usable endorphin-based painkiller. So the Nobel prize for the discovery of "the morphine within," no matter how well deserved, was relegated to a future time, when tempers cooled.

It was a time of fragmentation—within the families of scientists and among scientific families—but it was also a time of proliferation in the family of endorphins. By 1978, the number of opiate peptides had quadrupled from five to nearly twenty, and two new, giant precursor molecules had recently been discovered bringing the field to a point described by one researcher as "extraordinarily, almost hopelessly complex."

The first of these prohormones was pro-opiomelanocortin (POMC)—a huge (31,000 dalton) protein—which two young researchers at the University of Oregon, Richard Mains and his wife, Betty Eipper, first isolated in late 1976 and now claimed to be the parent molecule for ACTH, lipotrophin, and beta-endorphin. This was extremely mystifying since the known properties of ACTH—which stimulates adrenaline release, alertness, and hair-trigger reactions—are almost diametrically opposed to those of the opiatelike endorphins. Yet the two peptides seemed to emanate from the same elemental source—like yin and yang from the mind of the Buddha.

Sidney Udenfriend and his group working at a branch of the Hoffman La Roche pharmaceutical company devoted to pure research in Nutley, New Jersey, had quickly confirmed the Mains-Eipper finding. But by the following fall 1977, Udenfriend was sure that this giant protein was an even more intricate formulation of natural compounds than Mains and Eipper had originally suspected. It contained not only ACTH, LPH, and beta-endorphin, but possibly several different versions of melanocyte stimulating hormone (MSH). The precise function of MSH in higher animals was still unknown, but the coexistence of three discrete compounds in a single molecular source was reason enough for excitement and dismay. As Avram Goldstein has stated, "in biology one is a good number, two is a good number, but beyond that, you might as well have a million."

Udenfriend called the compound pro-opiocortin, a shortened version of its original name. "It made perfect sense," he recalls, "but it was the first indication that things were going to be a lot more complex than expected, because it suggested that beta-endorphin was acting in concert with ACTH and MSH. Here was one compound, POMC, being released from the pituitary to perform possibly three or more different functions." At a meeting that summer he enraged some of his more peace-loving colleagues by comparing the new compound to a multiple re-entry guided missile—"nature's own MERV."

Later that same year, another startling development began to take shape in Udenfriend's lab. Though Met-enkephalin was contained in beta-endorphin which was, in turn, contained in LPH and POMC, Udenfriend—like John Hughes—was sure that Met-enkephalin was not simply a breakdown byproduct of the larger peptides. Enkephalin maps in the brain did not correspond to maps for beta-endorphin and POMC, and the notable absence of the second of the original peptides discovered in Aberdeen—leucine-enkephalin—in any of the larger peptides was another conundrum. Where did the Leu-enkephalin originate? Udenfriend concluded that there had to be another molecular parent. His group had found hints of such a precursor in brain extracts but like Hughes, who was just starting on similar research at his new post at Imperial College, they could not isolate the compound in sufficient quantities.

Then, in 1978, a Swedish anatomist named Thomas Hökfelt made the discovery that high concentrations of enkephalins exist not only in the brain, but also in the adrenal glands—at the base of the spine near the kidneys. Enkephalin concentrations in the adrenal medulla were, in fact, significantly higher than those in the brain.

"It was a gold mine," Udenfriend recalls. His team of researchers began extracting cow adrenal glands, and by the following year, they had isolated and obtained enough information about a gigantic 50,000 dalton protein to leave Udenfriend "most amazed." The precursor, proenkephalin, was eventually found to contain six different versions of Met-enkephalin and one copy of the leucine peptide. Some of these intermediate-sized versions of Met-enkephalin—containing one to four extra amino acids—were hundreds of times stronger and longer-lasting than Hughes's original pentapeptides.

So, in addition to the many-splendored POMC, by 1979 Udenfriend and his colleagues were confronting "a vast network of enkephalin-containing peptides" originating from proenkephalin—differing in size, chemical characteristics, and, most likely, in their targets and function—which might vary not only according to the geography of their origin (in the brain, the adrenal glands, or in the intestine) but also according to their particular type.

Into this already complicated picture, Avram Goldstein added another jumble. Dynorphin was the name Goldstein coined for his new peptide—from the Greek root, dynamis, meaning "power." The name was appropriate since, in the guinea pig ileum assay, dynorphin proved fifty times more potent than beta-endorphin, nearly two hundred times more potent than normorphine, and seven hundred times more potent than Leu-enkephalin. Dynorphin, however, was unrelated to beta-endorphin or the enkephalins. It was, Goldstein reported, "in a class by itself."

The newest endorphin was a problematical brainchild. Goldstein had suspected its existence as early as 1975, when work at his Addiction Research Foundation focused on the pituitary opioid peptides (POP-1 and POP-2) isolated by Goldstein's collaborators, Brian Cox and Hansjörg Teschemacher. After realizing that POP-1 was identical to beta-endorphin, yet still wanting to make an original discovery of his own, Goldstein had shifted his attention to POP-2. It had only half the molecular weight of beta-endorphin; it was much more basic (as opposed to acidic), and did not wash out of the ileum as quickly. More intriguing still, this endorphin seemed unrelated to any of the longer Met-enkephalin-containing peptides which Sidney Udenfriend was finding. Goldstein had talked about his results at the Aberdeen meeting of the International Narcotics Research Club in 1976, but in a vague way that was quite uncharacteristic.

Over the next three years Goldstein stubbornly supervised research and reported on the substance—in the face of resistance from his friends and colleagues, particularly Roger Guillemin, who just as stubbornly insisted that Goldstein's finding was only an illusion. One researcher recalls that when Goldstein reported his scant results at the 1977 American Peptide Symposium held at the Salk Institute, Guillemin stood up with the dare: "Goldstein, I challenge you. If you have a peptide other than beta-endorphin, prove it!"

However, analyzing the chemical composition of the putative POP-2 endorphin posed some sticky technological problems—literally. "The substance would stick to the columns we were using, and we would never see it again," recalls

Brian Cox, Goldstein's lab director at the time. "It was a long slog to get it pure." Ninety-nine percent of Goldstein's material was always lost, adhering to the glassware each time his lab did an hplc run.

Problems in his lab were compounded by personal problems when, in early 1977, Goldstein was diagnosed as having Hodgkin's disease, a serious though not usually fatal cancer of the lymph glands. Through months of radiation treatment he struggled to stay in touch with progress on the new endorphin and to keep up with his duties as Addiction Research Foundation director.

The staff of the experimental drug treatment facility which he had founded on Welch Road had expanded to seventy strong by then, and full-scale clinical testing was underway of a long-lasting heroin substitute called LAMM, which, it was thought, might be a better alternative to methadone in the treatment of heroin addicts. The work was expensive and even after Len Cornell, a professional business fund-raiser, was hired to help with the Foundation's financing, Goldstein still found himself all too frequently on the road hustling for the money to support his projects and not in the lab.

At the same time a $4-million lawsuit was being brought against the Addiction Research Foundation by its neighbors after a series of nearby burglaries had been blamed on addicts being treated on the second floor there. Within a year this would force Avram Goldstein to close down the clinical part of his operation.

Given these distractions, the bulk of the dynorphin work fell to Louise Lowney, Goldstein's trusted, long-time assistant, and Shinro Tachibana, a Japanese postdoc, who found themselves frustrated by an inability to isolate enough of the new substance for even partial sequencing. In 1978, their entire supply of dynorphin consisted of 1,200 picomoles—.00000000012 of a gram—the combined weight of a few average germs. It did not seem that there would ever be enough, but that year, 1978,

Goldstein learned of a technological breakthrough by Leroy Hood and Michael Hunkepiller, two Cal Tech scientists who had developed an automatic protein sequencer which reduced the amount of material required for identifying the formulas of unknown proteins and peptides by a factor of one thousand. By early 1979, with Goldstein's minuscule sample, the Cal Tech researchers were able to decode the first thirteen amino acids—the active core of dynorphin.

Goldstein was exultant. "The greatest high I've ever experienced," he reflects, "was the period of a few hours after the call came from Hunkepiller with the sequence of dynorphin, when he and I were the only people in the world to know this absolute, undisputed fact—the sequence of a peptide that God had put here millions of years ago. We'd uncovered a secret of nature." There were twenty suggestions for names. It was, says Goldstein, "like having a baby."

This discovery took on added practical and commercial significance when his workers successfully mapped dynorphin concentrations and determined that the new peptide's geography was entirely different from that of the enkephalins or beta-endorphin—most plentiful in the spinal cord, rather than the brain. When the Chinese researcher J.S. Han demonstrated that the "new" endorphin played a crucial role in acupuncture analgesia, drug companies began to express interest.

"They were very hot on dynorphin almost from the start," according to Goldstein. "There was lots of money to be made in a painkiller as powerful as morphine that doesn't turn a person into a zombie. If you kill pain at the spinal level, you shut it off at the pass without affecting the thought processes and, since dynorphin mediates pain relief independently of the morphine system, dynorphin-type drugs may pose less risk of psychological addiction."

However, tests on lab rats revealed that, while dynorphin was a powerful painkiller, it had odd effects quite unrelated to analgesia. Goldstein called the behavior "barrel-rolling," and described it in a 1980 issue of *Life Science*:

> Dynorphin (1-13) treated rats exhibited self-imposed bizarre postures ... characterized by limb rigidity for about 5 minutes following drug administration, the rat extended its two limbs on one side in a completely horizontal position to its trunk. After this phase, the rat would lie on its side and bring the paws of its rigidly extended forelimbs together while rigidly extending the hindlimbs along the longitudinal axis of the body. This last phase lasted 5–10 minutes and was frequently followed by "barrel-rolling" (70 percent of 100 rats), a very rapid rotation of the rat along its longitudinal axis. The final phase was an opioid-like catalepsy.

Goldstein was hard pressed to fully explain either this phenomenon or one other—an uncharacteristically whimsical interlude, which interrupted his dynorphin research during what was a beautiful spring, in 1979. He had wondered if endorphins might cause that pleasurable tingling, the sudden desire to dance, when people hear melodies which stir them. So he charted the "thrill scores" of seventy student volunteers as they listened to their favorite recordings. Then he injected each of them with naloxone to block the effects of endorphins. For about half of the subjects the thrill was gone—suggesting that music to our ears is also music to our endorphins.

Sandy McKnight, a craggy-looking Scotsman with a nest of reddish hair and a handlebar moustache, had joined the Unit for Research on Addictive Drugs on October 4, 1976—his twenty-eighth birthday. He had come to Aberdeen as Hughes's assistant, replacing Terry Smith, who left the following January—partly because he had been offered a research job at Burroughs Wellcome and partly to get away from John Hughes.

After Hughes left in the fall of 1977, McKnight assumed the unofficial role of Kosterlitz's deputy. He had tremendous admiration for the old man, with whom he shared a common interest in single malt whiskys as well as opiate pharmacology, and he quickly became a regular, at the Prof's table by the window, in the Kirkgate.

For McKnight, the presence of Kosterlitz more than compensated for the practical constraints of work in Aberdeen. There was "nothing too flashy, nothing to knock your eye out," he recalls, except for the hplc machine and a few other technological necessities. Like many who visited the Unit after the enkephalin story had already become scientific myth, McKnight was initially surprised by the modesty of the famous third-floor labs at Marishal.

McKnight had begun by assisting Hughes on the search for precursors of the enkephalins. He was "never too happy" with the project, but had continued to work on it after Hughes left. A few months later, he had received a preprint of the Udenfriend group's first paper on proenkephalin. There was no way the Unit could compete with the kind of manpower and technological sophistication that Hoffman La Roche had put at Udenfriend's disposal. So since then, McKnight had been plugging away "piece by piece" on new endorphins. He and Kosterlitz were particularly interested in a fragment of dynorphin—dynorphin $_{1-8}$—which they suspected was the active core of the compound.

In 1978 Kosterlitz was elected a Fellow of the Royal Society. "It was an event-filled year," McKnight recalls. "John Hughes got contact lenses and 'Prof' was put on the Royal." Kosterlitz's energy was still astonishing—flying to the European Brain Research Conference in Warsaw one day, and straight on to the Committee on Problems of Drug Dependence in Philadelphia the next—or so it seemed to McKnight. "On one trip he went to Australia via Hong Kong, then hauled straight back, went to the office and took care of all the moderately urgent stuff right away, and had letters ready for typing the next morning. He was going at it frantically."

But with any seventy-eight year old, even someone as remarkable as Hans Kosterlitz, one always worried; and the subject of his age came up often over drinks between the younger staff members.

On a Monday morning in January 1981, Kosterlitz phoned in sick, something he never did; he said that he had a headache. Over the weekend he had become a grandfather for the third time, and Hanna was in Birmingham visiting their son Michael, his wife, and the new baby. Two days later, McKnight learned that Kosterlitz had suffered a stroke.

He was incapacitated for weeks, and had to teach himself to count all over again and learn to tell time, but he improved steadily during the following months and by spring, to everyone's relief, he fully recovered and was jetting around the world again—with only two concessions: Hanna insisted that she travel with him and that, when they were in Aberdeen, he come home every day for lunch.

In August he and Hanna attended the twelfth meeting of the International Narcotics Research Conference in Kyoto, Japan. The Narcotics Club had been rechristened the International Narcotics Research Conference, after a representative of the National Institute of Drug Abuse, one of the major sources of funding for opiate research, complained that the word "club" did not sound "serious" enough. At that conference the complete seventeen-amino-acid sequence of dynorphin was presented by Goldstein's former graduate student, Shinro Tachibana. And a young neurosurgeon from San Francisco named David Baskin announced that naloxone enabled stroke victims to move their paralyzed limbs.

Baskin, who was working with Yoshio Hosobuchi—the brain surgeon and collaborator with C.H. Li—did not know the precise reasons why naloxone worked. It might be counteracting the effects of endorphins which, he speculated, were shutting off the blood flow to the injured areas of his patients' brains. The resultant relief was brief (twenty minutes) and it worked only on some patients, but his announcement was a totally unexpected development, one with great therapeutic potential—which Kosterlitz, after his own stroke, found particularly intriguing.

Harry Collier, who was then teaching at Chelsea College, London, called that Kyoto meeting "The Conference of the Camera," since so many INRC members bought new Japanese cameras and flash attachments "with the effect of turning us into a swarm of fireflies." A garden party at Mount Hiei was the social highlight of the meeting, climaxed by a performance by traditional dancers dressed as a lion and a giant spider, in which the spider, ultimately, captured the lion in many silken threads. "While most of us were watching the contest, enthralled," Harry Collier recalled, "a few super loyal Brits stole downstairs to watch—on TV—a not entirely dissimilar happening, in which Lady Diana Spencer completed the capture of Prince Charles."

That October, Hans and Hanna Kosterlitz spent two weeks in China as guests of the Chinese Academy. There was a great deal of excitement over the endorphins and their connection to acupuncture in China, and despite swarms of cockroaches in one hotel bathtub, the visit was a memorable one. It was early winter, 1981, and Kosterlitz zestfully confessed to McKnight later that he had to wear "two pairs of long johns" at the Great Wall.

Life in the small set of labs in the Marishal College tower was quieter and more routine than it had been during the heat of the race to decipher the enkephalin formula, but this more subdued mood was not just characteristically Aberdonian. In general, the endorphin research field had, in Candace Pert's estimation, "mellowed out." The unforeseen complexity, the sheer number of endorphins, in part, prompted this change, as

did the less than successful first attempts to turn the discovery
into an overnight breakthrough in the treatment of pain and
mental illness. By 1981 it was clear that the careful, meticulous
hard work required to achieve these goals was, really, only
starting.

John Hughes's research aims at the beginning of the
1980s were typical of those of his colleagues. "It was time,"
Hughes recalls, "to look beyond the chemistry of the endorphins
to their wiring. To understand how these systems are controlled and what physiological functions they control, and
ultimately, how they contribute to behavior." Faced with these
new challenges, competition among the scientists had become
tempered by something like contemplation. They had slipped
beyond the moorings of their original expectations—into the
future.

RATS AND RUNNERS

If anything, controversy and heated open competition between top-level scientists that fueled the investigation into endorphins only served to attract other researchers to the fray. As Avram Goldstein said, "The field had an aura of excitement about it. The noise drove it; the hoopla brought scientists in." Despite setbacks and disappointments, by the early 1980s the ranks of endorphin researchers had grown as steadily as the numbers of endorphins, and new papers were appearing on the subject at the extraordinary rate of one per day.

The possibilities of breaking through on a nonaddictive painkiller or taking a bold stride forward in the treatment of mental illness still existed, but the long-term goals of many of the research groups involved in the work had shifted back to basics: toward the completion of a top-to-bottom, molecule-to-man profile of what the endorphins did. New paths of inquiry into the ways simple chemistry evolves into complex behaviors in animals and humans had brought the scientists to the cutting-edge of neuroscience, a new medical approach that increasingly merged the "hard" sciences—physics, biology, and biophysics—with the behavioral sciences, psychology, and psychiatry. It was, observed Candace Pert, "as if a lightning bolt had connected the two systems of knowledge into one system," synthesizing them into a single language. Along with many of her colleagues, Pert was now groping with almost esoteric questions concerning the distinction, or lack of it, between mind and body, physical and emotional states.

As for the researchers' original goals, much progress had been made. Desperately needed clues to the underlying causes of narcotics addiction had been provided. Using the endorphins as the basis for a new theory, scientists now felt that when addicts used heroin or other narcotic drugs, they might be shutting off their production of endorphins by artificially saturating opiate receptor systems. Once the drug wore off, without endorphins to slow them down, nerve fibers that were ordinarily excitatory became hyperactive, leading to the fear, anxiety, chills, and sweats characteristic of narcotics withdrawal.

The use of endorphins as a "cure" for addicts, however, remained equivocal. C.H. Li's associate Donald Catlin found that beta-endorphin appeared to stop the flulike side effects of withdrawal (stomach cramps, perspiration, muscle ache) in some subjects, but it had no effect on the basic mental and emotional mechanisms of addiction; even during beta-endorphin treatment, addicts craved narcotics. It was now also clear that endorphins, while quickly broken down under normal circumstances, could themselves be addictive if their action was artificially prolonged. Rats whose brains were infused with a seventy-two-hour supply of enkephalins or beta-endorphin exhibited the full range of sneezing, trembling, and jumping behaviors characteristic of rats going cold turkey once the dosing stopped. Drug company chemists, too, had observed that Met-enkephalin, redesigned to make it longer-lasting, would produce signs and symptoms of drug dependence, though to a lesser degree than morphine did.

The most clear-cut success had been achieved in the field of pain research. Candace Pert, along with others, had been able, by charting systems of opiate receptors and endorphins using autoradiography and other advanced mapping techniques, to develop a more detailed picture than scientists had ever possessed of the nervous system wiring diagram underlying pain perception. The new maps revealed three major pain pathways, all of them rich in endorphins. The first ran down from the gray area of the brain implicated in stimulation-produced analgesia to the nucleus raphe magnus in the back of the brain. It extended from there into the section of the spinal cord called the dorsal horn, where these descending nerve fibers met incoming neurons carrying pain messages from the body's extremities.

Opiate receptors and endorphins showed up in the spinothalamic tract, the so-called "fast" pain pathway running up the spinal cord and into the thalamus region of the brain stem, which is responsible for our almost instantaneous withdrawal from hot or sharp objects. They were also found in the spinoretricular tract, a slower, more diffuse neuronal network that conveys pain signals to the corpus striatum in the brain, from which they are in turn relayed to the hippocampus and cingulate gyrus, areas of the limbic system where emotional responses to pain are thought to be generated. At any point along these pain pathways, it seemed, the endorphins might play the crucial role of modulating pain signals or stopping them outright.

Yet, even from clusters of fluorescent specks on the new maps the scientists could readily "see" that the functional profile of the endorphins was likely to be every bit as complex as their chemical profile. "At first it seemed so simple," Avram Goldstein observed. "Morphine was a painkiller which functioned along nice, clear-cut pain pathways. But the receptors and endorphins were everywhere, in every neurosystem. Pain was just a part of it—it was a pervasive system involving every type of behavior."

High concentrations of endogenous opiates in the amygdala

and other limbic structures—where the euphoric effects of narcotic drugs were thought to be triggered—was a compelling indication that the endorphins also mediated pleasurable emotions; enkephalins in the vagal nuclei and area postrema of the back brain, where the cough reflex was controlled, might act as natural cough suppressants; in the gut, they probably slowed intestinal spasms—as Hans Kosterlitz had fathomed nearly twenty years earlier; Sidney Udenfriend's extended adrenal enkephalins possibly slowed heartbeat and respiration by modulating the release of adrenalin; and the presence of alpha, beta, and gamma endorphins in the hypothalamus and pituitary gland suggested that the "morphine within" played such disparate roles as influencing appetite, lowering body temperature, and—by countering the effects of ACTH—regulating not only physical and emotional reactions to stress, fear, and anxiety, but also responses of the body's immune system to injury or invasion by germs and viruses. The challenge was, and will be for years to come to trace these predicted effects from the molecular level to the living organism.

Rats provided many of the earliest clues. Because their organs and nervous systems respond in similar, predictable ways to those of humans, rats make surprisingly good test models. But a parallel group of investigations on humans was providing other, sometimes indirect, clues to previously unsought functions of the endorphins.

It was clear the endorphins produced analgesia in laboratory animals: pain responses—measured by the time it took rats to jump, or flick their tails away when exposed to heat lamps, hot plates, or tail clamps—were markedly diminished by injections of natural and synthetic endorphins.

Endogenous opiates also appeared to block pain in humans. When a Japanese team injected beta-endorphin supplied by Roger Guillemin into the spinal cords of fourteen cancer patients, all of them reported profound relief from pain, lasting an average of over thirty hours; in one case, more than three days. Guillemin, meanwhile, working with Floyd Bloom and Jean Rossier, had followed up Yoshio Hosobuchi's work on electronic brain stimulation, and found a two- to fourfold increase in levels of spinal fluid endorphins in a group of patients undergoing SPA. But the evidence was not restricted to scientists. More than 2.5 million pain sufferers in America had tried acupuncture successfully to relieve everything from "tennis elbow" to migraine headaches; and as a treatment for heroin addicts, acupuncture had been shown so promising that efforts were underway in the U.S. and Great Britain to apply the techniques to cigarettes, cocaine, and other addictions as well. David Mayer's groundbreaking experiments with acupuncture analgesia strongly implied that endorphins were at least partially responsible for producing these beneficial results.

Other surprising developments had widened the investigation of the functions of endorphins in pain perception. A case in point was the bold, firsthand experiment in 1978 by Huda Akil, which had established a link between endorphins and childbirth. For several months prior to the birth of her son, Akil had taken samples of his blood and her own for endorphin analysis. As she had already observed in two other new mothers and babies, plasma endorphin levels began to rise in the months preceding birth, reaching a peak—six times higher than normal—during labor. While Akil cautiously avoided speculation about the reasons for this phenomenon, others proposed that increased endorphins might be nature's way of easing the pain of labor. For Candace Pert—whose daughter Vanessa was born the following year—the evidence formed the basis of a new speculative theory. "It's interesting to think of a fetus floating around with its opiate receptors loaded with endorphins," she commented. "A fetus in that condition would be sleepy, would be calm, it wouldn't breathe. We don't want it to breathe when it's in the uterus surrounded by liquid. We want it to breathe when it comes out. It's fascinating to think about the fetus in this blissful state, mediated by endorphins."

At the same time, at the University of California in San Francisco, a researcher named Howard Fields had been drawn to the new endorphin field after seeing the "placebo effect" at work. Sugar pill remedies have been used by medical practitioners throughout the ages, and for good reason. Placebos—from the Latin "I will please"—produce beneficial results in about one third of all patients who try them.

In 1978, Fields was studying pain levels following impacted wisdom tooth extraction in volunteer patients. Over a third of the subjects obtained substantial relief from saline placebos, relief which Fields noticed would disappear after an injection of the opiate antagonist naloxone. Avram Goldstein later confirmed the results with a thirty patient follow-up study.

The tentative conclusion, that the placebo effect is based on the release of endorphins, caused Howard Fields, for one, to wonder how far the implications of the work stretched. "Can this system," he asked, "be activated voluntarily? That is, can people will themselves to feel less pain; or learn some mental trick to set the pain-suppressing mechanism in motion?"

Other behavioral studies supported a contention which C.H. Li had been broadcasting, that endorphins might be a kind of "happiness hormone" as well as a modulator of pain. John Liebeskind, one of the SPA originators at UCLA, observed that the EEG patterns of enkephalin-dosed rats revealed "funny waves" similar to those seen in satiated animals in a safe environment—patterns which other scientists dubbed "pleasure rhythms."

Larry Stein and James Belluzi, who had left Wyeth Pharmaceutical for teaching posts at the University of California at Irvine, described Leu-enkephalin as the "primary peptide of pleasure." Their lab rats bar-pressed only intermittently for Met-enkephalin, but the "animals went nuts for Leu," Stein recalls. He theorized that the natural functions of the two peptides might be different: Met acting as a pain modulator and Leu as a "euphorigen, a natural reward transmitter."

Simultaneously, a number of other researchers began to report that their rats were learning things more quickly on endorphins and retaining learned responses longer. David DeWied and his group at the Rudolph Magnus Institute in Holland reported that alpha- and beta-endorphins enhanced the ability of lab rats to learn and remember to avoid shock. Andrew Schally (Roger Guillemin's arch-rival) tested natural and synthetic Met-enkephalin and found that the ability of rats to learn how to run a maze seemed to improve. (Morphine, curiously, produced the opposite effect.) The combined observations bolstered the theory that, by providing internal reinforcing cues, endogenous opiates could be contributing to learning memory and possibly complicated instincts as well. A number of intriguing experiments based on tests with naloxone had been published by Jack Panksepp, a psychologist at Bowling Green University. Doses of naloxone reduced play and disrupted child retrieval in rats, broke up the schooling behavior of goldfish, and suppressed tail wagging in dogs. Panksepp argued that the negative effects indicated that the antagonist was counteracting the actions of endorphins underlying these complicated instincts.

Based on such evidence, it appeared to Candace Pert and other scientists that, in the human brain, the endorphins might play a dual role. They could block the transmission of messages along pain pathways by inhibiting nerves from firing but in a similar yet opposite fashion, the peptides could also be reinforcing the flow of information from the primitive centers in back of the brain forward to the higher thought centers in the cerebral cortex, by chemically rewarding behaviors, instincts, and memories. "When you look at it this way," Pert reflected, "the system seems to form a switching mechanism in which the receptors and endorphins act as sensory filters, perhaps having to do with selective attention—deciding what we pay attention to at any given moment."

*   *   *

Speculation that endorphins contributed chemically to the exalted feeling following running (or jogging) long distances combined both their assigned functions as pain modulators and pleasure peptides. "First you run until everything hurts, then it just gets so easy," was one runner's description of the euphoric state of effortless movement which had become something of a mythical goal—"the zone"—to his thirty million fellow jogging enthusiasts who were logging some twenty-six million miles in the U.S. alone every day. Others claimed to be "hooked" on running and complained of edginess, anxiety, and other "withdrawal" symptoms when circumstances kept them from their daily run.

These subjective descriptions were far from universal. "I think it's all a myth," an experienced New York marathoner scorned. "I don't feel good, I feel pain." But the discovery of endorphins raised the possibility that the accounts attesting to "runner's high" might have a basis in physical fact. A curious form of pain relief had been found to occur in rats exposed to "inescapable foot-shock." They were less sensitive to heat on the tail-flick test, and analysis of their brains revealed high endorphin levels. The phenomenon had been named "stress-induced analgesia." Possibly, runners were experiencing a similar effect, in which their endorphins were responsible for the sensation of breaking through the pain barrier.

In 1980, a study by Steven Gambert at the Medical College of Wisconsin in Milwaukee bolstered the "runner's high" theory. Analyzing blood samples from subjects who had run for twenty minutes on a treadmill, Gambert found an enormous increase in their beta-endorphin levels; in one case, a jump of over 400 percent.

Following up, one year later, Daniel Carr and Janet McArthur, two Massachusetts General Hospital researchers, completed an experiment designed to test the effects of a normal exercise routine on the endorphin levels of volunteer subjects. Blood samples were taken from several healthy but nonexercising women at the beginning, middle, and end of a four-month training program that consisted of one hour a day, six days a week, of vigorous calisthenics, stationary bicycle pedaling and running. The result was an overall increase of more than 50 percent in the women's beta-endorphin levels during the early stages of the program and, in addition, the Boston researchers observed that these levels were gradually elevated to nearly 80 percent as the training sessions continued. Conditioning seemed to augment the effect, which Carr and McArthur believed might account for the fact that the more exercise you do, the better you feel.

Studies elsewhere also revealed that running and exercise raised plasma beta-endorphin levels. However, scientists remained as divided as runners over the meaning of the new information. The problem was that since the opiatelike effects of the endorphins were known to occur in the brain not the blood, there was no way to connect the subjective experience of runner's high with even hugely elevated levels of bloodstream beta-endorphin. For although it is manufactured in the brain, once the peptide is released into the bloodstream, it does not seem able to cross back through the blood-brain barrier. Even if, as some scientists have suggested, the body has a special adaptation mechanism enabling beta-endorphin to be taken back up into the brain in highly stressful situations, there was no means of drawing firm conclusions from the circumstantial data about runner's high, short of "grinding and binding" the brains of joggers.

These drawbacks did not discourage attempts to further examine the subject, though. If endorphins are accumulating in the brain, Daniel Carr argued, "it may explain in part why people don't seem to notice injuries during strenuous exercise. It might also explain why people's moods improve if they do exercise regularly and why they feel bad if they are used to exercising and they have to stop." Yet the effect was variable.

Beginning joggers, interviewed by Michael Sachs, a sports psychology professor at the University of Quebec, almost never reported feeling euphoric after runs, and only half of the more proficient runners he questioned said they experienced the phenomenon. Among those that did, all agreed that being in good enough shape to stay on the road a long time—at least thirty-five minutes—was an indispensable criterion. No pain, no gain, and, apparently no runner's high.

In related research, Daniel Carr's colleague Janet McArthur began investigating the possible relationship between changes in endorphin levels and cases of amenorrhea—the lack of menstrual symptoms—among female runners. Experiments conducted by a Canadian research team at the University of Manitoba had already suggested such a connection. When the antagonist naloxone was administered to women who suffered from amenorrhea, the subjects showed significant increases in luteinizing hormone, a key regulator of ovulation. This implied that endorphins, ostensibly being blocked by naloxone, might be contributing to amenorrhea by lowering luteinizing hormone levels. For Janet McArthur's female runners, elevated levels of endorphins, while possibly pleasurable, might also have the negative effects of contributing to menstrual cycle disorders as well as increasing their risk of lowered fertility.

Based on her data and future studies, Daniel Carr hoped that easy-to-read charts might soon be developed which would help women plan their exercise programs. "A woman with a certain weight and height," he suggested, "might then be able to refer to a table which tells her that as long as she runs a certain number of miles a week, her fertility will be lowered by only one percent." Since some male runners complained of diminished sexual drive, charted guidelines for men, too, seemed a possibility to aid in planning exercise regimens.

Ongoing research such as that being done by Daniel Carr and Janet McArthur was providing at least some objective

measures of a phenomenon that could be of potential importance to health. While their work has not resolved the dispute
among scientists over the effects of exercise on endorphins, it
has demonstrated that under special circumstances, the
endorphin levels of some individuals can be dramatically altered.

Given the mounting evidence of a relationship between
stress and the endorphins, it was not surprising that researchers would also find intriguing connections between stress,
endorphins, and the immune system. But once again these
discoveries came to light via an indirect route.

The origin of the work was an investigation in the late
1970s by David Margules, a behavioral psychologist at Temple
University, of links between endorphins and obesity. When he
tested "Zucher fatty rats"—butterball specimens that gorged
themselves compulsively and grew five times heavier than normal rats—with naloxone, he noticed that they stopped over-
eating. Chemical analysis of their brains disclosed higher than
normal concentrations of pituitary beta-endorphin, which suggested to Margules that the excess peptide triggered the animals' gluttony and, logically, the obesity syndrome. He
speculated that similar endorphin imbalances might be opera-
tional, and that naloxone might be useful in treating human
obesity.

Though David Margules's original findings were heavily
criticized, by Roger Guillemin and Floyd Bloom among others, follow-up research had begun when attention was once
again drawn to his fatty rodents. This time, Margules reported
that genetically obese mice, in addition to having higher
endorphin levels were also resistant to tumors and had elevated counts of "natural killer" cells, disease-fighting white
blood cells, which instantly recognize foreign cells without
having been previously exposed to them.

Margules, Candace Pert, and others—including the popular author Norman Cousins—were suggesting that the endorphins, in the course of blocking pain, generating pleasurable sensations, or dampening down stress reactions, might also affect the ability of animals and humans to combat heart disease and the spread of cancer. The implication was that emotions, acting through the brain's neurochemical systems, could influence immunological responses, altering the ability to overcome illness.

In the wake of conclusions from several studies on human test subjects, the idea that emotional components like mood and attitude could be important to the causes and treatment of disease—a notion which until then had been regarded as almost heretical—began winning widespread support from the medical establishment. An increasing number of neuroscientists were using the term "psychoneuroimmunology" to describe the new mind-body link, and response to stress was their chief target of interest. Margaret Linn, a medical researcher at the Veterans Administration in Miami, for example, had conducted a five-year study of heavy smokers in an effort to distinguish if emotional factors played a role in the reasons why some of them developed cancer and others did not. She concluded that while divorce, family illness, job loss, and other traumatic life events were as prevalent among smokers who developed lung cancer as cancer-free smokers, clear differences could be observed between the attitudes of the two groups of patients. The cancer victims perceived these emotionally trying events to be more stressful, and regarded themselves as more responsible when bad things happened. The cancer-free smokers took stress less seriously. Among those patients with high perceived stress, Linn further noted, immunological responses were lower, even before cancer developed.

At Beth Israel Hospital in Boston, where similar experiments were completed on a group of healthy undergraduates, those who suffered more psychological symptoms of stress were observed to have only one third the normal levels of "natural killer" cells—the same type of white blood cell that David Margules was finding in abundance, along with high levels of beta-endorphin, in his tumor-resistant obese mice. Elevated endorphin levels had perhaps boosted the animals' immune responses, Margules suggested, by stimulating "killer cell" activity. "There's going to be a revolution, it's in the *Zeitgeist,*" he commented. "It's also scary, the need to keep the good vibes going . . ."

Questions far outnumbered answers, Candace Pert conceded, but she was convinced that the endorphins were "mood chemicals," which played an intimate role in the complex human healing process.

A final area of disputed interest was the proposed role of the endorphins in mediating sexual responses. Here, information ranging from the discovery by Jesse Roth at the National Institutes of Health that beta-endorphin acted as a reproduction cue in amoebas and other one-celled animals, to reports by drug addicts comparing the intense "rush" of heroin to orgasm, formed the basis for speculation that endorphin networks played a role in sexual drive and satisfaction. The results of experiments testing this possibility, however, were contradictory.

In early 1977, Lars Terenius and his Dutch collaborator, Bengt Meyerson, reported that when male rats received microdoses of beta-endorphin, and were placed in cages with receptive females, the peptide had a dismaying effect. "The treated male repeatedly approached the female and displayed all items of the precopulatory repertoire, but interrupted the performance just when he normally should have mounted the female. Those males who initiated mounting had a longer latency and low mount frequency compared to controls. Mounting was also performed in an abnormal way (no real clasp and thrust) so hardly any intromissions were achieved." This was a fancy way of saying that while the desire of the rodents was undiminished, their performance was sadly lacking.

Terenius steered clear of drawing any conclusions that would link abnormal beta-endorphin levels to human sexual dysfunction, but the possibility did occur to Jack Mendelson, Director of Alcohol and Drug Abuse Treatment at McLean Hospital in Belmont, Massachusetts, who lost no time in following up his suspicions. After a quick study, Mendelson reported that injections of naloxone, by presumably countering the effects of endorphins, increased the sexual urge of normal male test subjects and might, eventually, help to cure others suffering from impotence.

Such conclusions disturbed Avram Goldstein, from whose strict biochemical viewpoint most of the accumulating data on the functions of the endorphins in animals and humans amounted to a "magical mystery tour," signifying nothing. He quickly conducted and published his own study—"Evidence Against Involvement of Endorphins in Sexual Arousal and Orgasm in Man"—a backhanded rebuttal which, he hoped, would go beyond its specific subject to dampen "the wildfire of speculations that have recently plagued both the scientific and popular media."

Like Mendelson, Goldstein reasoned that if endorphins played a role in sexual drive, the opiate antagonist naloxone should alter these responses. A thirty-five-year-old male colleague volunteered to be the subject of an experiment and, in the course of twelve sessions—carried out on a weekly basis in "a secure private office"—he was injected with either naloxone or saline by Goldstein. After Goldstein left the room, the subject was instructed to masturbate.

To insure scientific accuracy, injections were delivered in a strict double-blind fashion and "no reading or pictorial matter or other artificial sexual stimulus" was permitted in the room. But the study was, admittedly, cluttered with other "unavoidable distractions." As a precaution—should there be any adverse reaction to the naloxone—the subject was to signal by buzzer once every minute, letting Goldstein know that he was all right. He was also asked to write down the approximate time of his full penile erection and orgasm, and to note whether the injection had "helped, hurt, or not affected" his responses.

In every case, the subject reported that there was no effect, and Goldstein trumpeted his negative results in the prestigious pages of the *Archives of General Psychiatry*. The debate over the functions of the endorphins, however, was unlikely to end there.

The proposed links between endogenous opiates and pain modulation, pleasure, learning and memory, stress, and immune system reactions, as well as sexual response, were unquestionably fascinating, especially as examples of ways in which chemical, physical, and emotional states could be integrated. But results in human and animal experiments remained controversial. Between the clear molecular event and the clear behavioral event lurked the shadow of thousands of discrete chemical and physiological subevents. And it was to these pieces of the puzzle that scientists were beginning to direct their attention as they waited for the next stroke of serendipity, the next breakthrough.

THE SYMPHONY AND THE ORCHESTRA

Shadowy figures walked the foggy Cape Cod beach, carrying umbrellas. It was early June, too early for the Cape, too cold. It had been raining all day, and the windows in the lounge of the Seacrest Hotel, where the International Narcotics Research Conference was meeting, were misted over.

Racing motorcycles whined on the TV as the scientists drifted into the bar from their rooms: Candace Pert, in torn blue jeans; Avram Goldstein towering over the others; John Hughes with a slim brunette, Julie Pennington, who had been, increasingly, his companion at recent conferences.

". . . we're sequencing alpha neoendorphin . . ."

". . . would have sent him the dynorphin one-thirteen if he'd only asked . . ."

". . . kappa one, kappa two . . ."

Snatches of conversation as cryptic as if the scientists were speaking in code described a simple discovery, which had become no longer very simple at all.

John Hughes could never have anticipated the tremendous expansion in the scope and scale of endorphin research. In the eight years since he had described "Substance X" to a handful of conferees in Boston, his original compound had been found to really be composed of two small peptides, methionine and leucine enkephalin. Alpha, beta, and gamma endorphins had also been discovered, and findings had so proliferated that his colleagues now contemplated three great endorphin families—of nearly twenty different subtypes. The endorphins came in short, medium, and long forms—each with its own characteristics and likely functions—forming, in part, an internal pain-modulating system, but also having implications which related to mental illness, acupuncture, appetite, immune responses, stress, and "runner's high." Endorphins performed, as one researcher put it, "real simple functions" —like heartbeat and temperature regulation—and "real fancy functions" having to do with emotions and drives.

"Busy compounds," as Huda Akil called them, they performed not in isolation, but by "coreleasing" and "comodulating" many other transmitter chemicals—acetylcholine, norepinephrine, and serotonin among them—to filter the babble of electrochemical nervous system messages into a coherent pattern of responses. Derrick Smyth compared the body's synthesis and release of endorphins to an artist's palette— "showers and mixes of different colors, varying according to the needs of the organism, to produce delicately complex effects." The accumulation of findings inspired another researcher, Arnold Mandell, to predict: "In the future, we will come to think of ourselves, our personalities, as a symphony of chemical voices in our heads."

The ways in which various endorphin peptides and transmitters, the players and instruments of the "symphony" orchestra, are synthesized according to information in our genes and molded by enzymes to produce their precise effects—how the conductor interprets the composer's score—remained a tantalizing mystery to the vast network of researchers, many of them quite young, drawn to the Cape Cod conference in 1982. It had been twelve years since Kosterlitz had convened the first "unofficial" meeting of the International Narcotics Research Club in Basel, attended by twelve scientists. Now there were nearly three hundred from a dozen countries and at least as many disciplines. Clashes of egos and ideas persisted, of course—the biochemical types and the behavioral types were constantly in disagreement—and the musical analogy which some were using to describe the ultimate implications of their work, described the scientists themselves. They were a large, out-of-tune orchestra, producing a strange yet captivating music.

The weather stayed bad, keeping the scientists indoors. No one seemed to mind. "You can always work," said one conferee cheerily. On the one day of decent weather, Candace Pert was breast-feeding her new baby boy—and third child—by the hotel's swimming pool. Brandon Pert had been born eight months earlier, on the living room floor in front of the fireplace at home, because Candace Pert believed that his endorphin levels would be higher in a natural setting. Since it fit into one of her current theories, that endorphins played a crucial role in mother-child bonding, she wanted Brandon to get his full neurochemical birthright. Her husband, Agu, who had assisted during the prolonged and difficult childbirth, now sat quietly by her side.

"In the beginning I worked on standard pharmacological problems," she said. "Now I study the biochemistry of emotion. . . . If the endorphins are 'pleasure peptides'—for the anticipation of pleasure—they go way back in evolutionary history. It's a primeval decision to use them that way. A leech has one enkephalin cell in the center of every ganglia cell— except the sex ganglia, where it has five enkephalin neurons. When you stimulate these cells, electrically, the leech has an erection. Helping the animal make basic decisions by rewarding things like sex and eating—that's basic emotion. Receptors are targets for emotions."

On the beach the scientists had organized their annual volleyball game. A lifeguard was scraping the remains of a headless eel from the steps of one of the beach-front cabanas. Candace Pert laughed as someone joked that one of her over-zealous colleagues must have mangled the creature to study eel-brain endorphins. "I wouldn't put it past some of them," she smiled acidly, then reflected. "The whole thing is like a science fiction fantasy," she said. "When I was an undergrad at Bryn Mawr—and Agu was my psychology instructor—we used to fantasize about finding a molecular basis for behavior and emotion. What has come true is a thousand times better. With the receptors and endorphins you can integrate down from a state of consciousness to a molecule."

John Hughes, fresh from a swim in the ocean, sprawled on a lounge chair nearby. Hughes had been having his prob-lems. His divorce had taken a toll on him, and he had fallen seriously ill with meningitis. Moreover, his high expectations for work at Imperial College had not materialized. Because he had been overburdened with administrative duties, his projects had not yielded clear results. His grants had been cut. So earlier that year he had accepted a new position as director of an exploratory research division of the Parke-Davis Pharma-ceutical Company in Cambridge, England. Yet, despite his disappointments, Hughes had become much more personable lately; friends said Julie Pennington was the chief reason. He seemed to be beginning to enjoy, for the first time, the trap-pings that went along with being a young and rather famous scientist.

At the Seacrest meeting, Hughes reported on the isolation of a huge "pre-precursor" for the enkephalins weighing in at some 90,000 daltons. More, ever unfolding complexities.

The goal of medical research, however, is the effective and humane treatment of disease, not confusion; and it is that ultimate achievement, one young scientist at Seacrest asserted, which creates the "pressure to hope" in the face of the most enormous difficulties.

In Lars Terenius's lab in Uppsala, Sweden, the pressure to hope had taken the form of a study of "neurogenic" pain—chronic, constant pain which lingered long after the injuries to patients had healed. "Phantom limb pain" years after amputations was only one textbook example; this syndrome, involving injuries of all kinds, was alarmingly widespread. (A 1982 NBC News segment estimated the number of sufferers in the U.S. to be as high as fifty million, and the estimated cost to society in the billions of dollars.) While the causes were often literally invisible, the pain was starkly real—as was the dilemma faced by its sufferers, for whom there was no satisfactory treatment. Chronic pain patients drifted from doctor to doctor seeking help; prescribed painkillers, even morphine, were ineffective.

Until the late 1970s, neurosurgeons treated such patients by severing the nerves responsible for carrying the pain messages to the brain. This approach had proven so ineffective—frequently worsening the condition—that the prominent neurosurgeon, W.K. Livingston, was led to bitterly remark, "the best neurosurgeon is one with no hands."

In 1982, the Terenius group tested a device called a transcutaneous nerve stimulator (TNS), which looked strikingly like a Sony Walkman—except that two padded electrode wires dangled from its metal casing, instead of stereo earphones. It had an effect similar to acupuncture, but with touch-pads rather than needles, and was effective in the treatment of pain from arthritis, migraine, and sports injuries. Several pharmaceutical companies—including Johnson & Johnson —were already marketing versions of TNS, for prescription-only use.

Terenius reported that three out of four neurogenic patients tested found the TNS treatment helpful. He suggested that the neurogenic pain syndrome began as a "decoding error" —stemming, in part, from endorphin imbalances. Endorphin levels in the cerebrospinal fluid of neurogenic pain patients were "very much on the low side." TNS, he observed, would raise their endorphin levels as the pain was relieved. Where opiates had failed them, electrically generated endorphins worked.

John Hughes's imminent move to Parke-Davis pointed to continuing interest in endorphins by the big pharmaceutical companies, but attempts by company researchers to create an endorphin painkiller superior to conventional narcotics had yet to hit pay dirt. At Eli Lilly, Robert Frederickson was still facing stiff management resistance as he tried to expand his metkephamid project; he had to prove that the enkephalin-based drug could do something that Demerol, the best-selling Sterling Drug narcotic, could not. The previous year, 1981, Frederickson had convinced the Research Management Staff Committee to fund a $5,000 study by Gary Devane, at the University of Florida, and when the results were in, they showed that metkephamid, administered to pregnant sheep, did not register in the blood of their fetuses; it crossed the blood-brain barrier to relieve pain, but not the placental barrier—as Demerol did. In fact, the standard *Physicians Desk Reference* contains a warning to this effect in regard to Demerol.

The experiment suggested that metkephamid might be safer for mothers during childbirth, and Frederickson instituted a hasty survey—conducted by the Lilly marketing department—at an obstetrics conference in Dallas. If a drug existed, they asked, with the advantages of metkephamid, would obstetricians use it? The response was favorable. Eighty percent of the doctors surveyed said they would switch from Demerol. Frederickson presented this survey, together with relevant extracts from the *Physicians Desk Reference,* to the Committee in January 1982. "The project was ready to be killed. It was too expensive, too unfeasible," he recalls. "The possibility that metkephamid might have an application in obstetrics was the breakthrough."

The obstetrics market was, by Lilly standards, just passable—in the 20- to 30-million-dollar range—but the Committee withheld approval to upscale the project until it was clinically established that the advantage of the compound applied to pregnant humans as well as sheep.

Frederickson wrote a new human testing protocol for the FDA and a study of thirty women during labor was completed with positive results. Expanded testing of two hundred more women seemed to be a certainty when Frederickson made his final presentation to the Lilly Committee before leaving the company in August 1984 to take a high-level research post at Monsanto in St. Louis. One of Lilly's marketing directors then told him bluntly, "Of course, you know, metkephamid is never going to be a drug. You're just wasting your time. Lilly's never supported it." Despite reassurances from high-level administrators that this was not the case, the conversation shook Frederickson.

After his last day of work at Lilly, as he left the Biological Research building and walked across the parking lot carrying a heavy carton of files, Frederickson still expressed optimism about the potential outcome of his decade-long efforts. But today the future of metkephamid—the first commercial endorphin painkiller—remains, at best, uncertain.

In March of 1982, Nathan Kline appeared in a courtroom in downtown Manhattan to sign a form that forbade him permanently from using "in any manner, whatsoever, any investigational new drug." The complaint had been filed in Federal Court by John S. Martin, Jr., the U.S. Attorney for the Southern District of New York, and accused Kline of violating the Food, Drug, and Cosmetic Act, claiming that he had treated twenty-three patients in 1977 and 1978 (nine more than he had reported) with beta-endorphin without obtaining government permission and, in a few cases, without the informed consent of the patients themselves.

Five years had passed since the Puerto Rico meeting, five years of "slow agony" for Kline, as his associate Heinz Lehmann recalls. "The summer after Puerto Rico we were called before an FDA panel. They slapped our wrists and told us not to do it again. But it didn't stop there. They took the extraordinary measure of bringing a criminal suit against him—a criminal suit! And his criminality, they alleged, was a sort of Mann Act violation—that he had seduced C.H. Li into supplying the substance across state lines."

Lehmann, says that, as a Canadian citizen, he was exempt from this prosecution, but FDA investigators had paid several visits to C.H. Li during the spring and summer of 1977. At first, Li recalls, they seemed to be "mainly interested in how beta-endorphin was made," but this pretext was eventually dropped. "They wanted me to give evidence against Kline," Li realized, "and I wouldn't do this."

It was Lehmann's impression that the FDA was ready to drop the matter—with a warning—that summer. The case, however, had come to the attention of Richard P. Kusserow, inspector general of the U.S. Department of Health and Human Services, who had taken up the investigation and, over the following years, pressed it with what seemed to Lehmann a determination to "get" Kline. As the case continued, Kline's lawyers' fees mounted to nearly $100,000. His practice was disrupted and, in private, he had told Lehmann that he felt "hounded," and complained of "vendettas."

On the afternoon of this court appearance, Kline issued a statement through his lawyer, Seymour Glanzer: "With this unfortunate matter behind me, I will serve my patients and the medical community with a continued commitment to relieve the suffering from the debilitating effects of psychiatric disorders . . ."

He seemed relieved, even optimistic, in the weeks and months which followed. As he swept back into his work, his energy level had not abated, but his career as an experimenter was over. "It was frustrating for him not to be able to function in an area where he had a valuable contribution to make," recalled his daughter, Marna.

Then, on February 13, 1983, Kline, in otherwise perfect health, suffered a ruptured aorta. There were no warning signals; the condition had been detected only hours before the crisis, and that night he died on the operating table. The endorphin court case was "a mean reward," Marna still feels, for a life of outstanding achievement and service. Nathan Kline was sixty-six years old.

Despite the sudden and sad developments of "Kline's caper," the possibility of links between endorphins and schizophrenia remained an open-ended question. At the Third World Congress of Biological Psychiatry in 1981, a World Health Organization–sponsored study concluded that naloxone did, in fact, produce a "significant improvement" in psychiatric patients who were already taking antipsychotic drugs. The two drugs—possibly working in combination on systems of brain cells affected by both endorphins and the neurotransmitter dopamine—produced a more dramatic result than either drug could produce alone.

The finding confirmed Lars Terenius's earlier suspicions, and suggested that naloxone, and other morphine antagonists, when used in conjunction with existing therapies might, indeed, be helpful agents in combating mental illness.

By the spring of 1983, the Terenius group was on the verge of announcing another exciting finding. The syndrome of postpartum psychosis, in which new mothers will ignore or sometimes endanger their babies, affects approximately one in every thousand women. The illness follows a strange course, erupting after delivery and subsiding, suddenly, eight months later. The fact that this time period coincided with the approximate duration of nursing had led Hippocrates, two thousand years earlier, to speculate that the disorder of postpartum psychosis was linked to mother's milk.

Now, it appeared, Hippocrates was right. That winter, Fred Nyberg, a newly arrived peptide chemist in Terenius's lab, had identified a mutant form of casomorphine—an endorphin normally found in the milk of nursing mothers—in the spinal fluid of women suffering from postpartum psychosis. While endorphins might normally be involved in maternal affections and bonding—as Candace Pert and others were saying—Nyberg thought this aberrant endorphin might be producing the tragically opposite result: psychosis on a molecular level.

The season changed into spring with an explosion of green leaves and mayflowers, as it always does in Sweden. Terenius found himself daydreaming at the window of the coffee room at the Biomedicum. He had spent the last few weeks away from the telephone and the responsibilities of the lab in Jerusalem, doing experiments on his own and, at the same time, escaping the dark and depressing final weeks of another cold Swedish April.

He was enthusiastic about Nyberg's latest findings. "They have revived our interest in schizophrenia," he said as he sat on a chair beside a portrait mirror of Marilyn Monroe in his office, quietly speculating about a study that he wanted to do. He had been reading the work of Lief Giessing, a Norwegian researcher from the 1920s whom he greatly admired: "Giessing operated a small hospital near a lake, where he treated only one type of patient with a syndrome which has come to be called Giessing's disease, a kind of catatonia. He followed his patients day by day, month by month, year by year, taking their temperature, measuring their pupil size, examining their secretions. He made a detailed map of all their behavior. He kept them on a standardized diet, mostly grains and fruit. It was like an animal colony. He'd also keep track of outdoor temperature, the air, water in the lake, wind, solar, and lunar cycles. And in the end, he could predict bouts of catatonia from any of these factors.

"The idea of a longitudinal study, where you could monitor the chemistry of model patients along with everything else . . . I'm very taken by that idea."

Candace Pert sifted through the crumpled wads of paper in her office wastebasket, searching for a lost note. One wall was taken up by bookshelves, another was exposed brick, scrawled with graffiti. There was a desk, a deskchair, and, for visitors, a chair with a sprung seat. The desk was cluttered with papers and blotched by coffee cup rings. Above the desk hung psychedelic posters and children's drawings.

Pert had not prepared the lecture she was scheduled to give that night; her secretary was quitting and she had to serve final divorce papers on Agu before he left on a cruise the next day.

Their divorce was amicable—a $500, uncontested "quicky." She had dressed for her lecture in a dark skirt and white satin blouse. Her toenails were painted in black, white, green, red, and blue stripes. On the way out of the building she spotted Agu; "I'm single again," she said to him jokingly, as the elevator door began to close, "maybe we can get together . . ."

She was feeling very "endorphinurgic," she said, because she had fallen in love with a young scientist and together they were going to discover the cause of lung cancer, using a bioassay she had designed for a peptide called bombasin, released by lung cancer cells. Her father had died of lung cancer, and she had tried to collaborate with his doctors until that became too difficult. Scientists in the field, she felt, were less interested in finding a cure for cancer than in "macho competitiveness."

Pert pulled her Fiat out of the parking lot. Later, in her "ivy-covered cottage in the 'burbs' of Bethesda" she spent the afternoon putting together her lecture out of a random pile of slides and papers spread out on a picnic table on the outside deck. Her children—Brandon, Vanessa, and Evan—came and went. The housekeeper was cooking chicken.

"Waxy rats," Pert chattered as she worked, "have little to do with analgesia or mental illness, and more to do with sex. It's lordosis, 'waxy flexibility,' the lordotic state. Female rats get it. They assume the lordotic posture during sex. Human females do too; they get completely passive. LRH, luteinizing hormone-releasing hormone, evokes it and endorphins affect LRH levels. That's why sex is addictive, uh huh . . . sexual dymorphism . . ."

She changed into her swimsuit and did stretching exercises in the yard before resuming work. "The best thing to turn endorphins on is sex, but sex with love, continuing over a long period of time. . . . You can deplete your neuropeptides. That's clear after sex, that feeling of being awash in these emotional chemicals. It's also true after a hard day when you don't know if you're coming or going and you have the lingering effects of all these different, often conflicting emotions, but then you just feel drained, flat. You can restore the balance easily through exercise or a good meal or a good night's sleep.

"We're machines, machines, machines," she insisted. "Receptors are targets for emotions. I'm sure that's the direction, even though I've been reluctant to be out front about it. Scientists are dispassionate. They aren't supposed to care how their work turns out. Of course, they do, but they often choose their work to avoid admitting they have emotions."

Candace Pert drove to Stone House, a nineteenth-century mansion on the NIH grounds, for her lecture, which was titled

"The Biochemistry of the Emotions—from Molecules to Mysticism." She told her audience how she had "agonized" that afternoon about using the word emotion at the NIH, where scientists were "the scariest and most brilliant in the world."

There was wine and cheese afterward. Her lecture a success, Pert drove back to her house laughing about what it would be like to compare the contents of the emotional centers of an English gentleman's brain with an African pygmy's.

The banquet menu started with poached salmon in avocado sauce accompanied by Pouilly-Fuissé 1979; the entrée was fillet of beef Wellington attended by a fine Bordeaux, Château LaHuiste 1976; dessert was Drambuie Syllabub, followed by small fishy pancakes called Aberdeen Nips; then the coffee and Grahams LBV port, cognac and, naturally, Glenmorangie. Gifts included a case of German wine from the Herz group in Berlin; and, from the INRC, a custom-designed, handcrafted, porcelain plate, its glaze garlanded with opium poppies encircled by strands of barley malt, and its back engraved with the coat-of-arms of Aberdeen University, ringed with a list of Hans Kosterlitz's numerous posts and honors.

A loving cup, with a similar pattern, was presented to Hanna Kosterlitz. The nearly two hundred scientists who had attended the day-long symposium on April 11, 1983—ten days short of Kosterlitz's eightieth birthday—now filled the large, lofty dining room at Churchill College in Cambridge. The dinner had been preceded by a prolonged sherry party, and accordingly the mood was festive. Half-a-dozen telegrams were read, including one from Reckitt and Colman, congratulating "a sage, yet exciting counselor."

Harry Collier, the master of ceremonies, composed a poem, based on Wordsworth's *Venice:*

To Hans Kosterlitz for his 80th birthday
O Hans! You're one of the uncommon few,
    Whose seventies show yet their fairest-flowers.
May now your next decade the last undo,
    Since you have learnt so well to stretch the hours.

The birthday celebration was an especially happy event, coming as it did after Kosterlitz's recovery from a second stroke—"a real bugger this time," Sandy McKnight recalled, anxiously. Kosterlitz had crossed the Atlantic eleven times in the preceding months. The January before the symposium he was in the Los Angeles airport with Hanna, waiting to board a plane back to London after a conference in Ventura, California, when he collapsed. His secretary, Mary Donald, took the phone call from one of their neighbors in Cults. McKnight called John Hughes, who, in turn, called Huda Akil in California. Hanna had already called Avram Goldstein—she was very frightened.

Kosterlitz was in intensive care for the first week after the stroke, and another tense week passed before he and Hanna could be flown home, courtesy of British Airlines. There had been a battery of tests in London and a long, irritable convalescence in Cults. Since the stroke, he had been blocking on names; it was a struggle for him to recall who had done a particular experiment. He could, however, retrieve a book from his shelf, open it to a specific reference, and locate the name quickly. His spatial memory was unimpaired, apparently. "If only I could be objective about it," he observed once, "this would be such an interesting phenomenon."

His doctors had forbidden Kosterlitz to drive, which was "a disappointing change in his life," one colleague notes, "but a blessing to Aberdeen pedestrians."

He was fully recovered physically, however, and it was obvious to all that the illness had not blunted any of the old man's spirit. Wearing a particularly natty, cream-colored jacket, he had been fielding congratulations in the Churchill college pub on the evening previous to the dinner. Hanna, in a pale flower-print dress, laughed and chattered while a Chinese postdoc from the Unit who spoke almost no English, tried to pose them for a photograph with Avram Goldstein, Eric Simon, and others.

"You can never predict longevity and energy," the old man remarked with a humorous glance, "but continuing to work, the excitement of events in Aberdeen, and my association with young colleagues have all been important to me."

The speakers on the day of the Kosterlitz dinner delivered twenty-minute summaries of progress in various areas of endorphin research, but invariably reminiscence intermingled with science. Gordon Lees recollected days in the frog room, while John Hughes described his gruesome recipe for pig-brain soup, and Lars Terenius, reflecting on the same period of "fantastic excitement" in Aberdeen, remembered a younger Hughes, "who was not as stylish as he is today," grinding up his brains in the back corners of the lab.

Huda Akil, in one of the most touching tributes, thanked Kosterlitz for giving his friends and colleagues so many "backward" days, when time would seem to stop and then march away from death toward the beginnings of all things.

Reminiscences, albeit of a somewhat less reverent nature, continued during the speeches at the dinner. Collier and Sydney Archer recalled with zest the original "Conference of the Cigar," and the disastrous meeting in Cocoyoc when Kosterlitz had let the cat out of the bag. William Bowman, the president of the Scottish Pharmacological Society, paid tribute to the Prof's intellectual virility with the "strictly allegorical" story of a very old Scottish professor who marries a twenty-year-old girl. A young doctor of his acquaintance, considering that the bride might find her new situation somewhat "lacking," suggested that the professor take in a lodger. A few months later they met: "How's the wife?" the doctor asked. "She's pregnant," said the professor. "Ah!" said the doctor, "and how's the lodger?" "Oh, she's pregnant, too," said the professor.

Finally Kosterlitz himself spoke and then, after a few remarks by Collier, the scientists all dashed out to the pub before closing time. Kosterlitz and Hanna stayed there until well past midnight when, despite her protestations for "more beer," they retired, leaving the others to fend for themselves.

Hans Kosterlitz's friend Harry Collier died that following summer, at age seventy-two.

Solomon Snyder's group was looking for marijuana receptors, while Snyder, with permission from Johns Hopkins, was going ahead with plans to form his own company, Nova Inc. He had recruited the Nobel prize winner Julius Axelrod to be on the board, and bought thousands of shares—literally for pennies. When stock in the company finally was issued at $1.50 per, Snyder became a millionaire overnight.

Avram Goldstein was beginning work which would lead, some months later, to his announcement of a substance found in the cow hypothalamus which was more like morphine than any of the endorphins.

David Mayer, a key contributor to the discovery of stimulation-produced analgesia and one of the first scientists to link endorphins to acupuncture, left in August for Sri Lanka, to study ritual fire walkers. He was curious to see if endorphins played a role in the phenomenon, and was planning to test some fire walkers with naloxone. "If they go up in smoke," he laughed, "we'll know how it worked."

Another year passed. Hans Kosterlitz was spending a few days at the Landsdowne Club in London with Hanna, following an International Narcotics Research Conference meeting—number fifteen—which had concluded in Cambridge the week before. It was a Saturday, when few club members stayed on there, and Kosterlitz sat alone in the salon, reading a custombound, leather and gold leaf version of the proceedings of his eightieth birthday symposium. The book had been presented to him as a gift at the conference's recent meeting.

The salon was an immense room, decorated with worn oriental carpets and comfortable antique leather "sleeping" chairs. The walls and moldings were pale green and peach, the ceilings were so high that voices echoed.

Kosterlitz had joined the Landsdowne Club years before; it was cheaper than a hotel, and the food was reasonably good. When they were in London, he and Hanna always stayed there, and she had stayed there with his nurse after the last stroke, when he was having tests done.

Adjourning to a table in the garden, Kosterlitz sat beside a greenish-looking fountain and ordered tea and hot cross buns. "When you are forty," he said, "you have to make a decision. One can be enthusiastic until then, especially if your teacher was. But then you have to think about the future. Will I be so successful that I will be accepted by the scientific community? If not, what shall I do? You can teach or work in industry. Scientists who have gone a little mad—like me—will continue doing research. I can't stop, but then I have been successful."

He looked across the garden, was silent a moment, then continued. "It is a question almost of God. Working on the enkephalins you get—without being religious—a commitment. You start to admire and wonder, how could that come about—that plants and animals share such structurally similar chemicals? How, even after a million years of evolution, could the earth, with all its plants and creatures, be so very simple and unified?"

He reminisced energetically for two more hours in the garden before Hanna interrupted. "This is the trouble with scientists," she teased. "They are uncouth, uncivilized. They don't know when to come in for a drink."

Their room was plain—twin beds, a polished dressing table and armoir, in which Hanna kept a supply of plastic cups, along with bottles of sherry and the Macallan unblended malt whisky. It was his habit, Kosterlitz said, to go back to work in the evenings with a small glass of whisky. "To sip it slowly," he said, luxuriantly, "with music . . . with Bach."

Hanna, opening bags of chips and peanuts, chattered on about shopping that afternoon. She was surprised by the number of Arab women she saw in one department store. "They look like beetles," she chortled. Kosterlitz sat near the window, with the sun streaming in, sipping his drink slowly.

"You have an alcoholic's nose," Hanna said. It was just a bit red from sitting in the sun, Kosterlitz replied. She searched in her handbag a moment, for her cosmetics case, drew out a compact and deftly powdered his nose.

"There," she laughed. "Men should wear makeup." The old man, with a smile pursed on his lips, stared out the window.

On the following Thursday afternoon, John Hughes was on his way to the Cambridge County Clerk's office to register the birth of his new daughter, Georgina Pennington Hughes. He was a father again and bleary-eyed to prove it; Julie, with whom Hughes was living, had given birth to the new baby just a few days before the INRC meeting. Katherine, Hughes's seventeen-year-old daughter from his previous marriage, was studying at Cambridge and spending several days a week with him, too. Attractive, bright, she was crazy about horses; Hughes had bought her her own pony on her sixteenth birthday.

There had been a second, severe bout of illness for Hughes as well, and a gall bladder operation. He had stopped smoking his pipe and taken up chewing gum; he was not sure which was the more "obnoxious." His new headquarters in the Parke-Davis Research Unit had been housed at first in a small, boxy, prefabricated building which looked like a forester's shed. It was built on struts, to keep the damp out, in a muddy, wooded field behind Addenbrookes Hospital in Cambridge.

Several months before, the entire structure had been gutted by a fire which had started in the lab.

"All that was left were John's chocolate digestives," recalled one of the lab workers. Miraculously, Hughes's early notebooks on the enkephalin discovery also survived. His unit had been transferred to temporary quarters inside the hospital until work on a new permanent facility could be completed.

Hughes and Julie Pennington were living thirty miles outside Cambridge, in a restored two-hundred-year-old farmhouse which they were beginning to furnish with antiques. Quiet millionaires—the "discreet" rich—lived in the other houses nearby. Some Hughes had already met: they were the sort of people "a small academic would never be exposed to." It intrigued him.

"You *can* have everything," he said, steering his Rover along the narrow, winding streets beneath the dreaming spires of the colleges. "I'm only just realizing it. There *are* such people and they *do* have everything."

He had never envisioned science as a way to riches, which is not to say he did not like being a modestly rich scientist. "If I had it to do over again," he reflected, "I would probably not be a scientist. A lawyer, maybe . . ." But, he added, thoughtfully, "the choice to be a scientist is not quite rational."

He was still painting (badly), and playing golf (again, badly) and gardening beautifully on the one-third of an acre plot of land behind their house. He would have liked to learn more about the chemistry of flowers. He was unlikely to do so. He knew that when he moved to Parke-Davis, he would not be able to pursue the sort of basic research projects he had been doing. Pharmaceutical companies wait for breakthroughs, they rarely make them.

Certainly things would never again be as simple and adventurous as they had been in his Aberdeen days. But Hughes was forty-two years old now, and he had made his own decisions. He was never quite as "mad" as Kosterlitz; he was not unhappy about that. But he could be just as driven if he had something to sink his teeth into. And as Parke-Davis Research Unit Director, he had that now. His labs and offices might be in temporary quarters at Addenbrookes, but, rimmed by work lights, in the woods behind the hospital, the new Parke-Davis facility loomed in the overcast afternoon like a giant, half-materialized specter.

It was five o'clock and Hans Kosterlitz was marshaling his troops.

"Do you think you'll be thirsty in half an hour?" he asked, popping into the staff office in the tower at Marishal College.

"Oh, aye," Sandy McKnight assured him.

The four others, all young researchers who shared the large staff office with McKnight, usually gravitated there by five-thirty, when the old man was due to show up again. Alan North and Graeme Henderson, visiting from an electrophysiology conference in Glasgow, arrived. Both of them were now at important posts: Henderson, his hair somewhat shorter than it used to be, was teaching at Cambridge; North, still "the handsomest scientist" in Hanna Kosterlitz's estimation, was at MIT. He had just been awarded a prize in Glasgow, "and," he told Kosterlitz proudly, "I owe it all to you." His prize was a bottle of Macallan, awarded in a whisky-tasting contest. Kosterlitz had a good laugh.

Kosterlitz was wearing a tan summer suit, while the younger people were all dressed more casually. It was August and the weather was warm. Henderson was wearing shorts, McKnight was in blue jeans and with a T-shirt printed with the initials of the Unit for Research on Addictive Drugs. He had had them made up for everyone in the Unit—including the Prof.

They all filed down the winding turret staircase from the

south wing to the first floor. In the parking lot, Kosterlitz pointed to his car, a big white and tan two-liter Ford Anglia. After a medical checkup which allowed him to renew his license, he was driving again, rhythmically scanning the road, on his way from home twice a day.

Hanna still insisted he come home for lunch. His last stroke had frightened her, and she was a bit less active now, too. They spent most of their evenings together; he waited until she went to bed at ten, before going back to work again, with a bit of whisky and Bach. She was seeing more of him and she liked it.

Kosterlitz dodged traffic, crossing the busy Queen Street intersection. Three doors down the block, at the Kirkgate Bar, he ordered his usual half-pint of McEwan's and, encircled by his young friends, launched into a discussion of food, language, and the Norman Invasion. "So many of the things we eat have French names," he observed. "You don't eat cow, you eat beef. *Boeuf,* beef. You don't eat sheep, you eat mutton. You never eat pig, you eat pork. You don't eat hen . . ."

The Kirkgate had changed little in the last ten years. Details of the past merged with details of the present. There was a dartboard in an alcove at the rear of the bar that had not been there then, and a piano, which was not there anymore. The brown tin ceilings, patched red leather benches, the photographs of past rugby teams, had not changed.

"This is how scientists think," Kosterlitz said, as a second round of drinks arrived. He had been searching, without success, for some early notebooks which the University library had requested for their archives. "In those days I wrote down everything," he reflected. "When you are young you write everything down. Partly it's a pretentious sense of importance. Later you don't. It becomes simple curiosity. You think only of the present and, a little, what you want to do in the future. In the case of the enkephalins I did not, originally, think it was the most important thing we were doing. When you think something is very important, you stop work, you become very famous. The discovery was just the beginning of something. If someone announces a sudden new development it is immediately suspicious. When people think they are making history, in almost every case, it is quite the opposite."

It was nearly seven when the group broke up. The Aberdeen granite facade of Marishal College, bits of steeples and turrets and domes of the strange cityscape, glowed a hazy silver in the lingering sunset. The roses were blooming in front of the college, the gulls were screeching; it was the end of another day. "It makes such a difference when the sun shines," Hans Kosterlitz remarked, as he stepped outside.

SELECT BIBLIOGRAPHY

Most of the landmark papers published in the scientific press on endorphins have been cited in the book. Of the hundreds of other books and articles surveyed in the course of my research and writing, the following were essential both in general and in the reconstruction of particular sections and incidents in the story.

Arehart-Treichel, Joan. "Winning and Losing: The Medical Awards Game." *Science News,* February 24, 1979.

Bloom, Floyd E.; Cooper, Jack R.; Roth, Robert H. *The Biochemical Basis of Neurobiology.* New York: Oxford University Press, 1982.

Davis, Joel. *Endorphins.* New York: Crown Publishers, 1984.

Eddy, Nathan B. *The National Research Council Involvement in the Opiate Problem.* National Agency of Sciences, Washington, D.C. 1973.

Goldstein, Avram. "The Search for the Opiate Receptor," *Pharmacology and the Future of Man,* Proceedings of the Fifth International Congress on Pharmacology, Karger, Basel, 1973.
———. *The Opiate Narcotics: Neurochemical Mechanisms in Analgesia and Dependence.* Karger, Basel, 1975.
———. "The Three-Dimensional Structure of Pharmacology." *The Pharmacologist,* 23, 1981.

Kosterlitz, Hans W. "The Best Laid Schemes o' Mice An' Men Gang Aft Agley." *Annual Review of Pharmacology and Toxicology,* 19, 1979.

Leff, David N. "Doctors Debate Brain," *Medical World News,* January 9, 1978.

Marx, Jean L. "Lasker Award Stirs Controversy." *Science,* January 26, 1979.

Melzack, Ronald. *The Challenge of Pain.* New York: Basic Books, 1983.

NOVA. "The Keys of Paradise." WGBH Educational Foundation, Boston, 1979.

Restak, Ricahrd. "The Brain Makes Its Own Narcotics!" *Saturday Review,* March 5, 1977.
————. *The Brain.* New York: Bantam Books, 1984.

Schmeck, Harold M., Jr. Opiate-like Substances in Brain May Hold Clue to Pain and Mood." *The New York Times,* October 2, 1977.
————. "Chemistry of Pain Begins to Emerge." *The New York Times,* May 1, 1979.

Snyder, Solomon. *Madness and the Brain.* New York: McGraw-Hill, 1987.
————. *Opiate Receptor Mechanisms* (with Matthysse, Steven). Cambridge: The MIT Press, 1975.
————. "Opiate Receptors and Internal Opiates," *Scientific American,* March, 1977.
————. "Clinical Relevance of Opiate Receptor and Opioid Peptide Research." *Nature,* May 3, 1979.

Strahinich, John. "The Endorphin Puzzle." *The Runner,* July, 1982.

Villet, Barbara. "Opiates of the Mind." *The Atlantic,* June 1978.

Wade, Nicholas. *The Nobel Duel.* Garden City: Anchor Press, 1981.

Yao, Margaret. "Loneliness, Sure, But Have You Tried the Beta-endorphin?" *The Wall Street Journal,* December 1, 1981.

INDEX

Free your hair, and the rest will follow.

CURLY GIRL

More than just hair . . . it's an attitude

A CELEBRATION OF CURLS:
HOW TO CUT THEM,
CARE FOR THEM,
LOVE THEM,
AND SET THEM FREE

·

by LORRAINE MASSEY
with DEBORAH CHIEL

·

WORKMAN PUBLISHING
NEW YORK

Copyright © 2001 by Lorraine Massey and Deborah Chiel
All photographs are by Anthony Loew unless noted on page 148.
Photographs copyright © by Anthony Loew
Illustrations copyright © by Bernice O'Regan
Design by Paul Hanson and Elizabeth Johnsboen

Library of Congress Cataloging-in-Publication Data

Massey, Lorraine
   Curly girl : more than just hair . . . it's an attitude :
a celebration of curls : how to cut them, care for them,
love them, and set them free / by Lorraine Massey with
Deborah Chiel
      p. cm.
ISBN-13: 978-0-7611-2300-2 (alk. paper)
   1. Hair—Care and hygiene. I. Title

RL91.M28 2001
646.7'24—dc21   2001026842

Workman books are available at special discounts when
purchased in bulk for premiums and sales promotions as
well as for fund-raising or educational use. Special editions
or book excerpts can also be created to specification.
For details, contact the Special Sales Director at the
address below.

Workman Publishing Company, Inc.
225 Varick Street
New York, NY 10014-4381
www.workman.com

Printed in the United States of America

First printing January 2002
10 9

In memory of A. Dance,
and for Kaih, Shey, and Dylan

ACKNOWLEDGMENTS

Many people helped us transform *Curly Girl* from dream to reality. We are very grateful to David Schiller, Lorraine's longtime client, who loved the concept so much that he insisted we bring it to Workman. Our heartfelt thanks also to Naomi Chiel-Bolzman and Kinneret Chiel, who recognized a great book idea when they heard it and knew that we would make the perfect "curlaborative" team. Peter Workman asked all the right questions and showed such faith in the project that we knew our book had found the right home.

Our editor, Ruth Sullivan, was unstinting with her advice, her hands-on shaping to create a book that fit her vision, and in her determination to push us to our creative limits. Jessica Firger helped us sort out inconsistencies and clarify murky instructions, chased down photographs, and kept us sailing smoothly through. Thanks, also, to Paul Hanson and Elizabeth Johnsboen for their artistic vision. Thanks to Güler Uğur, Rivka Hain, Patty Bozza, Elizabeth Gaynor, and Tiffany Lee for their input and curly girl spirit, and to Anthony Loew for his wonderful photographs. Jenny Mandel encouraged and advised us throughout the process. Carolan Workman's enthusiasm helped bring this all together. She is a true curly girl. Special thanks to Carol Kramer, who gave us a schedule, a structure, her editorial expertise, and the confidence that *Curly Girl* would actually become a book.

More than we can ever express, we applaud the entire staff of Devachan for their enthusiasm, support, and their amazing ability to cope with bright lights, construction sites, and crowds of curly girls. Special thanks to Carlos Flores and Ed Fagley, who have so totally embraced the curly girl philosophy. A huge bouquet of gratitude to Devachan co-owner, Denis DaSilva, and Shari Harbinger, multitalented artists who have contributed so much love, information, color, and creativity to our lives and our book.

Henry Dreher has straight hair but thinks curly; he gave us fabulous input, shared our highs and lows, and accepted our need for creative working sessions at odd hours and in all sorts of unusual venues. We especially thank Michael and Lorraine's children for their unconditional love and patience, and for putting up with their mother's endless phone conferences and editorial meetings. Kaih, Shey, and Dylan: Mummy promises to make it up to you.

Finally, to all the curly girls, young and old, who answered our questions, submitted to our scrutiny, smiled for the camera— this book could never have happened without each and every one of you. You have the curly spirit. More power to you!

—*Lorraine Massey
and Deborah Chiel*

I want to thank Lorraine, my hair spiritualist and dream co-author, for her unique vision and sense of style, and for all the wondrous twists and turns she's brought into my life.

—*D.C.*

Much love and thanks to all of my clients, who have supported me throughout the years and become my second family. Special thanks to Debbie, the best outreach curly girl.

—*L.M.*

Table of Contents

INTRODUCTION

C urls? The word sounds frivolous, too frothy to be the subject of a book. But we promise you, curls are serious business—and the horror stories you'll read in this book are shocking enough to, well, curl your hair. And so is the misinformation curly-headed women are likely to receive from hair care professionals.

For centuries, curls were considered a blessing, grace notes that added to a woman's beauty. But that attitude changed at some point in the twentieth century, and several generations of women grew up thinking their curls were not a blessing, but a colossal pain in the tress.

Most women with curly hair today have fought with it all their lives. They were teased in school and at home (usually by their straight-haired brothers). They searched for role models in fashion magazines and movies, only to see nothing but straight, lanky hair (usually blond). They've felt unsophisticated, silly, juvenile. Their hair frizzed up at inopportune moments, broke off in clumps if treated too harshly. They've imagined their curls holding them back from dates and jobs. They've been stereotyped, depending on the bias, as wenches or witches. They've spent a fortune on defrizzing products and other lotions that promised instant straight hair.

But the problem wasn't just one of attitude. There was literally no place for curly-haired women to go, because most hairdressers, especially in this country, have been just as tangled up in the hair stereotypes as the rest of the world. The catalog of curly hair crimes committed in many beauty salons is frightful:

disastrous haircuts, brutal brushing and blow-drying, chemicals that could straighten out a hardened criminal.

This book is meant to change all that—end the prejudice, celebrate the beauty of curls, but most of all, teach women with curly hair a whole new way of life. The program you're about to read is revolutionary: It will require an attitude adjustment, a straightening of the head, rather than the hair, if you will.

But the results will be astounding. Follow the routines in this book and your hair will be transformed. It will shine as never before, behave itself in public, even during typhoons, and frame your face with the world's most graceful beauty accessory, the natural curl.

OUR CURLS, OURSELVES

Finding Your Inner Curl

It's your head, not your hair, that needs straightening. And here's how to start.

Welcome to Curl Talk, a place where you can finally let down your hair. Chances are, if you picked up this book, you belong to the sisterhood of curly girls, women who've been fighting their curly hair for most of their lives, hiding it under hats, pulling it back, tugging at it with rubber bands, disguising it with braids, or flattening it out with anything they could find.

Depending on what era you were born into, you may have tried chemical straighteners, blow-dryers, irons, or gigantic juice-can rollers to straighten your hair. I know, just look at my picture on this page—the curls look pretty great, don't they? But they didn't always, and it took me a long time to learn to love and respect them. Now I spend most of my time, as the co-owner of a Manhattan salon, encouraging my clients to find their inner curl—an attitude that helps them accept their curls and make the most of them, straightening out their heads instead of their hair.

From the time I was born in the mid-1960s to just a few years ago, curly hair was made fun of more than it was admired. I hated my hair from the moment I was able to look in the mirror and see that, unlike my six brothers and sisters, whose hair looked appropriately lank and British, I had corkscrew curls that stuck out all over my head, making me look like Orphan Annie. By the time I was three, I was asking my mother for a straight-haired wig so I could pretend I was a Polynesian hula dancer. It was a strange request from a toddler living in a factory town in the British West Midlands. But for years I was sure that there'd been some mistake at the hospital and I'd been sent home with the wrong set of parents.

1965: I hated my curls as a kid.

I wasn't alone. As you read this book, you'll find the personal stories of many other curly girls who went through the same denial and despair I did. We all worried about humid days, when despite all our efforts our hair would frizz up. We were teased by kids in school ("Hey, Brillo, where'd you get that hair?") and made to feel that curls were inferior.

By the time I was four, I was watching the telly with my older brothers and sisters and admiring Mary ("Those Were the Days") Hopkins, a mod-generation pop star with stick-straight hair that swung back and forth as she played her guitar. If only my hair could swing, I'd think. I'd pull my sweater halfway over my head so that it hung down across my back. Voila!—I had straight hair, too.

As I got older and watched celebrities like Cher and Twiggy swing their long, perfect locks, I became more convinced that my curls were an aberration, a perverse joke played on some of us by a whimsical universe. A genetic mistake that the gods of beauty had planted in my DNA. I'd spend all day thinking up ways to make my hair stay flat and frizz-free. In my mind, the equation was simple: Straight was beautiful, curly was ugly. A sociologist might point out that for many people, this preference for straight hair was a subtle side effect of racism. Most of us have been influenced by stereotypes of beauty promoted in the last half of the twentieth century—the white Anglo-Saxon look, with straight blond hair and a pale complexion. Children could have curls—if they were golden—but they'd damn well better straighten out by the time they grew up.

I would go to bed at night, my hair tightly wound—imprisoned, actually—around gigantic rollers. I'd lie very still lest one should slip off and the curls spring cruelly and sadistically back to life.

So it was ironic, but maybe inevitable, that I decided to become a hair-dresser. I'd spent so much time fixing my own hair that I might as well try to make a living fixing others'. I served three years as an apprentice in London, then moved to Hong Kong for four years and became fascinated with my customers' straight hair. Next, I lived in Japan, where the only word of Japanese I learned in two years was *masuga.* It means "straight," of course.

Even after *Charlie's Angels* made long wavy hair fashionable in the 1970s, I kept mine short and straight. One year, I decided to wear it slicked back and short—remember that look? I think it was called a DA in this country. I was proud of it. But when I asked a not-so-diplomatic male friend what he thought, he said the back of my head looked like a "baboon's bum."

That was it. Like an addict who's bottomed out, I realized I couldn't fight my curls anymore. I started letting my hair grow. I stopped blow-drying it every morning. Meanwhile I read every scrap of information I could find about curly hair and how to take care of it. As it turns out, there is very little to be found on the subject. As the owner of a New York City beauty school told me recently, "Hair is hair, we treat curly the same as straight." No wonder so many people still straighten their hair.

Cleopatra wasn't the only queen of denial.

But I was determined to make my curly hair work. I began conditioning it regularly, experimenting with different products, upping the amounts of moisturizers. I let it grow out so that the soft *S*'s that are my hair's natural shape had room to develop. Eventually my scalp sprouted soft curlets that grew into ringlets, then tightened into thick corkscrews that spiraled down my shoulders. This was the way I was meant to look, my hair destiny, I came to believe. And I became totally politicized about curly hair. I saw it almost like an arranged marriage—not something I would have chosen for myself, but mine "till death do us part." I vowed that no one was going to straighten my hair or my mind again. "Free your hair, and the rest will follow" became my manifesto.

Unfortunately, while I had changed, the world around me hadn't. Straight hair was still the gold standard, especially in Beverly Hills. I had moved to California and gotten a job in a fashionable salon right out of *Shampoo*, the Warren Beatty movie about a hip hairdresser. I had been working there for about a week when the salon owner returned from a vacation. He looked at me, the new girl with politically incorrect curls, and went ballistic. "Someone blow-dry that girl's hair," he shouted. I left my post at the shampoo bowl and walked. Unlike Lot's wife, I never looked back.

I moved to New York, where, for the first time in the life of my curls, I was in the majority, surrounded by people who looked like me. Ethnic-looking people: Jewish, Italian, Latino, African American. Their hair was curly, too. I no longer looked or felt like an outsider.

A few weeks ago a friend jokingly accused me of living in a "curlocentric" world. That may be true—but it's also true that we still live

Pregnant, full and bouncy.

in a world where the WASP stereotype has a tremendous hold on our imaginations. Perhaps that explains why so many of us are still in curl denial, why cosmetology schools still teach stylists to "cut against the curl," and why so many hairdressers are intimidated by curly hair, preferring to blow it out straight rather than to work with its texture and shape. I attend many workshops and seminars around the country for hairdressers, but I haven't found one yet that features curly hair—or curly-haired models.

I'm trying to make up for that lack with this book and with my work as co-owner of Devachan, a salon in New York's SoHo neighborhood, where curly girls seem to find me like flocks of curly-haired homing pigeons. I've watched them learn to love their hair and work *with* it instead of against it. Finding their inner curl makes them strong, willing to stand up to stereotypical attitudes and prejudices.

Curly hair is the wave of the future. Sixty-five percent of women have curly or wavy hair. (Take the quiz on the following pages to see if maybe you are one of them.) For too long we curly girls have been at a loss about how to care for our hair properly or, worse, have gone through life pretending we are straight and mistreating our natural curls. I'm hoping that this book will revolutionize the way we look at curly hair. In it, you'll find a complete guide to curls, their origins, their problems, their special needs. You'll learn a radical and logical way to care for your hair, nurturing its natural curl. How to cleanse, condition, and style it, and how to have it cut well instead of sliced, carved, and butchered. You'll wear your curls proudly every day—even if you think you're having a bad hair day. I promise. It will change your life. So curl up (sorry) and start reading.

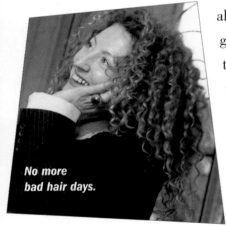

No more bad hair days.

Are You a Curly Girl?

Are you still hiding the truth from the world, maybe even from yourself? Take this simple question-hair to determine whether you're a member of the curly clan.

CURLY CLUES

☐ *1. Do you often wear your hair tied back in a ponytail?*

☐ *2. Does your hair develop volume in humid, hot, or wet weather?*

☐ *3. Does your hair make you feel out of control?*

☐ *4. Do you find yourself crying after every haircut?*

☐ *5. Look at old photographs and recall how you felt about your hair—and yourself—on the day the picture was taken. Was there a strong correlation between your hair and your mood?*

☐ *6. Do you almost always have a haze of frizz around your head?*

Michella L. : *still wears hair pulled back straight in a ponytail*

☐ *7. Do you blow-dry your hair so often that its texture is as dry and brittle as a piece of melba toast?*

☐ *8. Does your budget for products to straighten or relax your hair exceed your annual tax-deductible contributions to charity?*

☐ *9. Do you live in fear of humidity, sweating, spontaneous sex, a shower with your lover—or any weather or activity that might unmask you as a curly girl?*

☐ *10. Are you almost always unhappy with your hair?*

☐ *11. Do you worry about your hair before any big occasion, like a wedding or an important business meeting?*

If you answered yes to one or more questions, congratulations! You know who you are. You're a curly girl waiting to happen. Your hair is bristling with movement longing to break free, waves aching to curl, frizz begging for direction. Read on!

HAIR
The Inside Story

> On every curly-haired baby's head, there should be a care label reading: DELICATE. NO HARSH SHAMPOOS. NO MACHINE-DRYING. AIR-DRY ONLY. NEVER IRON.

I love care labels in clothes. They make me respect a fabric and think carefully about how I treat it. If only our hair came with a care label.

All Hair Is Fiber

There isn't much difference chemically between your hair and the fine wool that comes off a pashmina goat. The one hundred thousand or so hair fibers on your head stretch and absorb moisture, just like wool, which is composed of the same elements as hair: carbon, hydrogen, nitrogen, oxygen, and sulfur. Because hair is a fiber, it makes sense to treat it like one. How do you care for the precious fibers in your wardrobe? You should handle your hair as gently as you do your cashmere sweater.

You'd never dream of washing a good sweater with detergent. Yet most shampoos contain harsh detergents (sodium lauryl sulfate or laureth sulfate) that one finds in dishwashing liquid. They're great for pots and pans because they cut grease so effectively. Your hair, on the other hand, needs to retain some natural oils, which protect it and your scalp. Stripping them away deprives the hair of necessary moisture and amino acids and makes it look dry and dull.

I'd like you to try this simple experiment to see what detergent does to your hair. Go into your kitchen and pour a bit of dishwashing detergent onto a damp sponge and squeeze gently. Voila, bubbles! Now, hold the sponge under running water and notice that it seems to take forever to rinse it free of the lather. You never really get rid of all that detergent, do you?

Your curls react the same way to shampoo: because curly hair is so porous, it absorbs detergent like a sponge. The truth is that lathers don't cleanse at all—manufacturers put lathering agents into products so you'll buy into the joy-of-suds myth. You know, those women in TV commercials moaning in ecstasy as they lather up their heads in the shower, then reappear seconds later with wonderfully styled hair, shining with vitality. Well, forget the

Hair Facts

Hair grows at a rate of about a half inch a month. It develops under your scalp, in a tiny sac called the follicle. Inside the follicle it's alive. When the hair comes to the surface the fiber hardens. The follicle will keep growing the hair for three to five years. When it stops growing, it goes into a period of rest—a few weeks only while the root is released from the follicle—then drops out. You lose about a hundred hairs a day, not a bad percentage considering you have at least one hundred thousand on your head at any given time. Within days after a hair is shed, another hair starts growing to replace it.

advertising campaigns that put sudsiness right up there next to cleanliness, godliness, and sexiness. It doesn't work that way, and you don't have to buy into it.

I can't say this too often: *You do not need to use shampoo.* I'm not saying leave your hair dirty. As you read on, you'll see that I recommend cleansing the hair with . . . water and conditioner! My care routine for curly and wavy hair either cuts out shampoo entirely or cuts it down severely from your normal use. Whichever type of curly girl you are (see chapter 3), you're going to have to get out of the lather habit and end shampoo dependency—that ingrained belief that you have to wash your hair daily.

The Cuticle Is Critical

If you examine a cross section of a hair fiber under a microscope, you'll see that it looks like a worm. Growing around the worm's core are tiny scales, which cover the cortex or center of the hair like tiles on a roof. Those overlapping "tiles" are called the cuticle of the hair—and they're essential in protecting each strand and making your hair look good.

When the tiles lie flat, they reflect light and your hair shines. If the cuticle is ruffled, your hair won't shine because light needs to be reflected off a smooth surface. Detergents, heat, chemicals, or a hairbrush make the cuticle rough and scaly. Instead of lying flat, pieces of cuticle stick out and lock together like

A strand of healthy hair: the tile-like cuticles lie flat.

Velcro. So if you are using a blow-dryer to style your hair, stop, right now.

Lorraine's Shampoo Epiphany

In the bad old days, I would subject my scalp and hair to a vigorous lathering once or twice a week, for no good reason except force of habit. Afterward, for the first twenty-four hours, my hair would appear to float in space like a helium balloon, defying the laws of gravity, because I had ruffled the surface cuticle and dehydrated the curls.

Another three days would go by before my hair had recovered enough from its trauma that I was ready to admit we were related. Then we'd happily coexist for the rest of the week, until it was time—according to my self-imposed regimen—for my next shampoo. And the vicious cycle would begin all over again.

I followed this routine unquestioningly, because I'd never found any care instructions that addressed the specific needs of curly, as opposed to straight, hair. Then one fateful morning I looked in the mirror and realized my hair looked fabulous. According to my schedule, I was due for a shampoo, but I couldn't bear to mess with success. I dared myself to wait another day. One stretched into a second, then a third, until I'd managed to hold out for almost three weeks. My hair had never looked better, so I decided to initiate an experiment: I would declare my hair a shampoo-free zone and see how long I could refrain from washing it with detergent.

Now shampoo is a total no-no in my home. I don't use it at all anymore, not even a drop. I work up a sweat running most mornings, I eat in smoky European restaurants, and I swim in the ocean not far from my home. Yet my friends assure me that I pass the sniff test. My hair and scalp don't smell— and my hair has never looked better.

The high heat damages the cuticle. And if you still iron your curls to straighten them (not likely since that was a seventies fad), you're destroying precious fibers with the heat.

Why Curly Hair Is Drier

Most of us treat our hair and scalp as a single entity. But the scalp is very different from the hair. The hair is keratin; the scalp is skin and needs to be treated the way we treat our facial skin—by cleansing it gently and keeping it moisturized. Nature designs it that way: each hair follicle that produces the hair on our heads is also home to sebaceous (oil) glands, which release sebum, an oily substance that lubricates the hair. "Curly hair is so much dryer than other types of hair," says Dr. David H. Kingsley of the Institute of Trichologists, "because there are only about 100,000 hairs on a curly head, as opposed to about 120,000 straight hairs. And because there is less hair, there are fewer follicles and therefore fewer sebaceous glands to produce oil." If you have tight curly hair, the sebum sometimes has trouble getting to the ends, which tend to be especially dry. Those with corkscrew curls have to compensate with extra moisteners (see chapter 4) to replace the moisture that isn't getting to the ends.

It's possible to have dry hair and an oily scalp. Having combination skin (oily in the T-zone, but dry everywhere else) is one clue that you might have an oily scalp. The sebum and sweat, which your scalp produces, are sterile and clean, but they attract dirt and bacteria. These must be rinsed off regularly to keep the scalp healthy. But it's not necessary to remove all of the oils from your scalp; in fact, it's not healthy. You need a fine layer of sebum—called the acid mantle—to protect the scalp. My solution is to rinse the scalp daily, giving it a gentle rub and a good water rinsing. No harsh detergent is necessary.

It's in the Genes

If you look at a cross section of a strand of Asian hair (straight), you'll see that the shape of the fiber is round. (Think of toothpaste coming out of a tube.) A strand of curly hair, looked at in cross section, looks elliptical, with a slight curve in the middle (like ribbon candy). The center indentation makes it flex and spiral—in other words, curl. A strand of African American hair is flatter still than a strand of corkscrew curls, has the finest texture, and is therefore also the curliest. Wavy hair, on the other hand, looks oval under a microscope. Its spiral is gentler, and it bends very slightly. Your genetic inheritance determines whether your hair will be curly or straight.

The fiber of straight hair (left) is round; a strand of wavy hair (right) is oval.

As a rule, curly hair is very fine and straight hair is coarse and stronger. Someone with tight curly corkscrews may appear to have thick hair because it has such volume. That's an optical illusion. The spirals fill more space and create the impression of texture. Pull a strand of that hair out to its full length and it will be fine and very fragile.

The morning of my father's funeral, I had a really bad hair day. I don't mean to sound disrespectful, but this was my worst nightmare come true. All my life, I'd suffered because of my curly hair: bad cuts, ill-fated attempts to grow my hair long, hours spent straightening it with hideous-smelling chemicals, dates gone bad because my hair had morphed into a giant ball of frizz. Not to mention all the nights when I slept (or tried to) with my curls tightly twisted around giant orange juice cans.

I was a short, timid, skinny kid who entered a new school in the middle of ninth grade on a rainy day when my hair did everything it shouldn't have. Thirty-eight years later, I still believe I would have had a socially successful high school career if only the sun had been shining and the humidity low as I walked into my first class.

Hair straightened with orange juice cans

Worst of all were the Saturday mornings of my adolescence, most of which I spent in synagogue. My father was a rabbi, and I was expected to attend services every week. I would stand in front of the mirror, wailing because my hair had taken on shapes not known in nature. But my father refused to accept the frizz factor as a reason not to show up at services. I sat in synagogue week after week, hating my hair, myself, my life. I was convinced that I was the object of the entire congregation's collective pity and scorn. **I didn't have a bad hair day. I had a bad hair decade.**

After college, I became a school librarian. What better choice for a shy, bespectacled introvert who hated to be seen in public when the humidity was high? I started therapy, almost a residency requirement for the New York City neighborhood where I lived, and rehashed my childhood. I talked about how much misery my curls had caused me, especially as a teenager. **My therapist seemed to think that my unhappiness was related to other, more profound issues, but what did she know? Her hair was stick straight.**

Years passed. I quit my librarian job and went into publishing. I had my ears pierced, exchanged my glasses for contact lenses, began to emerge from my curl-related shell. Then came my father's unexpected death from a heart attack. On this most painful occasion of my life, when hundreds of people were expected to attend the funeral, I was furious because, once again, my hair had betrayed me. No doubt much of my reaction was misplaced grief, but my anticurl emotions ran deep and had a powerful hold over my psyche.

My story has a happy ending. I eventually met Lorraine, who encouraged me to stop fighting with my hair and cultivate my curls by growing them long. These days, I feel sexier, freer, more flirtatious, drawn to glitter and sequins. I am constantly astonished and gratified by my curls and people's reactions to them. My hair cascades down below my shoulders (and much farther when it's wet) in an explosion of corkscrews of varying lengths and textures. The curls change according to the dictates of the weather, and I love their many moods and shapes. They're easy to care for, now that I've given up trying to control them, and I never agonize about how my hair will look for a special event. I understand that as long as I treat my curls with respect (i.e., keep them well hydrated and properly nourished) and resist the urge to shampoo, blow-dry, or fuss, they won't ever embarrass me.

My hair gets lots of attention, which means I do, too, even more so as I experiment with different shades of color and highlights, depending on my mood and the season. Here's what I find most remarkable: I've become outgoing and friendly, a wallflower transformed into Miss Congeniality. I've discovered that basking in the limelight can be an emotionally uplifting experience. But having great curly hair is not without its responsibilities. I am frequently approached by curly girls hungry for information and moral support. **"If I can learn to be proud of my curls, so can you,"** I assure them, fulfilling my commitment to what Lorraine calls the curly girl mentoring program.

I've also had to revamp my wardrobe. A head of bouncy curls deserves better than T-shirts, khaki pants, navy blue blazers, and clogs. The safe, conservative outfits in my closet have been replaced by hip, free-spirited (or wild, depending on your point of view) clothes that are fun to wear and make me feel young. People tell me I look younger than I did before I became so well

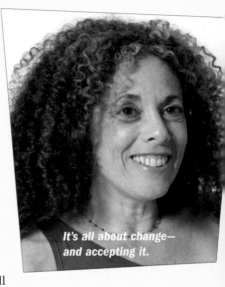

It's all about change—and accepting it.

informed about what my curls need to stay happy. I think it's "psycurlogical," a perfect example of curly girl mind-body unity.

Years ago, I found a card that showed a picture of Frieda, the redheaded, curl-obsessed *Peanuts* character, along with this wise-beyond-her-years statement: **People always expect more when you have naturally curly hair.** Now, finally, I am at one with Frieda. I have liberated my inner curl and let my spirit soar. I can meet any challenge. I am Curly Girl.

—DEBORAH CHIEL, WRITER

I would never have become a comedian if I'd been born with straight hair. Comedians need to have obstacles, and, boy, did I have them. Curls made my career. As I say in my book, "People who are successful take the good and build on it. I take the bad and build on that." It's what got me started in comedy clubs; all that anger motivated me. When I was growing up, I was the only one in my neighborhood stuck with curly hair. **People used to call me Brillo head.** They thought they were being original.

When I was really small, my mother used to brush out the knots in my hair with a wire brush that's normally used for grooming dogs. I screamed so much that she finally took me to a hairdresser at Best & Company on Fifth Avenue who had also worked on a curly-haired Italian princess in Italy. He cut my hair so short that it sat on my head like some sort of cactus. Not much different from a Brillo pad, actually.

In high school, I'd straighten my hair with chemicals so strong that I called them Agent Orange. It was the sixties and everybody then had to have "swinging hair." Kenneth, the hairdresser, became famous for giving people like Jackie Kennedy swinging hair. My hair does not swing. It springs. Or maybe it hops. On bad days it sinks.

My hair does not swing. It springs. Or maybe it hops.

In the seventies, I read that coffee separated curls and gave them weight. I'd brew coffee, wait until it was cold, then pour it over my head. My curls sagged, I looked awful, and I smelled of coffee. When I started doing stand-up comedy, I talked about how the hairdresser would pull my hair over giant rollers and spritz it with a ton of spray, so I'd look like an eighteenth-century composer. There I was, Beethoven with caffeine curves.

Now you should see how hard my hairdresser at *The View* has to work before a show. Everyone's afraid of curly hair on TV, because the light doesn't bounce off curls properly, or so they tell me. I think society needs to change its idea of what's pretty, but, personally, I still think I look better with straight hair. So sue me.

Before I go on The View, everyone works hard to straighten my hair.

—JOY BEHAR, COMEDIAN AND CO-HOST OF *THE VIEW*

THE THREE TYPES OF CURLY GIRLS

Which Curl Are You?

Curls are like snowflakes or fingerprints. No two are alike, making it difficult to generalize about curly hair. Some of us are born with tight corkscrew curls so relentless that not even Superman could stretch them out, so brittle that they break with the least resistance. Some of us have soft Botticelli curls that frame our faces with ringlets, making us look like angels in Renaissance paintings. And millions of us have varying degrees of curls and waves. Many of us fight them, straightening our hair with blow-dryers and rollers. In fact, some of us don't even know what our wave potential is. (See "Are You a Curly Girl?" on page 7.)

In order for you to know how to care for your particular curls or learn how to develop some waves, I've identified three types of curly girls—Corkscrew, Botticelli, and Wavy. For each type, I've used recognizable celebrities as identifying icons. Decide which celebrity and characteristics best match your hair, then go straight to the particular care routine for your "curl type" (see chapter 4) to learn how to nurture and encourage those curls.

CORKSCREW

Keri Russell   Gloria Reuben   Julianna Margulies

YOU KNOW YOU HAVE CORKSCREW HAIR IF YOU HAVE:

- [ ] Curls as tightly wound as a French poodle's if cut too short

- [ ] Lots of small coils of curls

- [ ] Superdry hair that crackles with electricity

- [ ] A high frizz factor

- [ ] Very dry skin

- [ ] Curls that tend to stand out from your head instead of lying flat

- [ ] Hair that soaks up as much conditioner as you feed it

Many Corkscrew divas believe their hair is thickly textured, but separate a single strand and you'll discover that it is actually baby fine and very delicate. That's why it breaks so easily, as African Americans can testify (see chapter 6). And because the cuticle stands out instead of lying flat, the curls catch and the hair snarls easily. Most tangles and snarls are found under the top layer of hair, at the nape of the neck.

Because Corkscrew curls are so very dry, your mantra should be moisturize, moisturize, moisturize. Hydrate your scalp as often as you apply moisturizer to your face and give your curls lots of TLC as you follow the care routine in chapter 4. African American curly hair is most similar to Corkscrew curls in fragility and dryness. But because it has special needs, I've dealt with it in a separate chapter.

If you follow the care routine on pages 30–38, you can have glorious Corkscrew curls that live up to their potential:

- Well-hydrated curls with spring and shine
- Low frizz factor, even in humid weather
- Short hair that keeps its shape
- Long hair with well-defined ringlets

BOTTICELLI CURLS

Sarah Jessica Parker Julia Roberts Nicole Kidman

YOU KNOW YOU HAVE BOTTICELLI HAIR IF YOU HAVE:

☐ Curls that vary in size

☐ Curls that fall gracefully down your head instead of sticking straight out

☐ Texture that is medium-fine

☐ Hair that is brittle and easily damaged

☐ Curls that sometimes cannot be coaxed into making an appearance because they're weighed down by the top layer of hair

Like people with tight curls, Botticelli curly girls have to keep their hair well hydrated with humectants and emollients (see chapter 5), but this kind of hair needs less conditioner for its daily routine. The curls are looser, in the shape of soft *S*'s. Follow the directions that begin on page 30 for Corkscrew and Botticelli curls, noting the differences in amounts of conditioner and how often you can rinse your hair. Once your hair has regained the necessary moisture (it takes two to three weeks), you'll probably be able to cut back on the conditioner.

Botticelli girls who want to live up to their name can have:

- Soft, cascading curls that look wonderful long or short
- Hair that can be worn in a variety of styles
- Hair that is very forgiving
- Well-defined curls released from beneath the top layer, or canopy

WAVY CURLS

Ashley Judd

Meg Ryan

Michelle Pfeiffer

YOU KNOW YOU HAVE WAVY HAIR IF YOU HAVE:

☐ Hair that you've always believed was straight

☐ Hair that on humid days is surrounded by a halo of frizz

☐ Hair that occasionally develops a natural wave, which you've tried to blow-dry out

☐ Hair that has a tendency to look unkempt

☐ Hair that is flat on the crown

☐ Had wavy hair when you were very young

I estimate that 65 percent of all women have wavy or curly hair, but many have never been aware of it or have been fighting their natural bent and misunderstanding their hair for years. Many of the women who fall into this huge category frequently wear their hair completely straight. The kinds of waves also vary greatly, even on the same head of hair. Some wavy hair can have a curl spring factor of five inches, while other wavy curls fall in extremely lazy *S*'s below the shoulders. Those wavy girls who think they are straight may be on too strict a haircut schedule, so that the waves are cut before they have a chance to develop. It's important to let wavy hair grow to its best length—giving the entire *S*-wave a chance to grow out. (See chapter 7.)

If you're a Wavy type and have always worn your hair straight and short, you may want to try to realize your curl potential. Check the characteristics on the facing page. Follow the directions on pages 40–44 for three weeks and you may be surprised to discover you're a curly girl, too. Treat your hair gently and bring out its full wavy potential:

- Loose, glamorous curls that need a minimum care routine
- Hair that is very versatile, whether short finger waves or an updated Farrah Fawcett look
- Wavy hair that shines with good health

The tightness of your curls (or spring factor) is a sure way to determine which type of curly girl you are. It's something your hairdresser should know or be told because it tells him or her how much to cut. Basically, the spring factor is the difference in the length of a curl when it falls naturally and when it's extended. Here's how to check yours: Pull a strand of dry curls down against your shoulder or neck to its full length. Leave your finger at the point where the strand touches. Now let go. With a ruler, measure the distance between your finger and where your curl naturally ends. The number is your personal spring factor. It will help you determine which hair-care routine to follow.

9- to 12-inch spring = Corkscrew curls
5- to 8-inch spring = Botticelli curls
2- to 4-inch spring = Wavy curls

If you have short hair, your spring factor would be about half as long as the figures above.

My first—and worst—hair trauma occurred when I was nine. I had very long, curly hair that fell halfway down my back, and I loved wearing it loose and carefree. My parents, who thought my hair looked unruly, announced that if I didn't start taking care of it, I'd have to get it cut off. One day, in the dead of winter, my mother made good on her threat and dragged me to a beauty parlor to get my hair cut in a short shag. I was so humiliated by the result that I decided to wear a knit cap to school until my hair grew back.

Don't even ask me what I went through in high school. It was the late seventies, when everyone but me had straight Farrah Fawcett hair. (I wonder if she has any idea how many curly girls suffered because of her hairstyle.) I'd wash my hair every night, blow it dry straight, and pull it back in a pony-tail. Then I'd wake up at 6:00 A.M. and wrap it around hot rollers to complete the treatment. The day of my senior prom, I was even more obsessed than usual with the weather report. We lived in Pittsburgh, Pennsylvania, where it is very humid, and the May mist is a nightmare. I was wearing a to-die-for, off-the-shoulder gown, and I wanted my hair to be equally sleek. When I woke up that morning, the weather was hot and humid,

and as the hours passed, the air remained laden with moisture. I gave up and let my hair do its thing.

When I emerged from my bedroom, my mother looked stunned. "Your hair looks beautiful," she said. "That's how you should always wear it." I was horrified.

I'd imagined myself as Farrah Fawcett, and I'd morphed into Shirley Temple.

When we arrived at the prom, I locked eyes across the ballroom with Mark, the boy I'd had a crush on since fourth grade. Like a scene from a movie, we walked toward each other, meeting halfway. "You look so beauti-ful," he said. "I can't believe what your hair looks like." We kissed passionately, right there in front of our dates. It was a magical moment. Then he threw up all over his shoes. He was totally wasted.

But he loved my hair.

—**SHELLEY OZKAN,**
FULL-TIME MOTHER

The Curly Life

Curls are so much more than just responsive little ringlets. They move, they breathe, they have attitude, they take positions. Curls embody all the qualities of freedom and fun that stir up our lives and stimulate our imaginations. In their resilience, in their ability to bounce back and find their own form, curls invent themselves over and over again.

You might even say (I have said it) that curls are revolutionary. They resist everything but their own impulses. Curls twist like Möbius strips, flex like flying fish, swerve like the circuitry in silicon chips, rise up like waveforms, and crackle like well-fed fires.

A curly girl is always a curly girl, even when her curls are hiding. My own curls were incognito for years, subdued by barrettes, braids, bobby pins, bows, sprays, and serious brushings. But curls are a Force of Nature and one wet summer Nature herself came down in a series of storms that transformed my strained and straightened hair into a cloud of cumulous curls.

I could hate my curls or I could love them, but I couldn't do anything about them. I decided not to hate them. It was like the first principle of riding a roller coaster: **Accept the curve, be delighted, and never look back.**

BY **JOAN SCHENKAR**

THE CURLY GIRL PROGRAM

Creating a Daily Routine

The program of daily hair care that's mapped out in this chapter is truly revolutionary. Adopting it means you'll have to give up a lot of assumptions you have about what constitutes good hair grooming. But if you've lived with curly hair all your life and put up with frizz, parched curls, and horrendous bad hair days, you're probably ready to start. I guarantee it will change your life.

Some of you—those I've classified as "Wavy" (see chapter 3)—will have to cut back on how often you shampoo your hair. But most curly girls will have to do something extraordinary—throw out every bottle of shampoo in the bathroom and get rid of your blow-dryer!

I'm going to show you how to keep your hair and scalp clean using only water and conditioner. Yes, conditioner. Once you break your shampoo dependency, you'll still be rinsing your hair daily, but in a way that will keep it shiny and healthy, instead of constantly stripping it of lubrication with the harsh detergents found in most shampoos. And you'll be letting your hair air-dry as well.

DAILY ROUTINE
FOR CORKSCREW AND
BOTTICELLI CURLS

Cleansing

Your daily curly hair routine starts every morning in the shower. (If you decide to skip a shower one morning, simply spritz, scrunch, and go. See "Curls on the Go," page 45.) About once a week, cleanse your hair and scalp with conditioner, as in step 2 (below). On other days, after wetting your hair thoroughly, go to step 3. While you wean yourself off shampoo, you may want to use conditioner to cleanse your hair twice a week. After that, once a week or every ten days is enough.

1 Step under the shower as if you're standing under a waterfall or are caught in a sudden cloud-burst. (The pressure can be moderately heavy.) Don't touch your hair yet. Let the water cascade through your curls in the way they fall naturally. Resist the impulse to start scrubbing your head and disarranging your hair's basic shape.

2 Take a half teaspoon of conditioner. It can be a regular or a leave-in conditioner, as long as it's rich in emollients and humectants. (See chapter 5.) With your fingertips and this bit of conditioner you're going to cleanse your scalp, loosening any residue that's accumulated. Believe me, the conditioner and the stimulation from your fingers will work as well as shampoo. Starting at the temples, rub gently down the sides, then move to the

top of your head, scrubbing gently toward the crown. Finally, move down the back of your head, finishing up at the nape. Now let the shower spray wash through your entire head, rinsing out whatever your fingers have loosened. Your scalp is clean now. Still worried about sweat and other buildup? Remember that sweat and sebum are sterile. But they do attract bacteria if left too long. However, friction is a time-tested method of cleaning (think of a washing machine churning), and it will remove everything that needs to be removed without harming your hair or scalp.

How Much Conditioner?

In general, the tighter or dryer the curl, the more conditioner you need. I suggest average amounts of conditioner here, but you are going to have to monitor usage on the basis of your hair's needs. If your hair has been damaged by coloring or too much blow-drying and chemical straightening, it probably absorbs conditioner very fast and will need more. You'll have to experiment with what amount of conditioner is best for your hair. If you apply too much conditioner, the worst that can happen is your hair will look overcoated and dull that day. Not a bad trade-off, considering you're making your hair healthier and shinier in the long run.

3 Now rub a half teaspoon of conditioner (a blob about the size of a quarter) between your hands and smooth the conditioner on the outer layer (or canopy) of your hair—the part that is most exposed to the elements. Work another half teaspoon under the hair at the nape of your neck, the spot most prone to tangles and knots. Be gentle because the hair there breaks easily. Using your fingers as a comb, gently comb through your hair from underneath, removing any loose hairs. Don't get nervous. Remember, it's normal to lose about a hundred hairs a day!

4 Spread another half teaspoon of conditioner through the hair at each side of your head, using your fingers as a comb. (Botticelli types may find that this is too much and weighs down their curls.) The point is to distribute the conditioner evenly through your curls so they don't fuse with each other, which, as you now know, can damage the cuticle.

Your hair should feel smooth and silky right now—almost like wet seaweed. Over time, you'll know instinctively whether or not to rinse out the conditioner at this point. If you do rinse, just let the shower spray fall over your head for a few seconds to evenly distribute the conditioner without removing all of it.

Bonus: At this point, you can rinse your hair just a little more and give it a wonderful lavender scent by spritzing your curls with some homemade Lavender Mist. (See "Lorraine's Lotions and Potions," page 53.) Comb it through with your fingers.

Spot-Cleaning

Just as you may clean a spot on a blouse, where perhaps you spilled red wine, you may occasionally want to spot-clean your scalp. If your scalp feels itchy or oily in one or two patches, put a dab of conditioner on your fingertips and scrub directly on the spot. Then rinse thoroughly. If you are still using shampoo, first coat the ends of your hair with conditioner, then spot-wash with shampoo. The spot-cleaning technique applies to all types of curly hair—Corkscrew, African American, Botticelli, and Wavy.

Drying

1   Step out of the shower and grab a hand towel. Bend forward and cup your hair loosely in the towel, then scrunch it upward toward the scalp to blot up the moisture. Do not wring or rub it dry.

2   Beginning at the back of the head, gently squeeze sections of hair. Continue all around your head, blotting any sections that are still dripping wet. Do it gently, going with the natural waves and without disturbing the hair too much. Remember the sweater analogy—after washing, you blot it dry in a towel so as not to disturb the fibers. And by now you know your hair is a precious fiber. Rotate the towel occasionally so that one section doesn't get sopping wet and lose its absorbency.

Styling and Air-Drying

Remember curly girl rule number one: Resist the temptation to blow-dry your hair at this point. Your curls need to recover their shape, not get blown out of proportion.

1 Take a tablespoon of a clear styling gel (see chapter 5) and rub it into your palms. Bend over to let your curls fall free. Starting at the ends, scrunch the gel in toward the scalp. I call this motion the accordion technique. As you are doing it, visualize the undulating waves and folds of an accordion as a slow tune is played on it. Start scrunching at the nape and work around your head, scrunching the top layer (canopy) of your hair last.

2 Now it's time to have some fun—and shape your curls. Go to the mirror. Scrunch sections of curls with your palms, pushing up and squeezing gently into place. For shorter or looser curls, twist the hair around a finger and clip. Or put a bit of gel directly on a clip before fastening it. This will help hold the front curls and give a little lift at the top.

Remember, your hair is still drying, so wherever you place your curls now, that's how they'll dry. Take another half teaspoon of gel and, ever so gently, graze your hands over the top layer of hair (don't be heavy-handed). This will minimize frizz.

3 To get the curls on the top of your head to stand a little taller, you need to lift and clip the hair at the roots. This method releases the top layer of hair from its own weight and allows it to dry faster.

Using a clawlike motion, lift a small amount of hair from the top of your head. (Hair should be pulled perpendicular to the scalp, neither forward nor backward.)

Place a clip at the roots where you pinched it and at right angles to the scalp. Make sure it's as tight as when you pinched it. Secure with a second clip (left). As a rule, you will need about six clips to "lift" the top of your hairdo—in front, at the crown, and between these two points.

If you want to disguise a part, take strands from either side and cross them over the part (right), then pin two curls on either side of it.

Once you've pinned everything you want lifted, leave your hair alone. Don't touch it for an hour. Let it dry, have some breakfast, get dressed, read the paper. Whatever you do, don't interrupt the curls or they'll frizz up. Remember, if you like the way your hair looks wet, you'll like how it looks when it dries.

If you don't have time to air-dry your hair, dry it with a diffuser (a shallow, bowl-shaped attachment that reduces the volume of air flow). You can control the effects of the diffuser by cupping your hand and lifting the section of hair that you're drying, so that the top layer of curls isn't blown every which way. To cut back on heat

Lorraine's Geography Lesson

We curly girls are natural weather barometers. Any increase in humidity, the slightest hint of rain or mist, and our hair gets big. I call this the east-west effect, hair that balloons out on either side of the head but lies flat on top, making you look a little like the Sphinx. (Think Gilda Radner's Roseanne Roseannadanna in *Saturday Night Live*.) Not a good look.

You need to train the curls on the top of your head to stand taller, so that your hair moves in a north-south direction as well. The easiest way to create this effect is to use what I call the Playtex bra technique because it *lifts and separates* the top layer of curls. Follow step 3 (see page 35), which explains how to use clips to lift your hair at the roots after you wash it. Then hang a "Do Not Disturb" sign for yourself on your head and don't touch it during the drying process.

Roseannadanna's east-west effect

Note: Well-informed curly girls—those who have healthy hair and a pro-curl attitude—often opt for a style that moves in a more east-west direction. You, too, may decide, once you get comfortable with your curls, to push your boundaries and be more daring. For a wilder, sexier look, place your fingers an inch or two above the roots on either side of your head and shake gently. You'll expand your hair in an east-west direction without sacrificing control or style.

Weekly Scalp Treatment
(for All Hair Types)

We know that exfoliating is good for improving the condition of your skin. Since your scalp is also skin, give it a special exfoliating treatment once a week or so. Exfoliating will slough off any dead skin cells or conditioner buildup, making your scalp healthier and relieving any itchiness. Mix up and apply the Exfoliating Scrub (below).

EXFOLIATING SCRUB

1 tablespoon brown sugar or quinoa (available at health food stores)
3 tablespoons conditioner

1. Mix together to create a thick consistency.
2. Wet your hair in the shower, then rub the paste on your fingertips. Apply to scalp and massage gently in a circular motion, starting at the nape of your neck and moving upward. Linger on any spots that seem tense or itchy.
3. Rinse thoroughly, then condition.

exposure, use a travel dryer, because its airflow is slower and weaker.

When your hair is completely dry, remove the clips gently. Look in the mirror. Bend over and shake your head a little. With your fingers, gently fluff your hair from underneath. Don't touch the top layer. If you still don't have enough height to suit your taste, you can use bobby pins and pin the curls just as you did with the clips. Get bobby pins the same color as your hair and you can wear them outside or to work. No one will notice. That's a great thing about curly hair—it hides a lot of scalp.

Second chance: If anything looks out of place, now's the time to make a quick fix. Use a couple of spritzes of a spray gel. Lift the curls you want to be higher, clip them as above, and wait until they dry before removing pins. If some curls seem too tight, clip a pin on the ends for a few seconds to loosen the coil.

When I was a little girl, I was so desperate for straight hair that moved when I turned my head that I begged my mother to buy me a bathing cap with a ponytail attached to it. For a while, my mother had my hair cut very short—I suppose to make it more manageable—and people thought I was a boy, which of course I hated. When it was longer, she'd tie it back in two tight pigtails, like the ones Kathy wore on *Father Knows Best*.

As a teenager, I tried everything to banish the curls. I'd slather Dippity-Do styling gel on my hair, then tape it down. I don't know *where* I got this idea, but somehow it made sense. When I'd remove the tape in the morning, I'd often strip away pieces of skin with it. Because I'm short and small-boned, I always thought I looked better with my hair up and away from my face. I wore it in a French braid for several years—until I threw my back out braiding.

Whenever I went to a hair salon, I'd get very uptight because I would always have to tell the stylist what to do with my curls. She didn't have a clue. I would insist that she leave it long enough to "put it back in a ponytail."

Patti and daughter, Dena, who loves her curls.

Then Dena entered my life. At age two my daughter would cry in front of the mirror whenever she looked at her mop of dark ringlets. She'd also clip handkerchiefs to the sides of her head to pretend she had long, straight hair. I worried that maybe she was learning this from me, and I began to wear my hair in curls—and not always tied back. Now that Dena is a teenager, she wears her hair long and curly.

It took me until my late forties to accept my curls. The fact remains that my hair will always be something to contend with. Given a choice, I'd still prefer straight hair that I could wear simple and short; it'd make my life and job easier—I own my own custom-made cookie company, so I always have to keep my hair tied back. But, for the first time in my life, I don't hide my ringlets.

—PATTI PAIGE, OWNER OF BAKED IDEAS

Curls banished with Scotch tape.

DAILY ROUTINE FOR WAVY HAIR

Where there's a wave, there's a curl; that's my motto. This routine is meant to get wavy hair into great shape (with extra hydration) and to encourage the memory of its natural curl.

Wavy hair lies flat against the scalp but has gentle *S* waves. It can be coarse or fine and the strength of the waves varies greatly. If you have this kind of hair, you've probably been blow-drying it straight. If your hair is short, the curl may not even be discernible. Every curl is in the shape of an *S*. Some are very loose, floppy *S*'s. You have to let your hair grow into the length of the second part of the *S* before it springs into place naturally. Sometimes the hair has to grow past your shoulders before this happens.

Wavy hair generally isn't as dry as really curly hair so you may choose to use shampoo— but only once a week. Check out the cosmetics and personal care section of your local organic or health food store for shampoos that contain little or no detergent. (See chapter 5.) The most radical changes for wavy hair are: when you shampoo your hair, always apply conditioner *first*. Stop using a blow-dryer to dry your hair straight. Never brush. Of course, if you get up and decide your hair doesn't need a complete wetting down, simply spritz with water, scrunch, and go. (See "Curls on the Go," page 45.)

Now, here's your basic wavy routine. On the days when you're not using shampoo, just follow steps 1 and 4.

Cleansing

1 Wet your hair under a gentle shower, letting the water simply flow through it. (You don't want to disturb any natural waves in your hair, so don't disarrange the basic shape of your hair while washing it.)

2 Now take a tablespoon of conditioner (see chapter 5) and, using your fingers, lightly coat your hair from the ends to the midshaft. This hair has been around longer than the hair at the roots and needs more lubrication. The conditioner protects the hair by not allowing shampoo to penetrate and dehydrate the shaft.

3 If you're using shampoo, squeeze a half teaspoon (no more) onto your fingertips and apply it gently to the scalp and roots only. Don't use your nails. Start at the forehead and work around the scalp. Then rinse thoroughly.

4 Add a half teaspoon of conditioner to your hair, and work it through with your fingers. Then rinse quickly, for just a few seconds. Now you're ready to blot-dry your hair.

Drying and Styling

1 Cup a hand towel in your hands and bend forward. Scrunch your hair toward the scalp in an upward motion. Blot the hair to get rid of moisture, but don't twist or wring the hair dry. Start at the back and gently squeeze sections of hair. Continue all around the head, rotating the towel so no one section gets sopped.

2 Rub a tablespoon of styling gel (see chapter 5) on your palms. You're about to encourage any natural waves that you have. Bend forward, looking at the floor. Scrunch in the gel, starting at the back of the head, then the sides. With both hands, scrunch the hair on the top of your head; then straighten up, still holding the hank of hair. Let go and you'll see the natural waves in the canopy.

Encourage them with more scrunching—always from the end toward the scalp. Look in the mirror—the way your hair looks now when it's wet is how it will look dry.

3   To prevent a flat top, you'll need to lift and clip some curls on the crown of your head. This separates the curls so they dry faster. (See "Lorraine's Geography Lesson," page 37.) Short-haired Wavy girls can use four 1-inch clips, lifting and pinning two sections at the back of the crown, two nearer the forehead.

If your hair is long and thick, you may need a couple of butterfly clips to lift and hold the waves. Simply clasp a wave in the clip and close it.

Playtex bra technique: lift and separate

4   Let your hair air-dry, if possible. If you're in a hurry, you can dry your hair with a diffuser. Instead of blasting your hair with a single stream of hot air, which can damage the cuticle and make the hair frizzy, you dry it gently without disturbing the waves. (Set the temperature on low.) Cup individual sections of waves, scrunching them a little to encourage the curl, and then aim the diffuser just on that section. Work around the head from back to side, to top.

5 If you want a curlier look, try the pin curl method. Starting at the crown, wrap a section of hair around your finger, slide your finger out, hold the coil with your other hand, and insert a clip at right angles. (The pin curls should stand out from your head, not lie flat.) Do your entire head in giant pin curls. Air-dry or, if time is short, use a diffuser set on low. When your hair is dry, gently pull out the pins or clips and loosen your curls with your fingers.

Those of you who are not yet believers in your curls will have to practice this method on faith. I promise that within two or three weeks you will find your waves are well established. They've been waiting for you to treat them this way for years!

CURLY GIRL *confession*

My husband thinks my hair matches my character. Before our wedding, we wrote letters, saying why we wanted to marry each other. During the ceremony, the rabbi read an excerpt from my husband's letter: "The physical attributes that first hooked me on Rikki—her eyes, her smile, her hair—still continue to thrill me. Rikki's hair reflects her personality: at times wild and unruly, because Rikki is spontaneous and alive; at other times controlled and strong, because Rikki can also be focused and determined."

—RIKKI LANE, DOCTOR

Curls on the Go

I f you wake up one morning and don't feel like showering or going through your usual hair care routine, use the Lavender Mist (see recipe on page 53) to refresh your curls quickly. Spray lightly—five or six spritzes at most—then take one curl at a time and twist it around your finger. Slide the hair off your finger and clip it horizontally at the root. The curls should be positioned around your head in soft

circles. For a quick fix, position about five curls on the crown of the head. If you have more time, use more. Let the curls dry for five to twenty minutes, then carefully remove the clips. Shake your head, loosen hair at scalp with fingers, admire your curls in the mirror, and go.

My hair is not curly; it has a wave to it. When I get out of the shower, and I let my hair air-dry, I have the most disgusting rat's nest on my head that anyone has ever seen. I used to have naturally wavy hair that turned into nice curls if I scrunched them and used lots of products. But I haven't trained it to be curly since I was sixteen.

For the last eleven years, I've been drying my hair straight to the point of destroying it. My hair is so brittle and won't grow past the middle of my back, because I'm always getting it cut. I use a hair dryer every day, even when I don't wash it, then I pin it up at night to keep it straight, so I don't wake up with knots in my hair.

I *know* I'm damaging it, but I'm insecure about it. **I know what I'm doing is terrible, but I still continue to straighten my hair.** I've learned to deal with all of my other body image issues, and I'm grateful for how I look. But my hair is the one thing left that I haven't accepted and I'd give anything to change.

—BERTHA BRACKEN, ACTRESS AND STUDENT

Before

After: curly conversion

PRODUCTS AND HOME REMEDIES

What's a Curly Girl to Do?

Curly girls tend to obsess about products, buying every new one that comes along in hopes of making their hair straighter, shinier, frizz-free, easier to manage. My care routine will get you out of that habit. *You'll need to buy only two products—a conditioner and a clear styling gel.* For Wavy types who will still shampoo their hair once in a while, I've suggested some alternatives to harsh shampoos.

I recently spent half an hour at one of my favorite beauty supply stores, checking out various brands of conditioners and gels. Here are some of the words I found on the packages: conditioning fixative, antifrizz lotion, texturizing creme, styling wax, forming gel, relaxing cream, moisturizing balm, hydrating cream, supporting liquid gel, nourishing cream, restorative cream, volume gel, moisturizing conditioner. Faced with all this jargon, what's a curly girl to do?

First, don't be fooled by the hype; if you read carefully, you'll see that many of the ingredients are identical from one brand to the next. But it's important to know what you're looking for in a product and how to read a label.

Talk to other women with hair similar to yours. Before buying, borrow or trade products with your curly-haired friends. Two or three uses should give you enough time to decide whether or not you like a particular conditioner or gel. If you've found a good stylist for curly hair, ask what she suggests for your hair. Hairdressers keep up with the latest advances in hair care products and experiment with different brands until they find two or three to recommend to clients. The information that follows is meant to help guide you through the product jungle, but ultimately you're the only one who can decide what keeps your curls happy and well nourished.

Shampoo

I've already talked about how harsh shampoos can damage your hair. The detergents seen most frequently on shampoo labels are sodium lauryl sulfate (the harshest), ammonium laureth sulfate (also harsh), and sodium laureth sulfate (a little gentler). Try to avoid products with the first two ingredients. It's best to water shampoos down with equal amounts of spring or distilled water or buy a product that lists plant extracts or buffering ingredients such as disodium EDTA or citric acid high up on the label.

What to Look for on a Label

Always look at shampoo labels before buying. As on a food label, ingredients are listed from most amount to least. Water is frequently the first ingredient, which means it's what you're spending most of your money on. Look for *cocamidopropyl betaine* on the label; it's the gentlest kind of cleaning agent and is found in baby shampoos. It doesn't lather as well, so it will not harm your hair as much as harsh detergents.

If you're shopping in a natural food store, look for *decyl polyglucose*, a natural cleaning agent, or shampoos made from olive oil or wheat germ oil.

You don't need shampoos with built-in conditioners. You're going to follow a different program, which involves applying conditioner to your hair before you shampoo, so that extra ingredient is unnecessary.

Conditioners

In general, leave-in conditioners don't contain enough emollients and humectants, so I generally don't recommend using them. However, as you'll see from my routine for Corkscrew curls, you will be leaving in a small amount of regular conditioner. Some curly girls, especially those who live in cold-weather regions, find that they need a thicker, richer conditioner during the winter months.

Reading the labels of conditioners can be confusing since so many ingredients just add to the thickness, fragrance, or look of the product itself and have no benefit for the hair. I suggest that you avoid conditioners with silicones. Although they do add temporary shine to the hair, I find they weigh down curly hair. (That means avoid using products with ingredients whose names end in -cone.) *The ingredients you absolutely need in a conditioner include emollients, humectants, proteins, and moisturizers.* Here's what to look for:

Emollients soften and smooth skin and reduce frizz in hair by smoothing the cuticle. There are hundreds of emollients. Shea butter is found in a lot in products for African American hair and it's excellent for most curly types. Others to look for include vegetable oils, wheat germ, olive and walnut oils.

Proteins coat the hair shaft and protect it. Look for plant proteins such as wheat, wheat germ, or soy protein on the back of the label.

Also, make sure your diet includes lots of protein because it's necessary for keeping your hair healthy from the inside out.

Humectants absorb water and hold in moisture. They are absolutely crucial in a conditioner for curly hair. Panthenol, vegetable glycerine, and sorbitol are just a few humectants to look for on the label.

Moisturizers add softness and control to curly hair. Amino acids and aloe vera are two great moisturizers.

Styling Gel

You don't need to know the chemical formula to buy a gel that's right for your curls, but here's what you do need to know. A clear gel is preferable; it's the last product you put into your hair before it dries, and you want your own color to shine through. (White or yellow-tinted gel can leave a film on the hair and, over time, make it look dull.) Look for a gel that doesn't contain alcohol and that has little or no fragrance. But it should contain the ingredients PVP (polyvinylpyrrolidone) and PVP/VA (vinyl acrylate).

I am a twenty-seven-year-old curly girl desperately in need of help. It's been a grueling journey: bad hair days; poor self-image and low self-esteem; a cabinet full of gels, mousses, and chemical straightening products; years of wishing for "beautiful, straight hair."

I wash my hair every day and plan my life around it. If I have a date after work but want to go to the gym in the afternoon, I worry about when I'll have the time to wash my hair. Forget about spontaneous—anything! Often, I prefer not to go out after work because I don't like the way my hair looks.

I'm a slave to weather forecasts and have a long list of life events—junior prom, graduations, Florida vacations—ruined by my bad hair. When my brother got married this past June, I had my hair cut and styled in an updo right before the wedding. What a nightmare! It was one of the hottest days of the summer, and I hated how my hair looked. I couldn't stop crying. Even today, I could cry looking at the pictures, and it wasn't even my wedding!

My bathroom is a product graveyard. I'll try a twelve-dollar gel once and decide it doesn't work, so I'll stick it under the sink. The truth is, I'd spend any amount of money to fulfill my fantasy of having straight hair. I'm a new woman when I get my hair blown out. I can walk into any room and feel like a queen. But I usually don't have time for that, except on special occasions.

My last boyfriend was very sensitive to my negative feelings about my curly hair. He always complimented me and told me how much he liked it. I hope that I can find another man who understands that **dealing with my curls is a major part of my existence**.

I don't think people realize the struggles we curly-haired women endure.

—BROOKE HIRSCHFELDER, CORPORATE HUMAN RESOURCES ADMINISTRATOR

When shopping for gel, do the skin test: if it feels sticky on your skin, it will feel sticky on your hair. You also want to avoid styling creams and waxes because they can make your hair look crispy and petrified, like ramen noodles.

If your hair is thick and wavy, you may need to use more gel, but a light hold works best for curly girls with fine hair. Spray styling gels are basically diluted versions of gels. They're especially good on loose, wavy curls because the mist gets lightly distributed through the hair without weighing it down. They're also a wonderful way to refresh all hair types during the day. (See "Curls on the Go," page 45.)

You can even make your own spray gel by combining 1/2 cup gel with 1 cup boiled water. Allow to cool, then pour into a spray bottle. If you think your hair needs a stronger hold, experiment by gradually adding more gel to the mixture until you achieve the consistency that works best for your curls.

CURLY GIRL confession

I used to live in Washington, D.C., where a person's political affiliation is a typical ice-breaker at cocktail parties. At one gathering, a man came up to me and said, **"I know you're a Democrat, because Republican women don't have hair like yours."** I realized he was right, and I wonder which comes first: having curly hair and being a Democrat, or the other way around.

When I was young, people thought I was wild because of my hair. Curly hair definitely has that aura about it. I now live in New York, where there's more ethnic diversity, and different kinds of hair are more accepted. I'm a graphic artist and exhibition designer, and I don't think my hair is a professional liability. In fact, it's probably an asset, because it's so memorable. But I'm still pondering the question of which came first, the hair or the political affiliation.

—KATHLEEN TOBIN-JONES,
GRAPHIC DESIGNER

LORRAINE'S LOTIONS AND POTIONS

If you hate putting all those chemicals from commercial products on your hair, try these homemade conditioners, rinses, and exfoliants that I've developed in my kitchen. You'll know they're fresh and natural because you make them yourself.

Lavender Mist

Lavender has cleansing properties, so this quick mist not only makes your hair smell like a lavender field in Provence, it's also indispensable for cleansing and reviving your curls. Make it in large quantities; keep a large spray bottle in your shower and smaller travel-size bottles in your purse, desk, and car.

1/2 gallon water
5 drops pure (not synthetic) lavender essential oil
3 empty spray bottles (available at most drugstores)

1. Fill a large pot with a half gallon of water.
2. Cover, bring to a boil, and simmer for an hour to get rid of impurities. (Check occasionally to make sure water isn't boiling away.)
3. Remove from heat, add lavender oil, stir, and replace lid.
4. Let steep until cool, then pour into empty spritz bottles.

Lavender mist makes a wonderful gift for friends, whether or not they are curly girls. Once you get hooked on the spray, you'll find lots of other uses for it. Some of my clients have told me that their husbands sprayed it on them in the delivery room, for a very calming effect.

Aloe Aroma Scalp Therapy

Aloe vera is a completely natural hydrating and conditioning therapy for your skin and scalp. The scalp is most responsive to this nourishing, cleansing treatment after it's been bathed in warm water and the pores are dilated.

After you've rinsed or shampooed your hair in warm water, apply 1 tablespoon aloe vera gel to your scalp. (Use the edible type of aloe vera gel, the kind that has to be refrigerated after opening.) Massage gently for several minutes. Rinse hair and condition as usual. Or leave in, as an alternative to hair gel.

Deep-Pack Chakra

A calming protein pack to soften your hair, create bounteous curls, and nourish your spirit.

> *1 tablespoon powdered egg (found in health food stores)*
> *1 tablespoon powdered milk*
> *½ teaspoon honey (combined with a few drops of hot water to soften)*
> *1–2 cups pasta water (for added nutrients) or plain boiled water*
> *3 tablespoons heavy cream (optional)*

1. Combine the first three ingredients to form a paste.

2. Add water (amount depends on the length and thickness of your hair).

3. Stir in fresh cream.

4. Pour the entire mixture over well-rinsed (but not freshly shampooed) hair.

5. Make a turban out of clear plastic wrap, wrap hair, and allow the rinse to penetrate for 1 hour or more, if possible.

6. Rinse well and condition, or shampoo and condition, depending on your hair type.

Lemon Aid

More clarifying and cleansing than any shampoo, this moisturizing and neutralizing tonic adds shine to your hair and removes buildup. It's especially good for very dry or damaged hair.

Combine juice of 1 large lemon with your usual amount of conditioner, then rinse through hair thoroughly.

Deep Endings

A revitalizing oil treatment that nourishes the ends of your hair. It's especially useful in winter, when hair constantly rubs up against wool and other heavy fabrics.

1–3 teaspoons olive, peanut, or sweet almond oil (amount depends on length and/or thickness of your hair)
2–4 drops pure lavender essential oil

1. Combine oils and apply to the ends of your hair.

2. Wrap hair with clear plastic wrap and leave on for 30 minutes.

3. Rinse thoroughly with the Lemon Aid (above).

Most oil recipes tell you to shampoo afterward, but I think shampooing undermines the benefits of this treatment.

Avocado Wrap

Another rich moisturizing hair treat to nourish dry ends.

1 ripe avocado
3–4 teaspoons honey
8–10 drops almond oil

1. Peel and core the avocado, then mix in a blender with other ingredients.

2. Apply to wet hair, concentrating on the ends.

3. Wrap hair with clear plastic wrap or a towel. Leave on for 20–30 minutes.

4. Rinse thoroughly with warm water.

Whattacurl Wants

The baking soda will remove heavy product buildup and leave your hair feeling shiny and clean.

1 tablespoon baking soda
1 cup warm water

1. Combine above ingredients in a spray bottle and shake.

2. Wet, condition, and blot-dry hair as usual.

3. Spray with mixture.

4. Allow to sit for a minute or so, then rinse with cool water.

5. Blot dry again, style as usual.

Flaking It

Excellent exfoliant for dry, flaking scalp.

1 cup heavy cream, beaten until fluffy (or Reddi Whip)

Pour into palms and then massage into scalp. Wait 5–10 minutes, then rinse well with cool water.

Fruit Smoothie

A moisturizing and tasty banana cocktail that adds shine and bounce to dry or unruly curls.

3 very ripe bananas
1 teaspoon almond oil
1/2 cup carrot juice

1. Mix all three ingredients in a blender.

2. Apply to wet hair, making sure that all strands are well coated.

3. Wrap a damp towel around your head and leave on for a half hour.

4. Rinse thoroughly with warm (not hot) water.

Love Is in the Hair

This sensual double dose of moisturizing oils acts as a refreshing tonic for dry, thirsty curls.

4 tablespoons olive or almond oil
4 tablespoons of your favorite conditioner
2–3 drops musk oil or other essential oil of your
*   choosing*

Mix well and apply to wet hair, combing through gently until your whole head is saturated. Use the entire amount for long hair, half the amount for short hair. Scrunch dry, then use clips to lift and separate the curls, as you would when styling. Leave in overnight or for several hours during the day. Rinse thoroughly with a combination of conditioner mixed with lemon juice and vinegar.

Curls from Ipanema

I was given this recipe by Ivone Da Silva, who has had over thirty years of experience as a hairstylist in Brazil. The potato starch–peach combination strengthens and revitalizes damaged, dry, or dull hair.

3 or 4 medium-size potatoes
2 cups water
1 peach (peeled)

1. Peel and wash potatoes, then cut them into chunks. Add water and refrigerate overnight in a covered bowl.

2. The next day, drain the water and save. (Discard the potatoes or add salt and pepper and cook for dinner.)

3. Puree the peach, then mix well with the potato water.

4. Apply the mixture to your hair and comb it through. Leave on for 20–30 minutes.

5. Rinse with water, and style as usual.

Glisten to Me

A gentle, all-natural hair spray that gives curls extra dimension and shine.

Vegetable glycerine (found at health food stores)
Distilled water (contains no minerals)
1 empty spray bottle (available at most drugstores)

Combine equal parts of glycerine and water in a spritz bottle and mix. Spray whenever your hair looks dull or needs a quick pick-me-up.

Hair Dressing

Here's a fabulous trick that adds shine to your hair and eliminates frizz; it works best for Corkscrew and very dry Botticelli curls. Pick up one of those sleek-looking oil spray misters at your houseware specialty store. Fill it with olive oil and a few drops of your favorite perfume essence, then spray hair after it's dry. I love the effect so much that I now use the spray mister every few days, or whenever my hair looks or feels especially dry. For best results, use olive, canola, or any kind of nut oil.

When I was living in Israel over twenty years ago, my greatest wish—shared by my first husband—was that I have long, straight hair. Once a week, I would wash my natural curls and commit an entire evening to a straightening process, then popular among Israeli women, called *abuagela*.

Using large clips to hold it in place, I would painstakingly wrap my hair around one side of my head and sit under a hooded hair dryer for forty-five minutes. Then, just as painstakingly, I'd repeat the process on the other side of my head. During Israel's five-month rainy season, all I had to do was step outside, and the results would be totally undone. When I married my first husband, I had the *abuagela* done by a professional. With the torrential rains that day, I was terrified that my hair would get frizzy and ruin the wedding. The wedding photos attest to the power of the *abuagela*—my hair remained straight, at least through the ceremony.

I freed myself from this wrapping-and-drying bondage one very hot summer when I was living on a kibbutz near the Lebanese border. I went to a beauty parlor where Moroccan and Yemenite immigrants —women with hair far kinkier than my own—had their soft, beautiful curls cut very short. I returned to the kibbutz a changed woman, much to my husband's disapproval. That may have been the moment our marriage started to fall apart.

At my second wedding, which also took place in Jerusalem, **I wore my hair curly.** Fifteen years later, I'm still married to the same man and wear my hair wild and free, all different lengths and shades of blond. The spiraling curls spring in every direction, uninhibited by the dictates of any artificially imposed style—a perfect metaphor for how I now try to live my life.

—NAOMI CHIEL-BOLZMAN, EDUCATOR AND CANTORIAL STUDENT

First wedding: hair subjected to the abuagela.

YOU GO, CURL!

African American Hair

*"Eventually I knew what hair wanted;
it wanted to be itself . . . to be left alone
by anyone, including me, who
did not love it as it was."*

—ALICE WALKER

Many of my curly girl clients are African American, and I tell them to follow my routine for caring for Corkscrew curls. They report particularly great results when they break the shampoo habit, which can cause serious damage to already dry hair and scalp that is a problem for the majority of African American women.

But I've also learned a great deal about curly hair care from them. For this chapter I've consulted with experts on African American hair and have asked a number of black women to tell their own hairstories. African American women have a lot to teach their curly-haired white sisters about hair care, including how often to wash it; how to hydrate very dry hair with conditioners and deep oil treatments; and what products to use.

Texturize and Hydrate

Joseph Plaskett Jr. is the co-owner of Joseph's, a family-run salon in Manhattan since 1958. Ninety percent of his clients are African American, but the shop often sees curly-haired white women, especially if they can't find a stylist who knows how to treat their corkscrew hair.

"If you want low-maintenance hair, natural is a good way to go," says Joseph. "If your hair is kinky, but you want a natural look, then you can soften and loosen the curl by texturizing it. We do a lot of texturizing in the salon, and the treatment does not damage the hair. I like an unstructured look, so if you have a good cut, you can just put some product in and rub your fingers through your hair—and let it do its thing.

"To keep hair healthy and shining, you need to hydrate the hair regularly with deep oil treatments, which most black women know because they grow up using pomades and oil treatments. At least once a week, apply vitamin E oil or an oil treatment to your scalp. (Any company that gears products to African Americans is going to have oil treatments.) Massage in, then comb through hair, using a wide-toothed comb. Preheat a heating cap and leave on for twenty minutes. Heat gives better penetration of the scalp. Then rinse thoroughly.

"In the salon, we like to do healthy things for African American hair," Joseph concludes. For example, instead of blow-drying hair or using curling irons, stylists roller-set the hair and put the client under the hair dryer. That way

Growing up, I was ashamed of having nappy hair. Both my grandmother and my mother always wore straight wigs, and I learned early in life that my looks were not acceptable. When I was a youngster, in the fifties, my mother used to sit me down in the kitchen every Saturday night and hold a hot comb to my head—we called this "getting our hair pressed"— so I'd look presentable for church. I don't have any childhood pictures with my hair in its natural state, only straightened.

In the sixties, I grew the biggest Afro I could, modeling myself after Angela Davis, whom I worshiped. I'd argue with people who called the Afro a "hairstyle." "This isn't a style, it's a way of life!" I'd say. Later on, I grew my hair into locks, which I call Nubian. I wore them for about seven years, until they were almost to my waist.

I'd been thinking about cutting off the locks for about six months. **First, though, I talked to my hair, because I believe that hair has living energy.**

I said, "You're very pretty, and I really appreciate all you've done for me; it was fun to see how long you could grow. Now I have to let you go."

My Afro wasn't a "style"—it was a way of life.

I now wear my hair cropped so close that you can see my scalp. When the hair starts to curl, I cut it off. (Actually, my husband cuts it with a pair of clippers we bought especially for this purpose.) I often ask myself, Why am I so intent on getting rid of the curls? Easy maintenance is part of it, but, also, I'm still caught up in ideas from my childhood of what hair is "supposed" to look like.

I used to obsess over having straight hair. I'm turning sixty this year, and now I'm working on not feeling that I have to look like someone else. **It's about attitude: if you're ashamed of your hair, you're not going to feel or look beautiful.** And as I start to appreciate myself as a person, I no longer see my hair as the summation of who I am. Like me, my hair is a work in progress.

—**BARBARA WALTERS,**
CLINICAL SOCIAL WORKER

you use less heat to style hair, as opposed to the huge amount you use blow-drying hair from wet to dry.

Khamit Kurls Care

Annu Prestonia, owner of the Khamit Kurls salon in New York City, has specialized in African American hair care for over two decades. "Unlike curly hair, kinky hair that's more than an inch long must be combed or brushed before it's allowed to dry," says Annu. Otherwise "the hair gets tangled up in knots and mats together." She recommends using a rubber vent brush or comb to get rid of tangled hair, but only after the hair has been thoroughly wet and conditioned. Brush the hair out in small sections, twist or braid each section, then allow it to dry.

"We are a subtropical people," says Annu. "Where there's sun and warmth, we don't have problems with our scalp and skin. But cold-weather climates (and indoor heating) encourage dry scalp." She suggests moisturizing the hair and scalp two or three times a week, with conditioners formulated from natural plant- and herb-based ingredients, such as honeysuckle, oranges, and rosemary, as well as shea butter and coconut, jojoba, and olive oils. Just as I tell my clients, Annu recommends using lots of conditioner after washing your hair—much more than what's suggested on the bottle. If you have the time, wrap your head in plastic wrap and leave the conditioner on for an additional twenty minutes. Then rinse thoroughly, because conditioner tends to leave a visible film on kinky hair. Annu also recommends that clients dry their hair naturally, if at all possible.

Eighty percent of clients at Khamit Kurls come in for hair extensions, which can be worn braided, twisted, or loose. Why do so many African American

I never had what was considered "good" hair among African Americans, because mine was kinky rather than curly. I'd go to my aunt's beauty salon, where we'd have our hair "fried, dyed, and laid to the side."

Then came the era of the gigantic Afro. My mother was horrified when I had my hair cut in a 'fro. Women of her generation had fought, at great personal cost, to look white, respectable, middle class. And there I was, flaunting my kinky hair, looking like a hippie—or, worse, a revolutionary.

By the late eighties, Afrocentric hair was more acceptable. Women's magazines featured articles on curly hair, and there was an influx of immigrants from the Caribbean and East Africa. Among them were professional hairdressers who showed us how to achieve a sense of personal style.

When I remember what a degrading and humiliating process getting my hair straightened was, I wish I'd had a hair support group. For the last five years, I've worn my hair in extensions. They're worth the investment of time and money because they're so much easier to care for. I feel much freer now that I wear my hair in braids. They have a lot of movement and a wonderful sculptural shape that complements my wardrobe and makes me feel confident about my appearance.

—**JANICE BURGESS,**
TELEVISION PRODUCER

women opt for extensions, which can be a time-consuming and expensive process? I ask. "Our hair is strong but fragile," explains Annu. "Daily grooming eventually wears away at its vitality. Our ancestors, in their genius, came up with styles that allowed the hair to rest for periods of time and still look beautiful. As far back as ancient Egypt, African women and men had extensions."

Today, African American women are just as likely to choose braids or locks because they want to preserve the health of their hair. And braids are a style whose time has definitely come.

When I do stage work I usually wear a wig, but when I go on auditions, I wear my hair natural. Most of the black women you see in commercials these days have curly hair—it's very "in" now.

I'm from a Jamaican background, where natural hair comes with a lot of stigma, but I'm not trying to make a political statement with my hair. (Though people often want me to.) A lot of black women get perms because they think it makes their hair more manageable.

A few years ago, when I had a perm, my hair was very thin and damaged and my scalp was very dry. My hair wasn't healthy, so **I started growing it out and wore extensions through the transitional period.** After I had two or three inches of natural hair, I took out the extensions and cut off the permed ends.

If I wash my hair and go, it tends to get really matted and I'm not able to put a comb through it when it's dry. I set my hair in straws as an antifrizz technique (see below). Since I've gone natural, my hair is much stronger. I wear my hair curly because I like the way it looks.

—SIMONE MOORE, ACTRESS AND MODEL

Simone's Straw Set

Simone Moore shared this straw set styling technique, which she uses to prevent frizz. It works best for short hair. (Hers is only three inches long all over.) You'll need: styling gel, plastic drinking straws (she cuts them in half; but if your hair is longer, you may want to use whole straws), and bobby pins.

After wetting and conditioning hair, comb it out using a wide-toothed comb, then apply styling gel to hair.

1. Holding the straw as you would a ruler, take a one-inch section of hair and gently roll the strand onto the straw, up and away from your forehead. Make sure you position the straw vertically, or at right angles to your scalp.

2. Insert a bobby pin through one end of the straw to secure.

3. Set hair in rows, working from the front of your head to the back. When you finish setting all of your hair, the straws will be in a pinwheel pattern. Allow your hair to air-dry or sit under a dryer for thirty minutes.

4. When you first take the straws out, the result may be too much of a Shirley Temple look for you, but then you can fingerstyle to loosen the curls. When dry, your hair is shiny and curly, rather than kinky.

My hair falls somewhere between kinky frizz and perfect curls. My sister, who has big, silky ringlets that I have always coveted, took charge of our hair when she was seven and I was five because my mother, whose hair is blond and straight, had no experience dealing with "mixed girl's hair."

My sister was very particular about doing our hair correctly. That meant putting it in two tight braids, the way all the other little girls—the black girls—put their hair up, and still do. But you didn't *just* put it in two braids; it was a real process. First, she'd part my hair perfectly—and I mean perfectly—down the middle. Then she'd use a brush specifically for coarse hair that made my scalp hurt. She'd use the elastic bands with the two colorful plastic balls attached and tie them extremely tight around the ends of both braids.

For a while we had a black nanny living with us. She was the epitome of everything I'd felt I was missing. Because I never had a black mom, I'd look to her for how to do my hair. We'd go to church with her, and she'd pull my hair back so hard that my eyelids would stretch and I felt as if my eyeballs would pop out.

At nine, I decided that I wanted to choose my own hairstyle, and

My sister took charge of our hair when I was five.

my mom brought me to a white-girl salon to get my hair relaxed. It was a big ordeal: they didn't know quite what to do with me. Once I started going to black hair salons the process turned out a little better—much straighter than the first time. I wore my hair straight, getting it done every two weeks, until my sophomore year of high school, when I attempted to wear it curly. When I got to school that day, one of my black friends told me that it looked like a dry Jheri-curl. Some white classmates said, "Your hair looks so cool." They thought that I had gotten a perm.

I really believe that when you wear your hair curly, everything starts falling into place. It's easier and natural. Today both African American and white people tell me they love my hair. **I'm lucky, because this is a good time to have curly hair.** It's considered cool now, and at twenty-two, I finally know how to take care of it.

—HILARY MITCHELL, TELEVISION PRODUCTION ASSISTANT

A CUTTING-EDGE PHILOSOPHY

A Crop of Curls

A stylist must approach each head and each curl as a separate entity with a mind of its own.

Getting a haircut is one of life's most traumatic moments for curly girls. No matter where you live, you've had at least one bad haircut in your life, maybe a lot more than that. You've asked for a trim and ended up completely shorn and looking like a skinned poodle; you've had an inexperienced stylist wet your hair down, then cut it as though it's straight, and you've ended up with mismatched and unflattering layers of angry curls. I've gone home in tears after a haircut, and so has almost every other curly girl in the world. So when a nervous customer sits down in front of me for the first time, I tell her I know where she's coming from. I explain her history so thoroughly, she thinks I've been spying on her. (Whatever our background, all curly girls share a common language about our hair.)

I begin by telling her that I'm going to give her a haircut that's just for her. Everyone's curly hair is different—in the tightness of curls, in how randomly the curls are distributed, and in how they grow naturally and frame the face. You'll never find the right cut in one of those books of styles that some salons pass around as if you're ordering a meal. You can't do that with curly hair.

In other words, there is no "style" for curly heads. I can't hand you a picture and say that's how you're going to look. You've been blessed with hair that has a mind of its own. Every strand is a separate entity that reacts differently to the scissors. The stylist has to approach each curl individually, considering its texture, its degree of curliness, and how it relates to the curls around it. I don't wet hair before a cut because I know that's a sure way to cut too much. Lopping off two inches all around on a curly head can leave the hair *five or six* inches shorter when the hair is dry. Cutting curly hair is about what you leave, not what you snip off.

Make sure your stylist listens to what you want.

I recently led a hair workshop for professional stylists on new and advanced styling and coloring techniques. Of the fifty or so men and women in the room, at least twenty-five had curly hair. I asked the curly heads how many of them had blow-dried their hair that day. At least ten people raised their hands. When I asked why, almost everyone said that blowing their hair straight was easier than trying to deal with curls. Finally, I asked how many of them *liked* their curls.

One woman stood up and said she could learn to love her curly hair if she could get it to look like mine. Most of the others nodded in agreement.

I wasn't surprised by their responses. I've yet to attend a hairdressing workshop in the United States that offered instructions on understanding and cutting curly hair, and I've seen very few curly-haired models participating in hairdressing seminars or classes.

In England, where the instruction is more comprehensive than what's offered in the United States, the emphasis is on cause and effect, explaining why certain techniques are preferable to others, and how every head

What lies beneath the canopy is a clue to what kind of cut a curly girl needs.

of hair requires an individualized approach. Each client has a different degree of movement and texture, a different hairline, a different cowlick. Curly hair is not predictable, which makes it impossible to categorize types of cuts. English and European stylists tend to cut hair dry, which makes excellent sense, for the simple reason that that's how we wear our hair. *It's also the only way to cut curly hair.*

My first-time clients are surprised when I don't send them off to have their hair washed immediately. Instead, I begin by asking the client to sit up straight in the chair, so I can examine her hair carefully. I pay attention to every movement, every contour, every characteristic. Is the hair frizzy? Overly dry? Stiff or crispy from too much gel or other products? Has it been straightened and dried out by blow-drying? Is the curl on the left side of the face tighter than the curl on the right side? Are the bangs begging for a trim? I listen to the client, but I also allow her hair to "tell" me its story, to let me know what its needs are.

I trim the curl a little at the ends to reduce frizz.

I next moisten the hair with lavender spray and scrunch it gently so that I can figure out the client's type of curl. Sometimes, especially if the hair has been blown dry, it needs a thorough wetting, so I have the client's hair washed with conditioner, scrunched, and dried under a heat lamp. Only then do I begin the actual cutting process.

Unless the client wants a much shorter look, which happens very rarely, most curly haircuts are about maintenance after the initial cut. Curls need to "read" their natural length. When I'm working on Corkscrew or Botticelli curls, I unfurl each curl and examine it as a separate entity, looking for frayed ends. I decide on the minimum amount that needs to be trimmed, then cut at the beginning of each curl to maintain its shape and avoid any

Magic Touch

An appointment with Lorraine is much more than a haircut. We talk about self-exploration and life issues, not just celebrity gossip. There's almost something magical about the way she touches my hair; I think it's because she really respects it.

—**NATHALIE WECHSLER, CLIENT**

Cut the curl at the beginning of each C.

dramatic spring-back. Think of a natural curl as an *S* shape. *S*'s are *C*'s reversed and sitting on top of each other. I cut the curl at the beginning of each *C*. While I'm cutting, I constantly shake the curls from the root to see where they lie and how they're going to fall when they're in motion, something you can't do when they're wet. And I try never to cut too much.

What's your natural length? It's that point when your curls flatter your face and fall gracefully. Some people need to grow their curls to shoulder length before the natural pattern of their curls emerges. Others have curls that can be cut shorter. I ask the client what length she's happiest with and try to accommodate her preference. In general, it's better for the client to leave the salon upset because her hair is too long rather than too short.

I start by pulling down the hair on either side of the face to make sure that it's even. I then look for pairs of curls or waves, which I call "Siamese twins"— a thick, heavy top layer of curls that is drooping and weighing down the curls beneath it. I divide a thick curl into two layers and trim one slightly shorter. The pattern and length of the exterior curl or wave is maintained, but it becomes bouncier because its load has been lightened. The newly shortened layer of curl pushes the longer curl outward and keeps it buoyant. In other words, the shorter curls support the longer curls and add volume to the hair.

To add volume: I divide a thick curl into two and trim one shorter.

This "super-in-position" method can also be used for curls that are top-heavy (i.e., all growing out at the same time).

You don't want bilevel curls, where the top layer looks as if it doesn't belong to the bottom layer. If the top layer of curls is still short, let it grow awhile. What you do want are seamless layers, which begin no higher than your chin. Tight curly hair tends to balloon out in an east-west direction, so that all the width of the hairdo is someplace around your chin. A cutter has to shape the curls carefully so this doesn't happen.

Above all, don't despair. If you find a stylist (see "Finding the Kindest Cut—and Cutter," pages 75–78) who's willing to listen to your hair needs and cut your hair dry, you will see a change. If a stylist has taken off too much, it may take six months before you really like your hair again. Be patient, follow my routine for conditioning and cleansing your hair—and your curls will heal themselves.

Finding the Kindest Cut
—and Cutter

You've come this far. You're a certified curly girl and you know how to care for your hair. It looks and feels better than it ever has. Now you have to find a good stylist, someone who can trim and shape your curls. Get the wrong person and all your hard work will be literally swept off the cutting room floor. Here are some of the things to think about and ask before you let anyone approach your hair with a scissors.

As every curly girl knows, finding a stylist who understands your hair is harder than finding a brain surgeon or a good defense attorney. The surest way, of course, is to see a haircutter's work. So when you spot someone with curly hair that looks wonderful, ask her where she has it cut. (Don't hesitate because you think it's intrusive; most people will be flattered by the question.) If you live in New York or Los Angeles, you might flip through

Curly Cut Dos and Don'ts

☐ *DO cut the hair when it is dry.*

☐ *DO avoid blunt cuts, which ignore the spring factor and stretch the hair to an unnatural state so it's too short when it dries.*

☐ *DO cut just before the crest of each curl.*

☐ *DO the top front of the hair last, and DON'T take too much off here because the curls are shortest and most fragile there.*

☐ *DON'T overly layer the hair.*

☐ *DON'T thin out fine curly hair. The gravity/weight of a strong curl is what gives hair definition.*

☐ *DON'T use a razor to cut curly hair. It isn't as sharp as scissors and can create badly frayed ends.*

magazines for a style you like, then check the credits for the name of the salon or stylist. Otherwise, keep asking around until you find someone whose hair looks great. Next step, phone the salon and ask the following questions:

- ☐ Is the stylist an expert at cutting curly hair?

- ☐ Does the stylist have naturally curly hair? Does she wear it curly? If so, this is a good sign.

- ☐ Will the stylist see you for a consultation? Don't be offended if the answer is no—it could mean she's so popular that she has no time. Some places charge for a consultation.

CURLY GIRL *confession*

For the last fifteen years or so, I wore my hair in long ringlets that cascaded down my back. **I cut my hair short twice—both times because I was involved with men who loved my hair long and they pissed me off. Men put so much value on hair.**

A couple of years ago, I was thinking about cutting my hair because my face had gotten thinner, I'd lost my chubby cheeks, and the long hair look wasn't doing it for me anymore. I'd been in a relationship for six years with a much younger boyfriend, a Frenchman, and we'd been trying to break it off for forever. When he went back to France, I did it. I had my ringlets cut off. The new, much shorter length felt cathartic and liberating.

Then my boyfriend called to say he wanted me to come to Paris for a visit. "You wouldn't want to see me," I told him. "I had all my hair chopped off." There was complete silence on the other end of the telephone. Finally he got up the nerve to ask why. "Because I can," I said.

—**LEONTINA LANGE, CLOTHING DESIGNER**

- [ ] Does the salon offer the option of drying the hair under heat lamps rather than with blow-dryers? Explain that you want to keep your hair curly.

- [ ] Does the stylist cut very curly hair while it's dry? If the answer is no, is he willing to listen and be open to a different approach? Unless a stylist can see how much spring there is in your curls, he won't understand your hair and he's likely to cut too much when it's wet, only to discover that fact after your hair dries.

- [ ] What products does the salon use? If you don't use shampoo and have a favorite conditioner, bring it with you and, politely, say that you prefer them to use it. Most stylists won't object, especially if your hair is in good condition.

Let's assume you got all the right answers and have made an appointment. But if, when you arrive, you're told to change and get your hair shampooed, a "bad hair" alert bell should go off. Instead, the stylist should sit you down, examine your hair, touch it, talk with you about your hair and what you envision having done—all before picking up the scissors. Pull a typical curl down to its farthest point and let go, so the stylist can see how tight the curl is. If your curls vary in tightness, show her which ones have a smaller spring factor. This is important so that she doesn't cut too much. Finally, explain that you'd rather leave your hair a bit too long than go too short.

Ideally, after the cut, the stylist should wet your hair and let it dry to see the finished results. This is the point when he or she makes those all-important final touches, picking up split ends that were missed the first time around or adjusting how the curls fall. You may want him to handpick and cut a few curls, especially around the front of your face.

Don't be afraid to talk to the stylist about your preferences, as long as you're polite. If this is a friendly neighborhood place, he may be happy to work with you and talk about curly hair problems. If this is a trendy big-city salon, your stylist may have an attitude problem, so be diplomatic but firm. After all, whose hair is it, anyway?

CURLY GIRL *confession*

People treat you more seriously when you have straight hair. They think curly hair is unprofessional. They want you to look tame and corporate, like an anchorwoman, with "anchor hair."

My five-year-old daughter, Josie, also has curly hair, but it's finer than mine and not as curly. She is thrilled when it's straight because most of her friends have straight hair. She also wants bangs, but if I let her have them, they'd curl up toward her forehead and look goofy, sort of like Hayley Mills in *The Parent Trap.*

I wear my hair curly when I'm rebellious and want to make a statement. It's my free-spirited, hippie look. It means I'm my own person, a solo flyer, and I don't have to conform to anyone's view of what a mother and working professional should look like.

—LUCY DANZIGER,
MAGAZINE EDITOR

COLOR ME CURLY

The Best Choices for Curls

By now, you're an expert on curly hair. You know how it differs from straight hair, you know that it requires special cutting and care, and you've learned how to live with it. Now that your daily routine nurtures your hair, you might want to shake things up a bit and experiment with your look by adding highlights or color.

Yes, color and curls *do* mix, especially now with the range of available color processes that can keep hair healthy looking. But you must take into account the special needs of curly hair and use color gently and sensibly. Curly hair absorbs damaging chemicals more easily because the cuticle around the hair shaft is open. "It also takes longer to recover from any damage, because the hair is so porous," says Denis DaSilva, the co-owner of Devachan. He and Shari Harbinger are the salon's color experts, and I consider them among the best colorists in the country.

Denis and Shari recommend using either semipermanent or demipermanent colors as the best choices for curly hair. "Semipermanent is not as damaging to the hair because it doesn't remove any of the natural color," says Shari. And the fewer ammonia-based products we use on our hair, the less dehydrated it becomes. Demipermanent color, however, is more effective on gray hair that may resist a milder coloring process.

At Devachan, we usually recommend that clients come back every four to six weeks for semipermanent color. Six weeks after the initial color treatment, we need to refresh the roots as well as the ends of the hair shaft. Beyond that period, most of the color will have faded or washed out.

Curly girls, especially those who have Corkscrew curls, should avoid dramatic color transformations overnight. Start with a demi- or semipermanent color that's close to your own, or two or three tones lighter. Live with it for a while before doing anything more drastic. Remember that all hair, but particularly curly hair, takes at least a week to recover from the trauma of being treated, and the depth and dimension of color will change as the curls return to their normal state.

As I often tell my clients, blond shouldn't be built in a day. If you do want to go from dark brown to blond, you need to build in the color over time. A couple of years ago, I decided I wanted a dramatic change. I waited until I knew for sure that my curls—and I—could deal with it, then chose a "good curl day"—a day when my hair looked great and I was feeling upbeat. I opted for a less caustic lightener and began by having just a few handpicked curls highlighted. I loved the results and the positive feedback I was getting, so I went for a full-blown lightening treatment. Now, I'm ready for a slightly different image; I'm going to introduce more "low lights," darker strands throughout the hair that will create contrasting colors. The result should be even more dramatic.

Even with semipermanent colors, the hair may lose some shine after coloring. Sometimes, after a color treatment, we use a gloss, a silicone-based product that restores shine and adds polish to the surface of the hair. We recommend glosses with a hint of color because they're more reflective and make hair richer and healthier looking. Glosses are a good choice, too, for gray hair that needs to look a little less yellow and more vibrant. They'll seal the cuticle, blend your gray hair, or make it shine like well-polished silver.

If you're in the mood for drama, you can have fun playing with highlights a few shades brighter than your natural color. At Devachan, we specialize in *pintura,* a highlighting technique invented by Denis. "The best way to highlight curly hair is to paint it on while the hair is dry," he says. "Painting is so visual that you need to see what you're doing to the hair."

"You're creating light on a canvas where there is no light," says Shari, "and you're defining the design of the cut." Curly hair is best for painting, because the colorist can pick out the more raised pieces of hair—the ones that best reflect the light. So you're guaranteed that you'll see the highlights exactly where you paint them. "If you paint the highlighted pieces too closely together," continues Shari, "you lose dimension, which curly hair needs. I leave a lot of space between each ribbon of light that

Pintura *coloring will give definition to your curls.*

After: *subtly brighter*

When I was growing up, I was obsessed with the story of Rapunzel and her long hair. I loved giving my long-haired dolls different hairstyles, because my parents forced me to keep my own hair short. They thought curls were meant to be tamed. **There is something about lots of curly hair that's very sexual, and parents don't like to see that in their kids.** My parents wanted me to behave like a nice, quiet girl from a good family. So I kept my hair "quiet," but I rebelled in *other* ways.

Then as soon as I was out on my own, I let my hair grow out and go wild. I now think that **my fascination with Rapunzel's hair has to do with becoming powerful and feeling in control.** Rapunzel's long hair gave her the power to escape from the tower. I grew my hair long when my parents were no longer able to control me—or my curls.

Today I work at an Internet company, where everyone else has tattoos and pierced body parts, so my wild hair is totally okay. In fact, people expect me to look unusual. People are fascinated by my curls; strangers stop me on the street, and many even ask to touch it. However, some things never change: even though I'm now thirty-six, my parents are still trying to "fix" my appearance. I'll be talking to my father, and he'll say in that tone, "Get your hair out of your face."

—NATHALIE WECHSLER, INTERNET COMPANY EXECUTIVE

I paint, so when the hair curls and sits away from the head, you see the contrast between the lighter and darker strands."

Before you have your hair colored, treat it very gently for a few weeks. Keep up the daily conditioning, and if you still shampoo, don't do it near the day of your color treatment. The harsh detergents in shampoos exacerbate the damaging effects of coloring. If you're opting for a new style, or getting your hair trimmed and shaped, get your hair cut first, then colored. After you get color, treat your hair with special TLC, using one of the moisturizing treatments recommended in chapter 5 (see pages 53–59). Remember that the more often you shampoo your hair, the more quickly the color will fade. (Another good reason not to shampoo!) You may want to use a color conditioner or mousse to minimize fading. Ask your colorist what he or she recommends. We sometimes custom-mix conditioning products for our clients, and your salon may offer a similar service.

Curls painted individually resemble ribbons of light.

Clients often ask me what I think about do-it-yourself coloring. Shari, Denis, and I all give a thumbs-down to the idea of home coloring. "If you have a discerning eye and artistic hand, it could work," says Shari. "But it takes longer for curly hair to recover from lost moisture than straight hair, so why take the chance?"

Denis agrees. "For curly girls, coloring kits can be a nightmare. The hair companies may call their products semipermanent, but the ingredients in home kits are the chemical equivalent of almost permanent color. Your hair is already dry and tends to frizz, so don't put it at risk by using overly strong solutions. You may think you'll save money, but if your hair is long, you'll end up spending more money than you might expect."

I grew up in a Turkish ghetto in Germany, one of eight children, and my mother used to give us all haircuts every six weeks. After I discovered that I had curls, I rebelled and started growing out my hair. By the time I was thirteen, it was thick and curly and reached to my hips. I have four very beautiful sisters, but I was the one with the beautiful hair.

My father used to taunt me, "If you didn't have your hair, you'd have to kill yourself, because you're ugly." His words hurt so much that one day when I was fourteen, I grabbed a pair of garden shears and chopped off all my hair, just to show him I didn't give a damn about beauty.

When I was in art school I went to my first hairdresser and had my hair dyed bright red, which was a real novelty in Germany in 1986. The other students, who loved to touch it, taunted me with the name *rote Hexe*—the red witch. But I liked that label.

Women in the German-Turkish ghetto where I grew up must ask their husband's permission before they can cut their hair. I've noticed that the first thing Turkish women do when they come to America is chop off their hair and straighten it. **When I moved to New York City, everyone told me to tie my hair back to get jobs, especially in the corporate world.** I straightened my hair only twice, and both times I got treated with more respect, as if I were a lady. My curly hair makes me more approachable, and men think they can talk to me in a freer way.

My curls tell a lot about me. Some days, if I don't feel good about myself, my hair just hangs there, as droopy as my spirits. Other days, if I'm happy or in love, my hair bounces and looks shiny. I've been getting a lot of compliments lately about my hair—things must be looking up!

—GÜLER UĞUR,
PHOTOGRAPHER

THE CARE AND HANDLING OF CURLY KIDS

Getting Kids to Like Their Curls

"**D**addy says that Amy looks like a little Greek goddess with her thick, black curls," is the very first entry in Amy Helfman's baby journal. I don't know what the later entries are, but I can guess one: "Amy's mom says that Amy's curly hair is driving her crazy." If you're the parent of a curly-haired kid, as I am, or if you've been one yourself, you know what I'm talking about. Curly hair can get into more messes than a two-year-old with a bucket of chocolate.

Kids are constantly running, tumbling, swinging, and jumping into mud puddles and piles of leaves. They throw sand at one another. They plop winter hats, dress-up hats, and baseball caps on top of their heads and never worry about whether their curls get matted or snarled. Until it comes time to wash those curls. Then oceans of tears get washed down the drain along with the sand and dirt.

I recommend treating kids' curly hair the same way I treat adults' hair. My younger son has very curly hair, and I stopped using shampoo on his hair

Best friends mirror each other; when Karly (right) stopped ironing her hair, so did Justine. Now they talk every day about their curls.

about the same time I stopped using it on my own. If I notice a dry patch on his scalp, I massage it gently with olive oil. He's never had cradle cap (a yellowish crust that often develops on infant scalps), and both his hair and his scalp look healthy and smell clean.

While baby shampoos usually are manufactured with detergents that are milder than most, it's still a good idea to *dilute the shampoo* with spring or distilled water before using it. Apply a small amount to the scalp and massage lightly. Resist the urge to work a generous amount of lather directly onto the hair, which will only ruffle the shaft and create even more snarls than already exist.

Ask your child to look up at the ceiling as you rinse the hair with water. Try to pour the water in the direction that the hair is growing, to help smooth the tangles and evenly distribute the shampoo. Continue rinsing until the water runs clear and you're satisfied that the shampoo has been flushed away.

Apply conditioner. If your child has baby-fine hair, use only a very small amount of conditioner, perhaps as little as a quarter teaspoon, or apply it only to the ends of the hair. Comb it through wet hair, beginning at the ends, and gently work your way up, using either a medium-toothed comb or your fingers to separate the tangles. (Never use a brush, which can turn the curls into a mass of frizz.) Rinse thoroughly, then reapply another quarter to half teaspoon of conditioner, depending on the texture and length of the curls.

Just Checking, Mom

My hair is like the waves, my hair is like the rug—curly zigzags. None of my friends has curly hair. My best friend has straight blond hair. I always ask my mom, "How do I get hair like that?" My mom's the only one I know who's curlier than me. She says she loves her hair. Some days I ask her, "Do you still like your hair?—Just checking, Mom."

Izzy (right) with mom and sister, Sophie.

—**Izzy Mandel, age 7**

If your curly-haired daughter insists on wearing her hair straight, comb it and put it in a ponytail to dry. Or braid the hair while it's still wet, which will help eliminate frizz. For curly styles, blot dry with a towel, apply a small amount of gel, and scrunch, as described in "Curls on the Go," page 45.

You can make your own detangling spray by combining an equal amount of water and conditioner in a spray bottle. This works wonders on curly kids' hair, which is healthier and more hydrated than ours so their curls usually don't need full-strength conditioning. Use your judgment: older girls with long, thick curls will need more conditioner than a younger child with short, fine hair.

What happens when your curly kid comes home with glue, paste, or a wad of gum in her hair? Rub the area with an ice cube until the sticky mess hardens and begins to crumble, then dab on a few drops of vinegar and about half a teaspoon of conditioner, depending on the size of the substance. Gently work it out with your fingers, rinse with the detangling spray, and comb through again, using more conditioner, if necessary.

My kids are used to my spritzing them with Lavender Mist (see recipe on page 53). It's great in the morning when they wake up with ruffled hair. I also use it to give their hair a quick rinse after a day at the beach. A little-known side benefit for school-age kids: the lavender spray is a great deterrent against lice.

Cozy Wolan, owner of Cozy's Cuts for Kids in New York City, usually assigns curly-haired stylists the job of cutting curly kids' hair. She and I agree that kids need haircuts that simplify

Cut #2: short bob with bangs

grooming. "Most kids won't sit still for more than two seconds when they're having their hair combed, so a child's haircut shouldn't require styling or blow-drying," she says.

I suggest two basic styles for curly kids. You can go for a very free and natural look, allowing the hair to follow its intrinsic shape, whether waves, ringlets, or smaller curls. This works very well for both girls and boys, although older boys are apt to resist a head of ringlets, no matter how charming it looks to you. For very easy care, cut your little curly girl's hair in a short bob with bangs. Keep the hair all one length, but allow a bit of an east-west direction—

Cut #1: free and natural

it looks adorable on little girls.

Getting Kids to Like Their Curls

Luckily for curly kids today, curls are in! Magazines that once showed nothing but straight lank hair now do features on how you can make your straight hair curly—quite a fashion reversal! But old prejudices die hard, and some kids are still made to feel that their curls are different, weird, funny. Cozy has tiny clients who come in regularly to have their hair blown straight. "I don't know where it comes from," she says. "But I see kids of five or six who are unhappy about their curls."

My own clients frequently tell me that they hated their curls from a very young age. And only a few years ago, I met a little girl who couldn't have been more than four years old whose father told me, "She hates her curls, so we try to point out women who have beautiful curly hair." The child had a head of gorgeous ringlets, but when I complimented her on them, she frowned at me and hid her head in her father's coat. It can be a casual remark, made in the child's company, or just the fact of making too much of a small child's hair. But children are quick to pick up on prejudices of all kinds.

Take advantage of today's trend to point out the benefits of curls to your own curly tops. But don't make a big deal out of it, or they'll figure something's up. Instead, once in a while, point out a woman with beautiful curly hair. Or talk about how much you like your own curls.

If you have straight hair and your child is curly, find her a curly-haired mentor—someone she can bond with over hair, its glory, its problems, and its orneriness. I might have avoided years of agony, especially during my adolescence, if only I'd known a curly girl to talk to. I'd spend hours in front of the mirror sobbing because I looked so hideous. When it was really humid, I'd wear my brother's balaclava, a woolen cap that fit skintight.

That's why I try to be a mentor to any curly-haired child or teenager who needs it. I think my teenage years would have been very different if only an enlightened curly girl had taken me under her wing and said, "Call me if you have any questions about how to take care of your curls."

If You're Straight and Your Kid Is Curly . . .

I'm white, and my husband is black. Our daughter, Naisha, has very thick, kinky hair. I didn't have a clue about how to treat her hair when she was a baby, so I left it short and curly until she was about a year and a half old. Then a friend said, **"You better learn how to take care of it, so people won't think you're a white mom who doesn't know how to deal with black hair."** About that time, a Caribbean woman started babysitting for Naisha, and she showed me how to create cornrows that kept her hair from getting matted. Generations of black women have taught one another how to care for their kinky hair. When you're grafted onto the culture, you have to find someone, as I did, to advise you.

Naisha is eight now, and my routine for maintaining her shoulder-length hair takes at least an hour and a half. After I shampoo and comb out her hair, using lots of conditioner, I set her up in front of a video and start sectioning the hair to make cornrows. It's a bit of an ordeal, especially as her hair begins to dry and gets tangled more easily. When we're finished, I often ask her, "Was it worth the pain? Would you want to do it again?" Up to now, her answer has been yes.

Although Naisha says she loves how her hair looks, she says if she had a magic wand, she'd give herself straight blond hair. That's so ironic, because as a little girl, I didn't like my hair because it was thin and stringy. I thought the black girls who wore the braided styles were really neat. Now I enjoy making cornrows, and I sometimes tell Naisha that taking care of her hair "is a privilege and a treat."

—PATRICIA HOGAN, OCCUPATIONAL THERAPIST

CURLY GIRL Q & A

No More Bad Hair Days

Q: What can I do for an itchy scalp?

A: This may sound flip, but my first answer is: Scratch it! An occasional itch is perfectly normal and doesn't necessarily signify a problem. Our skin constantly responds to stimuli in the environment. As I'm writing this sentence, the little finger of my left hand feels itchy, yet my skin looks perfectly healthy and rash-free.

If you're recovering from a longtime addiction to shampoo, your scalp will probably feel itchy a couple of days after you stop using it. An itch is often a sign that your scalp is healing, much like a scab does before it begins to heal. Though your scalp is starting to heal from a constant state of dehydration, an itch is a signal that it needs still more moisture.

If you have severely dry hair, make the Exfoliating Scrub on page 38. Wet your hair thoroughly, then massage in the scrub. If you tend to have combination skin and hair, wet the hair and give your scalp a massage without the conditioner. Start at the hairline using a circular motion. First, tackle the sides and crown and then move down to the nape of the neck. Repeat the treatment every three days for a week.

You can also try spot-cleaning (see page 33) or spritzing your scalp with Lavender Mist (see page 53), which contains natural medicinal properties that help cleanse the skin.

If the itching continues or becomes more severe, consult a dermatologist.

Q: My hair looks dull. How can I get it to shine?

A: First, how long have you been following my curly hair treatment routine? Give it two or three weeks before you expect miracles.

Your hair responds to the way you treat it. What are you doing to your hair that might cause dullness? Give up the myth that brushing one hundred strokes a night is good for your hair and donate your hairbrush to someone who needs it, maybe your cat or dog. Brushing can damage the cuticle of curly hair and rob it of its sheen.

If your hair really does appear dull, consider getting a semipermanent gloss for added shine. The gloss coats and seals the hair shaft so that it looks shinier than usual. You can get this treatment at a salon, and it will keep your hair shining for weeks. (See page 80.)

By the way, before deciding your hair is too dull, check out the light in your bathroom. We often judge ourselves based on what we see as we're standing in a small bathroom that's lit by fluorescent light directly above our heads. Try looking in a mirror when you're outside in natural light. This will give you a much better idea of the true state of your hair.

A: Hair grows half an inch a month, sometimes even as much as an inch a month. If you can't get to the salon when you need a touch-up, try camouflaging your roots by using the crossover trick:

Part your hair, then pick out two small sections of hair at the middle of the crown, on either side of the part. Cross the strands over each other, and pin

into place with a bobby pin. Continue working your way toward your forehead, until you've covered the part with three or four sections of hair. If you do this while your hair is wet, the sections will dry unevenly and cover up the part where the roots show. The idea is to create a landscape of mini hills and valleys that provides natural cover for your roots. In a pinch, you can use mascara on the roots. (They now make "hair mascara" in light and dark shades just for this purpose.)

A: I see many women whose hair is fuller and bouncier during pregnancy, but the front of their hair breaks more easily. You can restore the health of your hair after your baby is born by cutting off some of the length. About three to eight months after you give birth, or after you've stopped breast-feeding, your hair may show signs of breakage. Instead of your usual trim, cut off a couple of inches. This will decrease the weight pulling on the follicles.

If you notice that your hair won't grow past a certain point, it may have less to do with your pregnancy and more to do with your hair routine. Overwashing, brushing, or too much coloring can fray the ends and cause the hair to break.

Q: I swim in a pool three or four times a week. How is the chlorine affecting my curly hair?

A: You can judge how high a pool's chlorine levels are by how quickly the color of your bathing suit begins to fade. Imagine what that does to your hair. If you plan to spend the day at the pool, mix up a pint of distilled water with a table-spoon of conditioner and put it in a spray bottle. Spritz as soon as you get out of the pool.

You absolutely do not have to shampoo your hair after swimming in a chlorinated pool, because that just subjects your hair to more drying chemicals and dehydration. Instead, flush thoroughly with water when you shower, then use a tablespoon of conditioner or Lemon Aid (see page 55) to cleanse your scalp and hair. Rinse thoroughly, and reapply conditioner as you normally would.

Try to wear a hat in the sun. It will protect your complexion, as well as your hair, from harmful ultraviolet rays.

A: I love the way my hair looks at the beach—the combination of sea salt and ocean breeze is a tonic for my curls. The sea salt is good for your hair, so don't rush to rinse it off. The salt helps separate the curls and gives them definition, and the breeze helps your hair dry faster, so the frizz factor is reduced. Bring a leave-in conditioner with sunblock in a spray bottle and spray your hair after you get out of the ocean. At the end of the day, follow the conditioning routine described on page 94 to keep your hair hydrated.

Watery Beginnings

I often have the fantasy that curly girls are mermaids who have had to adapt to life on dry land. We come from the sea. The ocean is in our blood. It sings through our heart and lungs, our skin and hair. Our curls require the nourishment only a watery environment can provide. Both ocean waves and curly hair are forces of nature that can't be tamed. We can only accept and admire their power and beauty.

I often borrow from the vocabulary of the ocean when I talk about curls. Like the waves in our hair, ocean waves form consecutive *C*'s. The highest point of a wave is the crest or peak; the lowest part is called the trough. Tossed by the wind and the elements, the ocean waves ebb and recede like our curls expanding and receding according to the dictates of the weather and our states of mind. We can never transform their essential properties.

Being near the ocean feels like coming home to curly girls. Our hair and our selves thrive at the seashore. The combination of salt, wind, and water is a gift from the sea, a beckoning spray that feeds our curls and revives memories of our long-forgotten origins.

Q: How do I prevent hat hair?

A: Some curly girls think that wearing hats will make hair both flat and frizzy. But in fact, hats can reduce frizz; they act as a hairnet and keep hair in place as it dries. Before you put on your hat, use one of the pin tricks (see page 36) to keep the roots lifted.

When you take your hat off, loosen the curls by bending over, shaking your head a little, then fluffing them from underneath. To give the top layer of hair a quick lift, pick out a few of the flattened curls and spritz lightly with lavender spray or water. Twist each section around your index finger, then slide the curl off and either pin or hold it in place with your fingers for a couple of minutes. (If water isn't available, just lick your finger to create the proverbial spit curl.)

Q: I'm going through menopause. Can the hot flashes and night sweats negatively affect my hair?

A: While hot flashes may feel strange or uncomfortable, curly hair can actually benefit from the extra moisture that you're suddenly producing.

Sweat, as I've said earlier, is salt water, a part of the body's ecosystem and a natural cleansing agent. If the hot flashes are especially frequent or severe, you may want to wear your hair up, especially in situations when you feel you need to keep your cool. Be sure to carry a travel-size bottle of Lavender Mist (see page 53) in your bag and car for a quick refreshing spritz to your hair, face, neck, or wherever you need it.

Q: I'm having a bad hair day. Help!

A: *There's no such thing as a bad hair day.* Okay, I'll admit that some days are more challenging than others. You're rushing off first thing in the morning and forget to put in enough conditioner or gel. A strong gust of wind disturbs the topography of your perfectly well-defined curls. You go shopping, try on lots of sweaters, and leave the dressing room with your hair flying out in all directions. What do you do, short of plopping on a hat or pulling the curls back in a ponytail?

Spritz your hair with water or lavender spray, wrap a few curls around your finger for a couple of minutes, and clip them at the roots. You've restored your curls and re-created your hairdo.

Here's another "quick save" trick: Bend your head so that your hair falls forward. Place your fingers about an inch from the roots and give the bottom layer of hair a quick shuffle so that it reconnects with the canopy. Decide you can feel okay today about a slightly wilder style. Notice how much positive feedback you get from friends—and strangers. You're a curly girl, so even if your hair isn't behaving the way you'd want it to, love your curls and wear them proudly.

Fluffing from beneath

When I was little, my mother cut my hair very short—just two inches all over—so we wouldn't get into so many fights when she brushed it. I lived with that Bozo hair until second or third grade. It was the 1980s, and everyone had feathered hair. **I wanted to look like Daisy in *The Dukes of Hazzard*.** So I asked a hairdresser to feather mine. She layered both sides, which just made the curls tighter and frizzier and I looked like I was wearing earmuffs. It was mortifying. (Now I know enough about curly hair to never let a hairdresser layer my hair.)

Today I let my curls grow out, but if my hair gets wet and dries without conditioner, it will still frizz up and look like a dandelion gone to seed. Not a good look.

—**HEATHER CONWAY-VISSER, GRAPHIC DESIGNER**

Q: My hair sometimes looks stringy, not curly. Is this from too much product or what?

A: You're probably applying too much conditioner to the ends, which absorb products less readily because they're older. Also, combing your hair unnecessarily can cause a stringy, noodle-like appearance.

Try scrunching with a spritz of Lavender Mist (see page 53) instead, and you'll probably see a change. If your ends still appear to be weighed down, they may need a trimming.

Q: How can I reduce the number of products I use and simplify my hair routine?

A: Not only do all the bottles and jars take up shelf space, but they can lead to a vicious cycle of product abuse. You become more and more dependent on an ever-expanding assortment of treatments and products, instead of caring for your curls with a simple, natural routine. Resist the urge to buy new products that promise hair greatness.

Now that you've learned how to care for your curls, you can liberate yourself by throwing out most of the bottles and jars gathering dust in the bathroom. Reduce your collection to three simple basics: a conditioner (instead of shampoo), an herbal cleanser, and a styling gel. Our curls need very little more than TLC and moisture to flourish and look beautiful.

Q: I'm very rushed in the morning. Do I need to wet my hair every day?

A: Your hair will tell you whether or not it needs a daily dose of water to look its best. Some curly girls report that wetting their hair once every two or three days works fine for them. (This is almost never true for Corkscrew curly girls.) You be the judge. Remember, hair care is voluntary, but if you feel you don't have time even for a quick spritz in the morning, you may want to reevaluate your schedule—or your self-image.

Q: I travel a lot. How do I protect my hair from the changes in climate and water?

A: Your hair is a natural weather barometer, so trust what it tells you. Adjust your hair care routine, depending on where you are and how your curls are responding. You may need less conditioner in Los Angeles, because the weather is generally dry; more in England, where the frequent drizzle and fog can bring out the frizzies in even the best-behaved curls. Don't leave home without your conditioner and herbal spray, both of which will see you through almost any climatic situation. (In a pinch your conditioner can also substitute as hand cream or body lotion and vice versa.) Be sure to pack some herbal spray in your carry-on bag to hydrate your skin *and* quench thirsty curls on long flights. The friendly skies are never forgiving to your locks.

Q: What is clarifying shampoo or rinse, and does it restore shine?

A: You've obviously figured out by now that I don't put much faith in shampoos. I have even less confidence in specialty products such as après-pool or clarifying shampoos and conditioners. These products are merely another way to sell you more of what you've already bought and are often even harsher on the hair than regular shampoo. They strip your hair of any hydration, whether your own or that from the conditioner you use. Don't waste your money on one more cleverly packaged product that will inevitably wind up in the garbage.

A: Any of the above, alone or in combination, can have a profound effect on your curls. As a nonessential organ, your hair is at the bottom of the physiologic hierarchy, so it's likely to be neglected by the body when the immune system is fighting disease or depression. Even the mildest medications may have side effects, and your hair is not immune to these reactions. One client swears that when she takes decongestants for a day or two, her normally bouncy curls get dry and flat.

An emotional crisis can often result in a breakout of hives, pimples, or cold sores. It shouldn't be a surprise, then, if your scalp and hair also reflect your emotional state. If you lose your job or break up with your boyfriend, you're likely to eat badly, stay up too late, and lie in bed instead of exercising.

Your hair will bounce back as soon as you do. In the meantime, keep it tied back lightly, don't skimp on conditioner, drink plenty of water, and, above all, don't make any drastic changes in your hairstyle. Wait until you're recovered to experiment with a new cut or a different color. If you don't feel well, your hair won't look good, no matter what you do to it.

A: No, not if your intention is to straighten it. But if the weather is frigid, and you're in a rush to leave the house, you can use a blow-dryer with a diffuser, or a travel hair dryer, on the "low" setting. Dry slowly to protect your hair from singeing or getting overheated.

Q: How do I avoid a bad case of the frizzies?

A: Curly hair reacts strongly to every change in atmospheric conditions, whether it's high or low humidity, rain, sun, sleet . . . As humidity rises, very dry curls (especially the corkscrew variety) begin to move out in an east-west direction. On rainy or high-humidity days, be sure to wet your hair thoroughly, rather than giving it a quick spritz, and experiment with using extra conditioner. The additional residue will help pull your hair down and keep it moving south instead of east-west. And don't linger too long in a steamy bathroom after showering.

Another frizz-buster I recently

A cool rinse seals cuticles.

discovered is giving curls one last cool rinse to seal the cuticles before styling. Fill a bowl with cool water or seltzer and dunk your head in after you get out of the shower. Towel-dry as much of the moisture as possible, then put about half a teaspoon of gel on the canopy to keep it smooth. Don't touch your hair once you've applied the gel, no matter how tempted you are to pat the strands into place. This is a general rule for curly girls that becomes particularly important on frizz-prone days.

If you have a special date or meeting, you can protect your locks and encourage your curls to swell to their natural state by *loosely* covering your head with a light scarf for about ten minutes after you've finished styling your hair.

One more thought on the subject of frizz: It is not necessarily a bad

After chemically relaxing my hair for so many years, going curly was a life-transforming experience. I've learned to love my curls rather than be afraid of them. I've saved myself so much time and heartache in the morning, and I no longer hate my hair. **I've become such a huge advocate of curly hair that any time I see a curly girl, I make a beeline to her and say, "I have to tell you what I know!"** Then I'll tell her about how I wash and dry it, about the bobby pin trick—they always appreciate this.

For me, there's no turning back from being a curly girl. Sometimes I'll see girls with cute pixie cuts and wish I could carry off that hairstyle. But then I'll think to myself, that's okay, they'll never be able to wear their hair long and curly, like mine.

All my life I've been the tall girl with dark curly hair and I've *finally,* happily come to terms with it. **I love my crazy, tight, banana curls— straight hair just isn't me.**

I know that sometimes during pregnancy one's hair can change dramatically. I dread the possibility that someday my hair might lose its curl.

—**TRACY KESSLER, PRODUCER OF LIVE ENTERTAINMENT EVENTS**

thing. I personally prefer a gentle halo of frizz around my head to stick-thin, petrified curls so coated with product that they remain stationary when you move your head. As an advanced curly girl (and I have clients who feel similarly), I think that if hair is healthy and the curls are basically well defined, frizzy can be sexy. I've received so many compliments on days when I haven't fought the frizz that I now accept it as one of the ways in which my curls sometimes choose to express themselves.

Q: Why does the front of my hair never seem to grow as long as the back?

A: Nothing frames a face better than a few shorter, curly locks of hair. The hair around your face is a protective barrier for the rest of your hair. It is constantly exposed to wind, rain, heat, and other environmental factors, and therefore it has a shorter life span. So don't be surprised if you can't grow out your bangs past your chin.

However, you can mend and protect the tendrils around your face by treating them gently and nurturing them with extra doses of conditioner. Pay attention to the damage you may be inflicting unwittingly. Are you constantly pulling your hair, twirling your bangs, or running your fingers through the strands? Always handle hair with care, and *only when absolutely necessary.*

Q: Why are my bangs so hard to control, and how do I encourage the curls to emerge?

A: Many curly girls complain of problem bangs. Let me be perfectly frank: your bangs will never lie flat. Accept the fact that a Louise Brooks "fringe" on the forehead is not in your future. However, it is possible to have funky, cropped bangs, or two or three curls that form a kind of bang, to frame and soften your face. Be sure to have your bangs cut dry, and never cut them straight across. Between the sunlight, wind, rain, blasts of hot air from the oven, and cold air from the

My hair is on the frizzy side of curly. I wore it in pigtails when I was growing up, then blow-dryers came out and changed my life. I'd blow-dry my hair for forty-five minutes a day, five times a week. It was the seventies, and if I didn't do that, it would get bushy and stick out. I had lots of split ends. My sister would wrap my hair in orange juice cans. **I wore it long and straight, parted in the middle, trying for that Gloria Steinem look.** We had a swimming pool, but I'd never go swimming. It would ruin my hair.

Then I went to England, to study history at Oxford, and I cut my hair very

short—two inches all around. At Oxford, what you looked like said less about you than it does here. I really played with my hair there. I even dyed it pink.

Now, I love the fact that my hair is curly. Hairdressers still say, "It's too bushy, you need to go shorter or have it blown straight." But I ignore them. My daughter, who's four, has curly auburn hair. It's incredible. **I must have done something right: she loves her curls.**

—FRAN KELLNER, LAWYER

freezer, the hair around the forehead is the most delicate and weakest, so be kind to your bangs with regular conditioning. Finally, if your bangs simply aren't behaving one day, use the pin curl trick to keep them bouncy and well defined. Pull a curl out and place it where you want it. Put a clip at the root to hold it in place for a few minutes. Spray with water or a spray gel. Be patient. When it's dry, carefully remove the clip.

Q: How can I get rid of static?

A: Most curly girls don't have much of a static problem, once they throw away the hairbrush, use plenty of conditioner, and either eliminate or cut way back on shampoo.

If you do have severe static, however, I recommend using static-cling sheets: yes, the kind you throw in the clothes dryer. Pat gently across the top layer of your hair, and the static will disappear.

Q: Should I do anything special to my hair before I go to sleep at night?

A: If your hair is long, tie it back lightly to reduce tangling. You may sometimes also add extra conditioner or apply one of the moisturizing treatments I've suggested and leave on overnight. If so, be sure to use an old pillowcase or towel so as not to stain your regular cases with oil.

On other nights, use a sateen pillowcase or one with a high thread count to reduce friction and minimize split ends. The softer and more luxurious the cotton, the less damage it will do to your hair. And you may sleep better, too!

Q: What's the best way to tie back or put my curly hair in a ponytail without causing breakage?

A: Use a "scrunchie"—a ponytail holder that's covered with fabric—hair sticks or chopsticks, or a leather-covered clasp held in place with wooden sticks. Never use rubber bands or any other kind of elastic that could tug or tear your hair.

Tied in a Knot

Tie your curls back *with* your curls. To get hair off your face or for end-of-the-day-hair-droop, try this pretty solution.

First pull your hair back. Take a one-inch section of hair from behind each ear. Cross the two strands over the rest of your hair and tie. Then pull a couple of curls out around the front, to frame your face.

Q: I know I have to give up the blow-dryer habit, but I'm afraid that if I go natural, my hair will look terrible. How long will it take before my curls start to look good?

A: If your hair is wavy, you'll see more curls within three weeks; if you're a Botticelli or Corkscrew, you'll notice a difference in less time, possibly within two weeks. Although your hair will love going natural, *you* yourself may need some time to get used to your new look. Get over the notion that your hair will bend to your will.

Learn what it wants and needs to look good—maybe more gel on a humid day or more conditioner in the winter. Your curls will look great even if they don't conform to your exact vision. Trust me, that vision will change as you acknowledge that you're a curly girl. After all, if you don't accept who you are, how do you expect others to?

LOOKS FOR SPECIAL OCCASIONS

Easy Updos

I usually wear my hair down, because after so many years of hating my hair and feeling unattractive, I love to flaunt my curls. It's another way of telling the world that I'm proud to be a curly girl. I also enjoy the sensation of ringlets bouncing against my neck and around my face. But some days I wake up in the mood for something different, whether it's because the weather is hot and sticky or because I'm going out to dinner and want my hair to project that "special occasion" aura.

Your ringlets also have the unique ability to be delicately sculpted and piled high on your head. A simple updo will stay better—and endure for a longer period of time—on curly hair than on straight.

The first rule in any updo is to not over do. If a few extra ringlets fall out, leave them—an updo should show off your curls. Though ribbons, barrettes, and clips may dress up your hair beautifully, your natural curls will make any updo look romantic and classy.

Here are a few simple updos that are sexy, playful, funky, and, best of all, easy to create. Use caution when handpicking and parting the hair. You don't want to create snarls or knots.

Building a Foundation

Any secure building needs a foundation. When creating an updo, the same rule holds true. This technique gives you a solid base for the following two hairstyles, and it works for most hair lengths.

To build your base:

1. Part hair loosely in the center of the crown. Take a one-inch section of hair from the back of the crown (where your part ends). Lift it up and away from your crown, twisting firmly toward the forehead.

2. Roll the piece of hair around itself and into a tight, round coil.

3. Secure the first bobby pin diagonally, across the twist; then secure the second bobby pin so that it forms an *X* across the first pin. The

coil will stand out quite a bit from the scalp, which will give your updo some nice height at the crown. Now you're ready to build up from your base.

The "It" Curl

This romantic look for Botticelli curls works best with shoulder-length hair. Wait until your hair is dry and you've built a foundation (see facing page).

1. Beginning on one side of the part, pick up a small section of hair that falls in front of your ear, twist it firmly, starting at the root, all the way down to the end.

2. Bring the twist up so that it lies against or near your foundation. Secure it in place with a bobby pin. Repeat as above on the other side of your head.

3. Bring the twist up so that it meets the first section. Secure this piece with one or two bobby pins.

You may stop at this point for a simple version or continue with as many pieces as you'd like, building in "twos" (i.e., one section of hair from each side of your part). Gently tease out a couple of curly tendrils just at the hairline on both sides of your forehead, to create a soft, sexy frame for your face.

Curls' Night Out

For chin-length Botticelli or Wavy girls. With the variations below, this style can easily go from funky and tousled for day to a sexy after-hours look. First build your base (see page 110).

1. Beginning in the front at the hairline, twist a one-inch piece of hair back and away from your face. Continue making a loose, flat twist until it is possible to pin it to the foundation.

2. Repeat on the opposite side. Continue, working with equal amounts of hair from both sides of your head, until you've completely pinned up the top layer of hair.

3. Now take one-inch pieces from the nape of your neck, this time twisting up toward the top of your head.

4. Pin each piece at the crown but leave the ends loose. (Use two pins to keep your updo extra secure.) Pull a few ringlets out from the sides, near your ears, to frame your face.

You may want to clip a pretty barrette at the top to complete the look. Or, be a princess for the evening and don a tiara atop your crowning glory of curls.

Corset Curls

[or Viking Maiden Meets Native American Princess]

This grown-up version of a ponytail works best on long-haired Botticelli or Wavy girls. Use a thin thread of black leather, about eighteen to twenty inches long and one-quarter to one-half inch wide, for an edgy, sexy, downtown look.

1. Gather hair gently to one side and pull over your shoulder. Tie a piece of leather around once and knot, to create a ponytail. You can make a tie at the nape or lower, at the collarbone.

2. Crisscross the leather down and around the hair to make a series of *X*'s. At about two inches from the ends of the curls, tie the leather and let the ends fall free.

Knot for Everyone

This top-knot style looks great on all curly girls—Corkscrew, Botticelli, and Wavy. The knots create an eye-catching texture and keep your hair out of your face.

1. While hair is fairly damp (or moistened with lavender spray), part in the middle. Take a one-inch strand of hair from each side of the part. Lift straight up and, as if tying a shoelace, knot once but don't tie completely.

2. Next, pass each strand through once more to create a kind of rolled knot at the crown. Do this by bringing the left strand through (from back to front) and the right strand through (from front to back).

3. Now complete the knot by pulling the ends tight. I find that three or four top knots in a row look best, but you can tie fewer or more.

Goddess Curl

For long-haired girls with Corkscrew curls, this goddess updo is a great look when you're in the mood for something different. It can be dressed up for evening by following the suggestions on the next page.

1. Gather your hair at the nape of the neck and twist it gently, rolling the twist inward up the back of your head in the direction of the crown. This creates a crease or seam in the back. When you've twisted the strands as far as they will reach, hold your hair in place with one hand.

2. With your free hand, secure the twist to your crown by inserting two bobby pins in an *X*-shape at the top of the crease of the twist.

3. You may need to use several more bobby pins to weave the crease of the twist into the hair at your crown. Separate out a few of the curls to soften the look.

If you have short hair, follow the instructions above, but make the twist very tight, and use as many bobby pins as you need to secure the shorter strands of hair.

For a romantic twist on the "Goddess Curl," take a strand of colored ribbon or leather, lay it flat just behind the hairline so it looks like a headband, and twist it around your head.

1. Make a knot at the back of your neck, crisscross twice around the chignon, and bring the ends up to cross at the top of your head.

2. Knot or pin the ribbon in place with tiny sequined clips, leaving the ribbon to hang free. Or dress it up by inserting a fresh or dried flower at the side where the twist meets your crown or in the crease of the chignon.

Weight a Minute

How many times has this happened to you? You're about to go out for the evening, but it's humid and your curls have contracted to a third their normal length, and your best friend, who should know better, asks you whether you just got a haircut, because "Your hair looks so much shorter."

If you notice as your hair is drying that your curls are shrinking, attach a hair clip to the bottom of your curls at the back of your head and the sides for five or ten minutes.

You can also attach the clipped hair to your shirt or sweater. (It may sound silly, but it works.) The weight of the clip will stretch out the strand and naturally reduce the spring factor.

Nip 'n' Tuck

Sometimes it's fun to go short. If you're not willing to commit to a cut, fake it with a fetching faux bob, circa 1920s. This 'do works best on shoulder-length or longer curls.

1. Pull all of your hair back as if putting it in a ponytail. Wrap an elastic band around the gathered hair about 1½ to 2 inches from the ends.

2. Next, roll the tail under to whatever "length" you prefer. It will look best just around chin level.

3. Secure the hair with at least four bobby pins, using the crossover technique, and fasten under the hair, at the nape of your neck.

The Braided Bunch

For younger curly girls of any age or curl type, this style gives you lots of color and texture and it lasts for days. All you need is several spools of strong thread, either in bright, funky colors or in a shade that's close to your own hair color.

1. Cut a piece of thread about a foot long, halve it, and tie the two halves together in a knot. Choose a section of hair at random from the top of your head and braid it. Twist the thread around the bottom of the braid and tie it in a double knot.

2. For a fun variation: After braiding, tie the thread in a knot at the top of the braid, as close as possible to your scalp. Wind the thread around the length of the braid, finishing it off at the bottom with several wraps around the ends. Finally, tie the thread in a knot to secure. You can do several of both kinds for a funky, spring look.

A 12-STEP RECOVERY PROGRAM FOR CURLY GIRLS

One Shampoo at a Time

I t's not enough to admit that you're not straight; the compulsion to abuse products and your precious locks is deep seated and hard to shake. To help curly girls in recovery, we've invented a 12-step Personal Hair Growth and Recovery Program. Since sharing is a necessary part of the program, curly girls are advised to shift their obsession from product abuse to telling others about their curly conversion. When you feel the urge to shampoo or even brush your hair, stop first and call a friend.

The following steps are to be used only as life styling tools. Interpret them in the way that is most helpful to you personally and then follow them religiously. They have worked for millions of others who knew they were not straight. They can work for you. In the process of recovering your curls, you may recover other parts of yourself long since forgotten.

I ADMIT THAT I AM POWERLESS OVER MY TRUE NATURE—AND THAT MY CURLY HAIR WILL CONTINUE TO BE UNMANAGEABLE IF I DENY AND ABUSE IT AS I HAVE IN THE PAST.*

> *You can fight the truth for only so long. Make peace now, stop deluding yourself, and see your hair for what it truly is.*

Step Two

I WILL STOP TORTURING MYSELF WITH BLOW-DRYERS, BRUSHES, STRAIGHTENERS, ROLLERS, IRONS, AND OTHER DIABOLICAL WAYS TO STRAIGHTEN MY HAIR, AND I WILL REGAIN MY SANITY AS A CURLY-HAIRED PERSON. I WILL SEARCH MY BATHROOM FOR SUCH ITEMS AND DONATE THEM TO CHARITY OR SELL THEM ON EBAY.

Step Three

I WILL ADMIT MY ADDICTION TO GOING STRAIGHT AND ATTEMPT TO DISCOVER WHY I HAVE WASTED MY TIME IN THIS PURSUIT. I WILL ACCEPT THE NATURE OF MY HAIR AND CELEBRATE IT RATHER THAN FIGHT IT.

I WILL MAKE A DECISION TO TURN MY CURLS OVER TO A HIGHER POWER—THE POWER THAT CREATED ME AND MY HAIR—AND I WILL FIND A SPONSOR TO MENTOR ME AS A RECOVERING CURLY GIRL.

Step Five

I WILL GIVE IN TO THE FORCES OF NATURE, EMBRACING HUMIDITY, RAIN, AND WIND, FACING THE ELEMENTS CONFIDENTLY BECAUSE I AM NO LONGER ATTEMPTING TO GO AGAINST NATURE AND CONTROL MY CURLS.

Step Six

I WILL MAKE A LIST OF RELATIVES AND FRIENDS WHO ENCOURAGED MY CURL DENIAL WITH COMPLIMENTS ABOUT MY STRAIGHT HAIR. I WILL FORGIVE THEM AS WELL AS HAIRDRESSERS WHO ABETTED MY HABIT.

Step Seven

I WILL ACCEPT THAT THE SCALP AND THE HAIR ARE TWO DIFFERENT ORGANS WITH TOTALLY DIFFERENT NEEDS, AND I WILL TREAT EACH ACCORDINGLY.

Step Eight

I WILL GIVE UP FOREVER SHAMPOO DEPENDENCY AND LEARN HOW TO KEEP MY HAIR CLEAN WITHOUT TURNING TO PRODUCTS THAT HARM ME.

Step Nine

I ADMIT THAT IT IS MY RESPONSIBILITY TO TAKE CARE OF MY HAIR IN THE BEST WAY POSSIBLE. I WILL LEARN HOW TO DRY IT WITHOUT HARMING IT, AND I WILL LET MY CURLS GROW TO THEIR FULL POTENTIAL.

WHENEVER I AM TEMPTED TO GO STRAIGHT, I WILL CALL A MENTOR OR FRIEND WHO HAS EMBRACED HER CURLY DESTINY AND SEEK HER ENCOURAGEMENT IN LIVING AN HONEST CURLY LIFE.

Step Eleven

I WILL CARRY THE MESSAGE OF CURLY HAIR TO OTHER WOMEN STILL LIVING IN CURL DENIAL.

Step Twelve

I WILL PRACTICE THE PRINCIPLES THAT I HAVE LEARNED EVERY DAY OF MY LIFE.

TIME LINE

A Cavalcade of Curls

IN THE BEGINNING

Curls are God-given and divine. There were no bad hair days in Paradise.

CURLS ON HIGH

Artists through history have depicted angels with curly hair. They are probably right. Curls are celestial.

GODLY CURLS

All the Greek and Roman gods had curls—from the sculpted marble locks of the Apollo Belvedere (in the Vatican) to the fusilli curls of **Botticelli's *Venus*** in the fifteenth century. Diana, goddess of the hunt and the moon, was especially honored for her curly head. Women washed their hair once a year—on Diana's birthday, August 13.

2000 B.C.: ANCIENT EGYPT

Archaeologists have found evidence in Egypt of hairpins, combs, and curlers being used as far back as 2000 B.C. The curlers could create crimps (for fullness) or curls (for beauty). Curling irons and contraceptives were introduced around the same time, which makes sense. Curling tongs in the British Museum that date from the fifteenth century B.C. have attached blades—for trimming split ends.

The upper classes wore wigs decorated with elaborate braids and curls, and arranged like tiles or puffed out into beehives. Their tightly plaited wigs resembled some popular contemporary African

American hairstyles, such as extensions and dreadlocks. The ancient Egyptians worried about frizz. But instead of Dippity-Do, hair was coated with beeswax and twisted around heated metal rods.

1500 B.C.: ANCIENT GREECE

The natural look was fashionable in Greece from 1500 to 650 B.C. Women wore their hair long, letting their curly locks cascade down to their shoulders in corkscrews or spirals. They used mud and pomades to "set" the curls, and ribbons and bands to hold them in place. The looks were amazingly contemporary.

70 B.C.: ANCIENT ROME

The Romans didn't begin to curl their hair or use wigs until about the third century B.C., when they started to copy the Greeks with great enthusiasm. Intellectuals found the trend ridiculous. "I will tear from your head those curly perfumed false locks you have so carefully arranged," says a character in one Plautus play.

But elaborate curls caught on. Around 70 B.C. Roman matrons were getting their hair curled with a device called a calamistrum—a hollow stick made of bronze. Ivory, gold, silver, and bone hairpins held the curls in place.

In the early part of the millennium, Roman women started wearing even more elaborate hairdos, arranging their phony curls around a crescent-shaped wire called an orbis. It was probably an attempt "to get some height," the same impulse that gave rise to the beehive—1,950 years later.

SECOND CENTURY A.D.: ROMAN EMPIRE

Hairstyles got more elaborate and thick, with false curls, expensive wigs, and hair dye (black or blond). These enhancements infuriated the early church fathers. St. Clement of Alexandria inveighed against all the "frizeling and curling of

Haire" and ruled that if you were wearing a wig when blessed, only the wig got the blessing. He was on to something— the barbarians were at the gates.

A.D. 500–1200: DARK AGES

They don't call these the Dark Ages for nothing. Few images remain. Many women kept their hair covered to show modesty.

In Byzantium, the head could be decorated with jewels. **Empress Theodora** is shown in mosaics with an elaborate headdress with beads shaped like long spiral curls. But you can't see her hair.

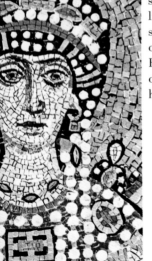

FOURTEENTH AND FIFTEENTH CENTURIES

Hair came out of the closet. A high forehead was a mark of beauty, so wealthy women plucked their foreheads and wore their hair in elaborate coiled braids, which disguised any natural curls. Sometimes hair was rolled, but curls were rare.

SIXTEENTH CENTURY

Queen Elizabeth I, who was bald, loved wigs of tight red curls. Mary Queen of Scots wore her tresses straight and smooth. She lost her head.

In the latter part of the century, wealthy women started waving and curling their hair. Even when they wore tight caps, they frizzed whatever hair was left showing. Curly wigs made a comeback.

SEVENTEENTH CENTURY

The Baroque era, excessive in all artistic expression, produced grandiloquent hairstyles. Wigs for women became more elaborate, although kings like Louis XIV could wear their naturally curly hair long and free.

In the first half of the century, women frizzed their hair for a fringe across the forehead, then used heated *bilboquets* or *roulettes* to curl their hair, letting the curls fall loose below a chignon or bun.

By the last half of the century, curls were so hot that a language of curls was developed, which included the high curle, open curle, drake tail curle, and snake curle. Hair was frizzed or crisped. Women wore towers of false curls, called a *tour*. *Confidentes* were small curls near the ears, while *creve-coeurs*, or heartbreakers, were curls at the nape of the neck.

The **hurluberlu** (above) became the most popular hairstyle, both in England and in France. Madame de Sévigné thought she was too old for it but recommended it to her daughter. The hair was parted in the middle, then curled with short, fat ringlets all over the crown and sides. Some hair was left long so graceful locks could fall coyly down each side to the shoulders.

The *fontange*, in which the hair was piled extraordinarily high on the head, was invented by the **duchesse de Fontange,** who was sleeping with Louis XIV. Out hunting with Louis one day, the duchess lost her hat and tied up her curls with a lace-edged garter. Louis found this tousled look delightful and declared it the style of the moment. The duchess allegedly used a wire frame to hold it up and egg whites to keep the hair in place.

How did other women keep all these curls in place? One beauty book of the time advised making a paste with gum arabic and water, then using a curling iron. After mixing the ointment over a "gentle fire," you rubbed it on your hair for a style called "Curiously Curled." Indeed.

EIGHTEENTH CENTURY

Hair grew simpler for the first half of the century—Louis XIV had tired of his mistress and her hair. But hairdressers became so adept

at constructing towers of hair that the fad came back with a vengeance in the last half of the century.

Hairdressers created towers of curls and filler—scraps of wool, flowers, pompoms, ribbons, feathers, pearls, even miniature ships. Legros de Rumigny, the Alexandre de Paris of his time, gave classes in Paris in the construction of such coiffures. He recommended beef fat as a pomade. Newspapers made fun of the styles and complained about the stench coming from hairdos that hadn't been changed for months. Mites and other vermin were reported escaping from the hairdos.

The height thing became ridiculous. Marie Antoinette,

it was said, had to remove her headdress before getting into her carriage. Other women just stuck their heads out the windows for the ride. As the hair grew higher, the curls took a backseat, although in England women had the ends of their hair frizzed in a style that was called **the hedgehog.**

Alas, at the end of the century, many of those hairdos came off, along with their owners' heads.

NINETEENTH CENTURY

For a time, inspired by the Revolution, Frenchwomen adopted short bobs, sometimes with their natural curls showing at the neck. The idea was to look as Republican as possible. Those evolved into Grecian styles—like the coif of **Madame Récamier,** a turn-of-the-century Parisian

trendsetter whose hair was pulled up but softened with curls around the face. Women achieved this look with a fixative called "antique oil." If weather caused their stubborn tresses to lose their spring, they resorted to curly hairpieces.

In England, women let their ringlets fall naturally. Hair would be tied in a topknot or chignon, but spirals of curls would fall gracefully over the

shoulders. Across the ocean, the elite adopted the same styles.

Eventually the topknot came down and women wore their hair smooth on top and cascading into long spirals, sausages of curls, or, like the young **Queen Victoria** (above), in coils of braids.

It became fashionable to have a lot of hair, so much so that, in 1848, Britain imported 8,766 pounds of French hair. Hair would be piled high on the head, with ringlets and

"frizettes" framing the face and trailing down the back.

Curls continued to be fashionable for the rest of the decade.

1852: THE MARCEL REVOLUTION

In 1852, a Frenchman named **Marcel Grateau** invented an instrument that changed the world. Rather than crimping the hair as past curling irons did, his instrument created soft, natural-looking waves. He called the effect moiré, or watered, undulations. But eventually his achievement was named for him, and the marcel wave took hold for the next eighty or so years.

Grateau introduced a new simple style of soft, **Pre-Raphaelite** waves. Opera singer Nellie Melba and Caroline "La Belle" Otero, a famous actress of the period, would come to him for their marcels. Now the hair could be pinned up or pulled back, but soft, natural-looking waves could soften the effect.

1900–1919: POMPADOURS AND GIBSON GIRLS

Hair was long but worn up in soft waves and curls, with fringes of bangs or a "rat," which was a roll of hair covered with an invisible hairnet that was placed high on the forehead and covered over with the

owner's natural hair. The result was a **pompadour**. The sides were softly waved with the marcel curling iron. **Gibson girls** frizzed curls on their foreheads.

1904: THE PERMANENT WAVE

A German named Karl Nessler devised an **electric permanent waving machine** in 1904, but it took twelve hours to get a permanent—and it was a huge contraption of a machine. The device didn't become popular until after World War I.

1920: THE BOB

When dancer **Irene Castle** bobbed her hair after the war, she set off the first major hair trend of the twentieth century. We think of the bob today as a short straight style. But in 1920, to bob your hair meant simply to cut it short. Whether it was curly or straight depended on your genetic inheritance. Women thronged to barbershops to be shorn. It was a boon for permanents. Many women felt they couldn't just have short straight hair— they'd look like men.

"The bob of today . . . is based on the wave," pronounced *Collier's* magazine in the 1920s. "Straight hair is something so infrequently seen that it must be classed as a personal idiosyncrasy." But short, neatly defined wavy hair—just like Irene's—was flattering and easy to wear. And accessible, if you could afford to get a permanent wave (which cost about $35 at the time).

If you were a siren, say, like Wallis Simpson going after a king or like **Josephine Baker,** the toast of Paris, you affected ultra-sophisticated, almost sculpted marcel waves. The duchess of Windsor wore marcel waves for thirty years, finally adopting the bouffant in the 1960s. The look didn't require a permanent, just some well-placed wave clips inserted into the hair when it was still wet.

1930S

The curly or wavy bob look lasted for most of the 1930s. **Myrna Loy** in the *Thin Man* series, **Irene Dunne, Sylvia Sidney,** Rosalind Russell . . . all had curls, via permanent waves, nature, or pin curls.

Meanwhile, a curly-headed **Shirley Temple** danced her way onto the stage and into the national consciousness, forever establishing curls as cute—but maybe not sophisticated anymore. Gradually, as the decade wore on, grown-up women let their hair grow a little longer. It was curly or not.

But then two movies changed everything. The first was *Gone With the Wind,* in which **Vivien Leigh** portrayed Scarlett with long and wavy raven tresses.

1940S

Then, in 1941, **Veronica Lake** (right), a sultry blonde with soft curls, appeared in a B movie called *I Wanted Wings.* Lake's signature S-shaped wave of hair covered one eye and fell

seductively to her shoulder. Suddenly everyone was attempting the look. Defense plants complained it was endangering Rosie the Riveter types, but the style persisted.

For most of the 1940s, hair was worn flat on top and parted on the side, falling gracefully into a few well-placed waves.

But **Rita Hayworth**'s long lanky look was mostly for younger women. Moms tended to wear short curly hair, regularly permed to perfection. The cold permanent wave was invented in 1947, and suddenly you could do it yourself. A lot of frizz and fumes resulted, but the hair was easy to maintain.

1950S

Curly hair dominated the first half of the decade, and **Lucille Ball**'s almost poodle-cut curls became a national institution. They went with Dior's "New Look": the long bouffant skirts and wasp waists required neat, sculpted hair with careful curls and waves.

Grace Kelly

1960S

In the 1960s African Americans wore their hair in Afros as a political statement, and many women aspired to look like **Angela Davis** by letting their hair grow into 'fros.

But most white women's hairstyles were straight. Hippie men who couldn't be bothered let their hair frizz out like Albert Einstein's. Hippie girls tended to wear theirs natural and the longer the better.

In 1961 Charles Schultz introduced curly-mopped **Frieda** into his *Peanuts* cartoon strip. While most girls in the '60s were trying to go straight, Frieda lived comic strip life by her inspired dictum: she could do anything because she had "naturally curly hair!"

If you were chic and avant-garde, you copied Audrey Hepburn's existentialist pixie in *Funny Face* (1957) or adopted the gaminlike looks of Fellini's wife, **Giuletta Masina**.

Less rebellious types ballooned up with beehives and bouffants. "Visible waves are absent," wrote *Chicago Tribune* fashion editor Eleanor Nangle in 1963, describing the latest trends in hairdressing, "and there isn't the trace of a curl."

Back-combing or teasing, which hadn't been seen since before the French Revolution, reappeared. Women with curly hair learned to iron it or blow-dry it out straight.

1970S

This was the decade that many curly girls still remember, in agony. They ironed their hair or rolled it in orange juice or beer cans to get it straight. The only possible variation was the **Farrah Fawcett** look—long and

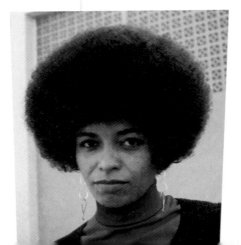

basically lanky, with feathery waves. These had to look phony; real curls wouldn't work.

1973: MOST HUMILIATING MOVIE MOMENT FOR CURLY GIRLS

A lot of curly girls still recall the movie moment that truly betrayed them and their hair. It was in *The Way We Were*, the 1973 movie starring **Barbra Streisand** and Robert Redford. In college, Barbra's character let her corkscrew curls go natural, and Redford never looked her way. Cut to five years later: she's a knockout with ironed hair, and, yes, she got the guy. For some curly girls, Streisand didn't make up for this politically incorrect moment until 1983, when she proposed to a Botticelli-haired **Amy Irving** in *Yentl*. Barbra, who was

masquerading as a guy, hid her own curls in this one.

1980S

The **Dorothy Hamill** straight, short wedge was the most ubiquitous style of the early eighties, but renegades were starting to appear. Amy Irving in *Honeysuckle Rose* won Willie Nelson's heart with her Botticelli curls. And even Dyan Cannon, who'd straightened her hair for earlier movies, let her curls show in this one.

The 1980s was also the decade of "big hair"— you remember, the teased-and-sprayed, helmet-head, mall-mama thang.

1982

Cute curly carrot top **Orphan Annie** in the seventy-five-year-running comic strip appears in the Broadway musical *Annie*. **Aileen Quinn** plays Annie in the film adaptation.

1990S

The pendulum swung the other way to hair that was flat and broomstick straight.

By the late 1990s stick-straight hair lost its cachet, and the new century is a curly millennium.

TV actresses with curls are making waves: **Dyan Cannon,** who had straight hair in 1969's *Bob & Carol & Ted & Alice*, is the definitive older curly girl of the millennium.

2000

When *Felicity* star **Keri Russell** lopped off all her curls, ratings for her show *Felicity* plummeted. The upshot: Russell's new contract with WB includes the proviso that she not cut her hair for the duration of the show.

Suddenly everyone is clamoring for curls. The tide has turned, and everyone wants to catch the wave. Straight-haired women are resorting to pin curls and scrunch, rollers and permanent waves. It's finally our turn and it's about time.

2001 AND BEYOND

According to *InStyle* magazine, many celebrities, like **Sandra Bullock**, are faking the must-have look for spring—curly hair! "After their hair is curled," reports one stylist-to-the-stars, "they feel more flirty and feminine."

Curly girls protest the release of Disney's *The*

Princess Diaries, a modern fairytale flick that features an ugly duckling teenage girl who is transformed into a swan—via brush and blow-dryer. The founders of the Web site www.naturallycurly.com boycott the film.

"Hairstories" premieres at Jacob's Pillow in Becket, Massachusetts, by the **Urban Bush Women Dance Company**. Blending choreography, music, and videotaped interviews with black women, the show explores and celebrates the once pejorative term *nappiness* and the culture that surrounds black women's hair.

The *Mademoiselle* September 2001 issue asked men to rate the hairstyles of fifty women. Among various lengths, straightnesses and textures, the curliest girl came in *first!* According to the judges, she looked the most "playful," "sexy," "chic," and "touchable."

Elle magazine features a cover story on the power of curls, along with information on curling your hair, using setting lotion, and scrunching. The headline:

UPWARD SPIRAL: THE SEASON'S MOST GLAMOROUS COIFS ARE ANYTHING BUT STRAIGHT. WHETHER TEASED, CURLED OR WAVED, MODERN HAIR IS FINALLY TAKING AN INTERESTING TURN.

We couldn't have said it better.

Minnie Driver

IT'S A CURLY WORLD

The curly hair look is *in!* All those celebrities with the natural ringlets are letting their hair go free. Curly girls are the ones to watch this season—from stars like Nicole Kidman, with her fabulous Botticelli ringlets, to Minnie Driver, whose cascading corkscrew curls turn heads and land roles, and Meg Ryan, whose tousled, sexy bed-head look has replaced Jennifer Anniston's as the look of the new decade. Below are just a few of the curly girls who have become fashion's new role models.

Meg Ryan

Nicole Kidman

pe Cruz

Lisa Nicole Carson

Sarah Jessica Parker

lsea Clinton

Christina Aguilera

Charlize Theron

Ananda Lewis

ASTROLOCURLS
A Horoscope

Aries
MARCH 21–APRIL 19

As spring stirs, the season of renewed life and the start of the sun's annual cycurl, fiery Aries symbolizes beginnings. You are full of fixed ideas, so your boundless curls may threaten you, to the point where you may butt heads with the herd. If you don't rise to the occasion, your hair will. Submit. After all, the part of the body ascribed to Aries is the head.

Taurus
APRIL 20–MAY 20

Taurus signals the rites of spring, and spring is in the hair. Taurus types who cultivate their gardens willingly may be inclined to get stuck in the mud and might dig in their heels and resist change as a result of many bad hair experiences. Don't be closed to new information. Seek a logicurl approach: you are known to be the goddess of the past. But don't be a has-been. Be the goddess of the now and try a new look.

Gemini
MAY 21–JUNE 21

Gemini brings in the mellow breezes of the summer—and, yes, with it, the humidity. As a twin, staring at your reflection, you have a need for individuality. But you have to accept that going straight and going curly is not always a heal-thy option. If your hair shows any sign of damage, you, as the embodiment of the quickening of human intelligence, must accept its truths. Once you get to know your hair's natural state, it will present itself differently every day. How can you be bored?

Cancer

JUNE 22–JULY 22

The sun has reached its highest point over the Northern Hemisphere. Open to new ideas, you must nevertheless set limits as a mother must for her adventuresome child. You do not readily accept others, so you may be in need of a worthy hairdresser to guide you right. Being moody with your hair won't solve a thing. Coexist; it's worthy of you. Curl up with *Curly Girl*, then pass it on to another Cancer curlfriend.

Leo

JULY 23–AUGUST 22

At the heat of the high summer, with its intense solar rays, curls are running rampant. It's time to explore your *S*-sence. When dealt with properly, your mane will inspire radiance and you will become a leader, encouraging other curly girls to emerge from their dens. If you deny your curls and slink off to try to smooth away the frizzies, by high noon, the untamed will of the frizz will persist.

Virgo

AUGUST 23–SEPTEMBER 22

At the beginning of the fall harvest, Virgo's humble awareness equips you early in life with an understanding of your hair's potential. But with your quest for perfection, you need to remember the old saying "It's not perfect, but it's perfect for you." Life's too short to be dissatisfied with one stray frizz. Look at the big picture, and stop fussing; otherwise you'll have big hair. Remember, while your hair is drying, do not micromanage.

Libra

SEPTEMBER 23–OCTOBER 23

This is the fall equinox, when the sun enters the sign of Libra, a h'air sign that holds an invisible thread connecting us all. Libra rules relationship, one to one, and you are often one with your hair. If not, you may pay too much attention to the counsel of others and not be in touch with your inner curl. But you will eventually arrive at your hair's true state of harmony. With the right *Curly Girl* bible, you'll be one of us.

Scorpio

OCTOBER 24–NOVEMBER 21

As the nights grow longer, with a suggestion of winter, you consummate the bond with your hair with intense experimentation. Together, you must confront its *S*-sence in pursuit of the hairy truth. The unbound curl emerges and is understandably a challenge to pursue daily, weekly, monthly, yearly. Scorpio is attuned to the cycurl of death and rebirth, choosing to weather all weather conditions, since we have no choice in the realm of our hair. Scorpio tails will make your hair curl—if it's not already.

Sagittarius

NOVEMBER 22–DECEMBER 21

Born in the winter months, you Sagittarians need your hair to be as carefree and easy as you are, as long as you have a hair routine to follow. You sometimes come off sounding self-righteous, so lighten up, curlfriend. You're the perfect outreach curly girl, especially at holiday party time, since people are always asking you about your hair. It's all about your hair-itude, sweetie.

Capricorn

DECEMBER 22–JANUARY 19

Capricorn is born in the heart of winter, a product of the longest nights.
Capricorns have their own particular vision of the world, so you may at
first rebel against your curls. You typically need to be on top; you are
determined to overcome all obstacles, and your hair may be one of them.
Let down your guard, reach out to a curlfriend, and unite. Remember,
your hair is on top, not you.

Aquarius

JANUARY 20–FEBRUARY 18

Aquarius is the ruler of the h'air wave. Winter has been too long,
and as the water bearer, curls R U. You usually confront your hair
frustrations, but if you're slightly insecure, you may demand that
your hair change according to your perception of the situation. If you
reject your curls, you reject your *S*-sense. Curl now, or forever hold
your hair piece.

Pisces

FEBRUARY 19–MARCH 20

The days lengthen and thaws begin as Pisces moves beyond
herself, always following the movement of the ocean currents
and the current trends. You are easily swayed, which is both
your strength and your weakness, and this trait also applies
to your hair. Sometimes overwhelmed by what's current, you
flounder in the face of your curly hairitage. If you can just
ride the wave, you can be on top of anything.

There was a little girl
  Who had a little curl
Right in the middle of
  her forehead.
When she was good
She was very, very good,
But when she was bad,
  she was horrid.

—Henry Wadsworth Longfellow

Curly Diary

First curly haircut (date) _____

Day 1 _____

Day 2 _____

First week without shampooing _____

_____

_____

_____

Gave away hairbrush and
blow-dryer _____

_____

I found my inner curl. I am a:

Corkscrew ☐   Botticelli ☐   Wavy ☐

Comments about my new curls _____

_____

_____

_____

_____

_____

My curly hair makes me feel like...

Bad hair day and how I coped

Number of days without shampooing

Saturday. Big date. Tried new homemade
conditioning recipe. How hair felt

Boyfriend's (husband's) response to my new curls

Another curly girl asks for advice about caring for her curls

Curly girl support group

Let hair grow out for two months

Appointment with stylist. Her comments and suggestions

Four months since
last shampoo, but who's counting?

Photo Credits

Front cover: *(main image)* photographer/Güler Uğur, model/Heather Conway-Visser; *(top image)* Marc Dolphin/ Getty Images/Store; *(bottom)* Anthony Loew

Back cover: *(all)* Anthony Loew

Page iv: Photofest

Page vi: Photofest

Page viii: The Art Archive/Galleria Nazionale dell'Umbria Perugia/Dagli Orti

Page x: Tricia Meadows/Globe Photos

Page 11: Oliver Meckes/Photo Researchers, Inc.

Page 15: *(left)* John Durham/Science Photo Library/Photo Researchers, Inc.; *(right)* Biophoto Associates/ Photo Researchers, Inc.

Page 18: *(left)* John Spellman/Retna Ltd.; *(right)* Rose Hartman/Globe Photos

Page 20 *(left to right)*: Fitzroy Barrett/Globe Photos; Marion Curtis/DMI/Timepix; Steve Granitz/Retna Ltd.

Page 22 *(left to right)*: Tricia Meadows/Globe Photos; Marion Curtis/Timepix; AP/Wide World Photos

Page 24 *(left to right)*: Fitzroy Barrett/Globe Photos; Nina Prommer/Globe Photos; AP/Wide World Photos

Page 37: Photofest

Page 95: Kobal Collection/Gainsborough

Page 124: Photofest

Page 125: *(The Fall of Man)* Historical Picture Archive/Corbis Images; *(Archangel Gabriel)* The Art Archive/ Galleria Nazionale dell'Umbria Perugia/Dagli Orti; *(The Birth of Venus)* Erich Lessing/Art Resource; *(Egyptian Dancing Girl)* Erich Lessing/Art Resource

Page 126: *(Vabia Matilda)* The Art Archive/Museo Capitolino Rome/Dagli Orti

Page 127: *(Empress Theodora)* The Granger Collection, New York; *(Bartolommeo Veneto)* The Granger Collection, New York; *(Queen Elizabeth I)* Victoria and Albert Museum, London/Art Resource; *(Eleonore-Marie Louise)* courtesy of the New York Public Library/Picture Collection

Page 128: *(Queen Marie-Louis)* The Art Archive/JFB; *(Marie Angelique Fontage)* courtesy of the NY Public Library/ Picture Collection; *(De la Parure des Dames)* courtesy of the New York Public Library/Picture Collection

Page 129: *(Hedgehog style)* The Art Archive/Musee Carnavalet Paris/Dagli Orti; *(Queen Victoria)* Giraudon/ Art Resource/NY; *(Juliette Recamier)* Erich Lessing/Art Resource; *(M. Marcel Grateau)* Hulton-Deutsch Collection/Corbis Images

Page 130: *(Rossetti's La Pia)* Art Resource/NY; *(Karl Nessler)* Photofest; *(Irene Castle)* Photofest

Page 131: *(Josephine Baker)* CSU Archives/Everett Collection; *(Myrna Loy)* Photofest; *(Irene Dunne)* Photofest; *(Sylvia Sidney)* Photofest; *(Shirley Temple)* Photofest; *(Vivien Leigh)* Photofest; *(Rita Hayworth)* Photofest; *(Veronica Lake)* Photofest

Page 132: *(Lucille Ball)* The Kobal Collection; *(Grace Kelly)* The Kobal Collection; (Peanuts *cartoon*) Photofest; *(Giuletta Masina)* Everett Collection; *(Angela Davis)* Corbis Images; *(Farrah Fawcett)* Everett Collection

Page 133: *(Barbra Streisand, both)* Photofest; *(Yentl)* Photofest; *(Dorothy Hamill)* Everett Collection; *(Annie)* Photofest; *(Annie, cartoon)* Photofest; *(Dyan Cannon)* Mirek Towski/DMI/Timepix

Page 134: *(Keri Russell, left)* Armando Gallo/Retna Ltd.; *(Keri Russell, right)* Jerry Dabrowski/Zuma/Timepix; *(Urban Bush Women)* Jennifer Lester/Urban Bush; *(Sandra Bullock)* Andrea Renault/Globe Photos; *(Minnie Driver)* Corbis Outline

Page 135: *(Penelope Cruz)* Andrea Renault/Globe Photos; *(Chelsea Clinton)* Kevin Lamarque/Reuters/Archive Photos; *(Nicole Kidman)* AP/Wide World Photos; *(Lisa Nicole Carson)* Mark J. Terrill/AP Photos; *(Christina Aguilera)* Fitzroy Barrett/Globe Photos; *(Sarah Jessica Parker)* Tricia Meadows/Globe Photos; *(Charlize Theron)* Fred Prouser/Reuters; *(Meg Ryan)* Nina Prommer/Globe Photos; *(Ananda Lewis)* Fitzroy Barrett/Globe Photos